W   N

Acoustics of Music

The

PRENTICE-HALL MUSIC SERIES

DOUGLAS MOORE, Editor

Acoustics of Music

By

WILMER T. BARTHOLOMEW, M.A., M. MUS.

Fellow of the
Acoustical Society of America
and Instructor in the
Peabody Conservatory of Music

ILLUSTRATED

PRENTICE · HALL · INC.
Englewood Cliffs, N. J.

Copyright, 1942, by

PRENTICE-HALL, INC.
Englewood Cliffs, N. J.

First Printing..........May, *1942*
Second Printing......October, *1945*
Third Printing.........July, *1946*
Fourth Printing....September, *1947*
Fifth Printing.........April, *1950*
Sixth Printing..........July, *1952*
Seventh Printing.....March, *1956*
Eighth Printing.........July, *1960*
Ninth Printing......February, *1963*
Tenth Printing ....June, *1964*

Printed in the United States of America
00285—C

To My

MOTHER AND FATHER

Preface

The Taj Mahal, that dream of architectural loveliness, seems to our entranced vision far removed from such mundane things as the measurement of angles, the stresses and strains of building materials, and the chemistry of pigments. But is it not related to these matters as the harvest is to the seed? Beethoven's Ninth Symphony, that last mighty dream of a stormy soul, or *L'après-midi,* that more delicate dream of fragile beauty, seems to our transported ears to have no connection with such prosaic things as the compressibility of air, the reflection of sound waves by walls, or the mathematics of Fourier analysis. But there is a connection, unrecognized and scorned though it be by many. We are usually unconscious of it during the emotional experience of listening to music. But whether or not we like to admit our dependence on such material things, there is no art capable of rearing high its magic towers of beauty without building them on the strong foundation of the established and immutable laws of "the-nature-of-things," or science. This is usually recognized in such an art as architecture, but frequently unrecognized in such an art as music. For example, an undiscriminating writer has said, "The soul of the piano transcends all investigation." Such a statement is patently incorrect, since the soul is not in the piano but in the pianist—and I hope it will there continue to transcend investigation. That which is essentially imponderable cannot be weighed or analyzed very far. But it is quite possible to study the action of sound waves, the action of the piano, and the actions of the muscles of the player, and draw certain conclusions that may greatly aid the pianist in the expression of whatever is in his soul. And if the results of such investigations, based on facts instead of traditions alone, were in the hands of piano teachers, how much better chance would some struggling piano pupils have of eventually expressing whatever is in their souls worth saying. And what is true of the piano is true of other instruments.

The musical mind has often not been an analytical mind. The composer, in the throes of creation, needs to grasp large outlines before they fade, and *later* weigh, criticize, and polish, after the heat of inspiration has passed. The performer, in the midst of an inspired rendition, has no time for analyzing what he is doing; the attempt to do so will frequently dispel all inspiration. And even the listener probably does not get the keenest enjoyment from those moments in which he listens analytically. Thus there seems to be a need for a book *for music students and musicians* that will clarify some of the foundational matters of acoustics, and give to musicians in readable form the materials and the spirit for analysis of their problems of composition, performance, teaching, criticism, and appreciation.

This book, therefore, is written from the musician's standpoint, in the hope of answering the questions that music students and performers might ask. Many texts have appeared which show an indifference to musicianship, with all that that implies, and an ignorance of the vast and important domain of aesthetics. This text attempts to supply a need not supplied by these other books. However, although written from the musician's standpoint, and with, I hope, a constant awareness of aesthetic factors too subtle and tenuous to be caught in the scientist's sieve, it does eschew the typical pseudo-mystical misinformation that weakens so many texts written by musicians lacking either scientific training or a true mysticism. It does not go far into the scientific realm, but it attempts to be correct, up-to-date, and truly scientific in spirit as far as it does go.

Thus the book is an attempt to bridge two fields, and herein lies perhaps a weakness, but also whatever value it may have.

It should be readable and informative to a musician on the one hand, since it omits all except the most elementary mathematics, while explaining in simple language many of the phenomena with which he deals. On the other hand, it should be both informative and readable to a scientist, since it does not go into the niceties of tonal modification and instrumental technique, while at the same time it does make the tie-up between the physical principles of sound and their artistic flowering in the tone qualities perceived by the hearer from musical instruments.

The book, however, is not a text on instruments per se. This need is provided for by texts designed especially for courses in instruments or orchestration. Thus the characteristics of the various instruments (except possibly the voice) are not treated exhaustively, one by one, in any one place, but frequently by groups, as they illustrate this or that acoustic principle.

Similarly, various topics usually to be found in an orthodox book on sound are here touched very lightly, or even omitted entirely, as having no particular bearing on practical music. For example, there is no mention made of singing flames, or of Lissajous figures. Certain other topics are omitted because of their complexity and the unsettled state of the research done on them to date. Thus, for example, the anatomy of the ear is only suggested lightly, and the controversial subject of comparative hearing theories is omitted entirely.

I have, however, claimed an author's privilege in going into considerable detail on the subject of the voice, in its physical and physiological, and even somewhat into the pedagogical, aspects, since these have been the fields of research in which I have specialized. Furthermore, no other aspect of music is so greatly in need of clarification. If a conscientious interchange of opinion and sympathy could take place between the fields of acoustic science and voice teaching, and if the contempt so often felt by each group for the other could be alleviated, all would benefit. But what a great "if" this is, implying as it does a certain capacity for humility.

Throughout the text I have attempted to observe carefully the distinctions between physical and psychological terms. Occasionally, however, for one reason or another, this has been relaxed, and "loudness" may appear for "intensity" in places, "pitch" for "frequency," and so on.

Certain sections, either of less importance or of greater difficulty, have been set in smaller type, particularly in the discussion of the voice, and of harmony and scales. These sections may be omitted without destroying the continuity of the remainder.

In the preparation of such a text as this, necessitating the study of many references, it is difficult to give credit to every source to which credit is due. Some authors are mentioned by name in the body of the text. Manifestly, others have necessarily been omitted therefrom in the interest of coherency of style, although these, and in fact most of the works consulted or quoted, together with certain other selected references, are listed in the bibliography. In particular I wish to express my indebtedness to Sir William Bragg's delightful little book, *The World of Sound*, upon which I have drawn heavily, especially in the introductory sections, and in such things as the use of a spring to illustrate air-column vibration. His method of presentation is so lucid that I fall back frequently on his phraseology, unable to find a better way of stating the idea.

For the use of Figure 40 and related material, I am indebted, as are all authors and students in this field, to the far-sighted research program of the Bell Laboratories, and to the growing significance of the Acoustical Society of America, now in its thirteenth year of existence. These two influences continue to bear most worth-while fruit in the rapid development of the new acoustics, formerly the step-daughter of science.

My thanks are also due to Mr. Louis Cheslock, Mr. Frederick Weaver, and Mr. Hayward Henderson for suggestions, criticisms, and corrections; to various others of my colleagues and students who have helped in one way or another in the preparation of the text and its illustrations; and to my wife, Elizabeth V. Bartholomew, who has assisted in the reading of proof. I shall be happy to be apprised of whatever errors or omissions remain.

One word remains to be said. It can be said briefly, but none the less gratefully. This text would never have been commenced eight years ago, let alone travailed with and now completed, without the enthusiastic and inspiring encouragement, the active cooperation, and the kindly criticism of one man—Otto Ortmann.

W.T.B.

Baltimore, Maryland

Table of Contents

CHAPTER   PAGE

PREFACE vii

TABLE OF ILLUSTRATIONS xv

INTRODUCTION 1

1. PRELIMINARY SURVEY OF THE NATURE OF VIBRATION, AND ITS
   RELATIONSHIP TO MUSIC 3

   Elasticity and momentum. Simple harmonic motion. Natural
   period. Frequency and pitch. Amplitude and loudness. Harmonic series, partials, overtones. Complex vibration. Inharmonics. Vibration form and tone quality. Harmonic and formant theories of tone quality. Tonal attributes summarized.
   Vibrato.

2. SOUND WAVES AND THEIR CHARACTERISTICS 27

   Resonance. Transverse wave motion. Longitudinal, or compressional, wave motion. Diffusion. Reinforcement. Velocity
   of sound in air. Wave-length. Sound waves in other media.
   Graphic recording of sound waves. Harmonic analysis. Principle of superposition. Interference. Beats. Difference tones.
   Reflection, types of echoes. Uneven distribution of reflected
   sound. Reverberation and absorption. Insulation. "Good
   acoustics." Diffraction. Refraction. Doppler effect.

3. VIBRATORY SOURCES OF SOUNDS USED IN MUSIC 85

   A. *Stretched Strings* 85

   Traveling waves. Transverse standing waves, loops, nodes.
   Plucking. Bowing. Striking. Harmonics. Pitch. Loudness.
   Tone quality. Duration. Instruments.

   B. *Air Columns* 103

   Traveling waves. Compressional standing waves, loops, nodes.
   Wave-length. Edge tones. Reeds. Open and stopped pipes

CHAPTER   PAGE

contrasted. Overblowing, harmonics. Wood winds and brass
winds contrasted. Pitch. Loudness. Tone quality. Duration.
Instruments.

C. *Percussion* 129
Stretched membranes. Rods, tuning forks. Plates. Bells.
Instruments.

D. *Voice* 139
Manner of production. Pitch. Loudness. Tone quality, placement. Physiological and psychological aspects of good voice
quality. Duration, breath control. Song and speech contrasted. Whispering.

E. *Noise* 159
Noise in percussion instruments. Noise elements in all instruments. Noise and health.

4. HARMONY AND SCALES 163
Relation of consonance and dissonance to harmonic series. Evolution of diatonic scale (true or "just" intonation). Need for
temperament. Equal temperament. Equal temperament contrasted with just intonation and Pythagorean intonation. Tuning procedure in equal temperament. Characteristics of different
tonalities.

5. HEARING 199
Mechanism of hearing. Pitch limits and sensitivity. Loudness
limits and sensitivity. Duration limits and sensitivity. Binaural
sense. Deafness. Distortions of hearing. Analysis of complex
sounds.

6. ELECTRONIC RECORDING, REPRODUCING, AND SYNTHESIZING OF
SOUND 223
Limitations of early phonographs. Electronic recording and
reproduction. Limitations of loud-speakers. Electronic instruments.

BIBLIOGRAPHY 231

INDEX 239

Table of Illustrations

FIGURE   PAGE

1. Recording of sine curve from pendular vibration   4

2. Vibration forms of a rope   8

3. Harmonic series on C   9

4. Harmonic and formant theories of tone quality   16

5. Four instants during one cycle of a voice vibrato   22

6. Formation of circular water wave   29

7. Formation of air wave by vibrating string   31

8. Simple sound waves with graphs of pressure variation   48

9. Complex sound waves with graphs of pressure variation   49

10. Oscillograms of different instruments sounding A–440   50

11. Change of tone quality in the oboe with increasing pitch   52

12. Analysis of complex wave into two partials   53

13. Analysis of complex wave from organ pipe into twelve partials ..   53

14. Interference of waves from tuning fork prongs   57

15. Beats from two tuning forks   59

16. Reflection of sound waves by plane wall   64

17. Reflection of sound waves by curved walls   66

18. Diffraction of sound waves   77

19. Refraction of sound waves by temperature gradient   79

20. Refraction of sound waves by wind gradient   80

xv

FIGURE   PAGE

21. Successive refraction and reflection over water 82

22. Traveling waves on a rope 86

23. Vibration of string in octave form 87

24. Vibration of plucked string 88

25. Graph of vibration of a point on a bowed string 89

26. Simple and complex forms of string vibration 93

27. Longitudinal vibration of a spring 105

28. Eddies formed in water flowing past an obstacle 108

29. Cross-section of organ flue pipe 109

30. Open and stopped pipes producing fundamentals 112

31. Open and stopped pipes producing harmonics by overblowing ... 113

32. Effect of end correction on pipe length 122

33. A group of flue and reed pipes of various types and qualities,
    all tuned to Middle C 125

34. Vibration of membranes 130

35. Vibration of rods 132

36. Vibration of plates 134

37. Vibration of bells 135

38. Relation of meatus resonance to high formant in male voice 146

39. Good quality contrasted with poor quality in male voice 149

40. Throat positions 151

41. Relative sizes of intervals in Pythagorean intonation, just intona-
    tion, and equal temperament 174

42. Equal loudness contours between the threshold of audibility and
    the threshold of feeling 208

Acoustics of Music

Introduction

As human beings, we are so accustomed to the phenomena of sound that it never occurs to us to inquire into their causes. What makes sound?

We live in a world of things—material objects—which we cannot help shaking or moving slightly when we touch them or when we move around. Our footsteps shake the floor a bit. If we drop a ruler on the table, both ruler and table are given a slight quivering movement, called *vibration*. Such motions are usually too small and too rapid to be seen, but they are nevertheless present.

In addition to living among these more obvious surroundings of material things, we live at the bottom of an ocean of air. As Sir William Bragg says in his book, *The World of Sound,* we are constantly stirring this air, since we cannot move anything, not even our bodies, without moving the air in contact with them. If we strike a table, not only does the table quiver, but the air in contact with it receives a quiver which, once started, travels through the air in all directions in a way somewhat similar to the way a disturbance on a water surface will travel away in all directions on the surface till it becomes weakened and dies away.

Now, since we can hardly move without setting up a quivering motion in bodies, and through them in the air itself, it is natural that man and other forms of life should have been provided with sensitive organs to detect these air tremors, in order to warn them of approaching danger, if for no other reason. These organs are our ears, and when they detect an air tremor, we say we hear a sound, and we know that somewhere or other a quiver was imparted to the air, probably by some material body. Different material bodies impart different types of tremor to the air, and by recognizing these different types we know what kind of a body produced the tremor in the first place. Thus we easily distinguish between the sounds of a pistol, a streetcar, a violin, or a voice. We even distinguish between voices, and between various words spoken by a single voice, and between various emotional or physical conditions in a single voice as it pronounces a single word. And when we are deprived of this marvelous sense of hearing we are afflicted indeed, and feel ourselves isolated from our fellow men.

These small quiverings or tremors in bodies or in the air we call *vibration,* which may be broadly defined as any form of to-and-fro movement.

Sound is a sensation produced by vibration. More specifically, it is the sensation experienced when vibrating air particles touch our eardrums. Naturally, therefore, three things are needed to produce sounds: (1) an instrument to produce vibrations; (2) a medium (usually, though not necessarily, the air) which conveys these vibrations away from the source to the receiver; and (3) a receiving instrument, the ear, which transforms these vibrations into a sensation called sound. However, the term *sound* is frequently not limited to the sensation heard, but is loosely extended to include the atmospheric quivering responsible for it, or even the vibration of the sounding body itself, whether there is anyone present to hear it or not.

Acoustics (the word is from a Greek verb signifying "to hear") is the science or physics of auditory vibrations—that is, of those vibrations which can be heard by the human ear. It is therefore the study of the physical basis of music. Helmholtz, a German physician who became interested in the physiology of the eye and ear and in the whole field of sound; Koenig, a scientist and instrument maker in Paris; and Lord Rayleigh, an English mathematician and physicist, contributed much to the early modern development of acoustics in its musical aspects. Many other names need to be added to this list in more recent times.

I

Preliminary Survey of the Nature of Vibration, and Its Relationship to Music

---

Elasticity and Momentum

THE principles which underlie all vibration, and therefore all sound, musical and otherwise, are: (1) the tendency of a body to return toward its rest position if it be displaced therefrom, and (2) its tendency to overshoot the rest position, becoming displaced in the other direction. Usually these are called *elasticity* and *momentum*. Thus, if a diving-board be pulled downward by someone below it, its inherent elasticity tends to pull it back upward toward its normal position of rest. If released, it will fly upward, and once in motion, its momentum carries it *past* the rest point, and causes it to be displaced above the rest point. Because of this, its elasticity again tends to restore it, and it bends downward again but again overshoots the rest point, and so on, so that it remains in a state of to-and-fro movement, or vibration, until frictional forces bring it finally to rest. Another illustration is that of a swinging pendulum, where the restoring force is the force of gravity. The pendulum falls for the first half of each swing, but overshoots and climbs on the other half.

In bodies which vibrate fast enough to produce sound, the action is similar, although the actual motion is often too rapid, as well as too small, to be seen by the naked eye. For example,

3

the prongs of a sounding tuning fork may be moving back and forth only a thousandth of an inch, but very rapidly. Even though the movement is so small as to be practically invisible, if some tiny object suspended on a string be allowed to touch one prong, it will be bounced violently away, and if the fingers touch the prongs very lightly, the tickling sensation indicates that motion is present.

Simple Harmonic Motion

The simplest possible type of vibration which a body may have is known as *simple harmonic motion,* abbreviated to *S.H.M.* It is approximately illustrated by a swinging pendulum. Insofar as the pendulum-bob departs from a straight-line motion (that is, swings in a curved arc), does it depart from true S.H.M. Simple harmonic motion has been described by Miller,[1] as follows: "It takes place in a straight line; it is vibratory, moving to and fro; it is periodic, repeating its movements regularly; there are instants of rest at the two extremes of the movement; starting from rest at one extreme the movement quickens till it reaches its central point, after which it slackens in reverse order, till it comes to rest at the other extreme." To this should be added the statement that the restoring force is always proportional to the displacement from the rest position.

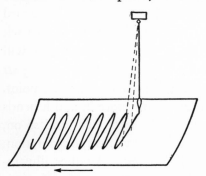

Fig. 1—Recording of sine curve from pendular vibration.

If a pendulum is set swinging, its motion can be graphed (recorded for the eye) by causing it to record in some way on a surface moving at right angles to the direction of vibration, as shown in Figure 1, where the recording surface is moving to the left.

[1] Miller, Dayton C., *The Science of Musical Sounds,* page 6. New York: The Macmillan Company, 1916.

The result is a curve, regular and symmetrical, and this graph of S.H.M. is called a *sine curve*. If some vibrating body should vibrate in S.H.M. at a rate rapid enough to produce sound, the result would be a simple or "pure" tone. Probably no instrument produces a tone that could be called absolutely pure (produced by an absolutely true S.H.M.), since, as we shall see, material bodies persist in vibrating in several ways at once. However, the following tones are quite near this ideal, and are therefore called simple or pure tones: tuning fork tones (especially when aided by a resonating box), falsetto "oo," and the tone produced by blowing against the edge of a bottle.

Natural Period

Every material body which can vibrate has a time of vibration most natural to it, dependent on such factors as its size, its weight, the elastic forces that it is under, and its distance from points of support. Thus, for example, the long pendulum of a large clock takes longer to complete a vibration than a short one in a small clock. This time is called the *natural period,* and is the length of time required to complete one to-and-fro movement.

Frequency and Pitch

Naturally, a body having a short natural period can complete a greater number of vibrations in a second of time than one with a long natural period. Thus bodies having short natural periods vibrate with higher frequencies, *frequency* being defined as *the number of cycles per second,* meaning the number of complete vibrations to-and-fro per second. Bodies vibrating very slowly do not produce the sensation of sound, but when their frequency reaches about 20 or more per second, we begin to hear a very low sound, and as the frequency continues to rise we hear sounds of higher and higher pitch, until finally at a point roughly around 20,000 vibrations per second we cease to hear sound. Such vibrations are literally producing tones too high for us to hear, although other forms of life may be able to hear them.

Some insects appear to employ frequencies even as high as or higher than 50,000 per second. "Violin A" is produced by a vibration occurring at the frequency of 440 per second, "Middle C" by a frequency of 261.6.[2]

Since the period is the time required for one complete vibration, the period of the vibration producing Violin A is 1/440th of a second, that of Middle C approximately 1/262nd of a second. In other words, the period is the *reciprocal* of the frequency.

It is clear therefore that *frequency* and *pitch* are closely related. The first is a physical term, the second a psychological one. The E-string on a violin vibrates with a greater frequency than the G-string, producing a higher pitch in the mind of the hearer. The vocal cords of a soprano vibrate with greater frequency than those of a bass, producing a higher pitch. No matter in what way we produce vibrations, provided only that they are fairly regular, and that the number of them in a second of time is roughly between 20 and 20,000, the ear hears a tone, whose pitch depends on how many vibrations there are in a second.

This fact—that *pitch depends on frequency*—may be made very evident by the simple experiment of passing the fingernail or the edge of a card across the teeth of a comb or the ridges in the cover of a book. If done slowly enough, each individual tooth or ridge may be heard. If done a little faster, a tone of low pitch will result. If the speed (and therefore the frequency) were exactly doubled, the pitch would rise precisely an octave. If flicked very quickly, a high-pitched squeak would result. Many other illustrations will suggest themselves; for example:

---

[2] It is of course understood that the frequency is a *rate*. Thus, if 220 vibrations occur in a half-second, we shall hear the pitch of Violin A, but lasting only a half-second.   Violin A has not always been at this rate of frequency. In Paris at the time of Mersenne it was as low as 374 per second. At other times and places it has been at various points, sometimes as high as 500 and more.   In the time of Bach and Handel it was around 422. At one time secular music was played at "chamber pitches" considerably higher, sometimes several semitones higher, than "church pitches."   There seems to be a tendency for the pitch standard to rise, in order to secure greater brilliancy, until it becomes so high that it must be brought down again, whence it starts to rise again.

the effect of phonograph speed on pitch, or the rise in pitch of the hum of a siren or an electric fan when turned on, which is caused by the increasing frequency of the impulses given off to the air by the fan blades. If something moves 262 times a second, one will hear Middle C. Conversely, whenever one hears Middle C, unless it be one of the "subjective tones" to be considered later, it is quite certain that some material body somewhere is vibrating about 262 times a second. The fundamental pitches produced by musical instruments lie mostly between 40 and 4000 cycles in frequency, although, as we shall see later, the "overtones" may be above 4000, in fact up as high as the limit of audibility, around 20,000.

Amplitude and Loudness

It should be clear, furthermore, that the *amplitude* of vibration (the distance through which the body moves for each to-and-fro movement) is related in a similar way to the *loudness*. The first is again a physical fact, the second a psychological sensation. The wider a piano string is caused to move during its vibration (through a heavier blow by the hammer), the "louder" is its sound perceived in the mind of the hearer. The wider a clarinet reed is caused to vibrate, the louder its soun´ will be. Many other illustrations will suggest themselves.

Harmonic Series, Partials, Overtones

If a long rope be stretched between two supports, and then slowly jiggled at one end, it can be made to swing up and down in the manner shown in Figure 2a. If the speed of jiggling be then doubled, it will take the form shown in 2b. An apparent point of rest will appear in the middle, and the string will appear to be divided into two vibrating parts, called segments. If the speed of jiggling be tripled, as in 2c, three segments will occur, with two points of rest. These points of rest are called *nodes,* and the moving portions *loops.* This process can be continued.

It indicates that bodies may vibrate as a whole, or in a certain number of parts, all of which vibrate at a faster rate. In the case of a long rope the vibrations are all too slow to produce sound. However, the stretched strings of a violin, piano, or other stringed instrument can divide up in this same manner. And, as we shall see later, the air columns which form the vibrating members of all wind instruments divide up in a similar

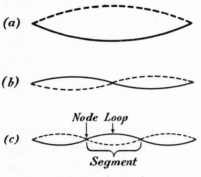

Fig. 2—Vibration forms of a rope.

way to produce segments vibrating at higher frequencies.

If a vibrating body, such as a stretched string, vibrates as a whole, in S.H.M., the tone it produces is called its *fundamental,* or *first partial.* If it vibrates in two parts or segments, as when a string player lightly touches the string at its midpoint, the vibrating length is only half as long as in the original, and thus it vibrates twice as fast. It is as if each half of the string were vibrating by itself in S.H.M., and at twice the former frequency. The tone produced in this case is the octave, or *second partial.* If it vibrates in three segments, the vibrating length is only one third as long as in the original, and the frequency is therefore tripled. The tone produced in this case is the perfect twelfth, and is called the *third partial.* If it vibrates in four segments, the double octave is produced. If in five, the tone two octaves and a major third above the original is produced, and so on. These partial tones make up a *harmonic series,* as it is called. The tones above the fundamental are sometimes called *harmonic overtones,* or *harmonics.* Naturally, however, since the fundamental is called the *first* partial, the first *overtone* will be the *second* partial, the second overtone the *third* partial, and so on.

The first sixteen partials of the harmonic series constructed on C_{16} (C two octaves below Middle C),[3] are as follows, although the harmonic series does not end with the sixteenth partial. Theoretically it may continue indefinitely, even beyond the limits of hearing, its members usually growing weaker and weaker, the higher they are. The tones in brackets are only approximate in pitch, number 7, for example, lying between A_{49} and Bb_{50} of the piano, and number 11 lying between F_{57} and $F\#_{58}$:

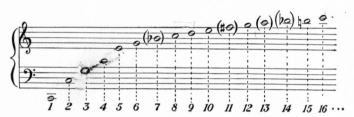

Fig. 3—Harmonic series on C.

Without changing the length of the tube, the player of such an instrument as the trombone, by changes of breath pressure and lip and tongue position alone, can produce seven or eight of the tones of a single harmonic series. And by changing the tube length he can vary the fundamental and thereby secure other harmonic series. Other instruments can produce even more than eight. In fact, number 16 of the series is possible on a French horn.

The harmonic series gives us the ratios of the frequencies of the various intervals. The ratio of the octave is 1:2—in other words, the upper tone of an octave always doubles the frequency of the lower tone. Thus we see in Figure 3 that the five C's are represented by the numbers 1-2-4-8-16, the G's by the numbers 3-6-12, the E's by 5-10, and so on. Similarly, the ratio of the major third is 4:5, that of the major second 8:9, that of the major

---

[3] In accordance with standard acoustical terminology, the tones of the piano keyboard are indicated by their respective letter names followed by a subscript number indicating the number of the particular tone, counting upwards from the lowest A. Thus the lowest A would be A_1, Middle C would be written C_{40}, and the highest tone of the keyboard, C_{88}. This scheme has been used in this chapter, but it has not been found practical to maintain it throughout the remainder of the book.

sixth 3:5, and so on. These matters will be considered in greater detail in Chapter 4.

Complex Vibration

Mills has given us the illustration of a canary swinging on its perch in a cage which is being swung back and forth by a man who is walking back and forth from one end to the other of a car in a shuttle train running back and forth between Times Square and Grand Central Station. Obviously, the motion of the bird is the complex resultant of at least four different motions. Although it is difficult to realize how it takes place, a sounding body may also vibrate in two or more different forms *at the same time.* Thus, the single soundboard of the piano responds (vibrates) to two or more tones played simultaneously. A single phonograph needle can transmit from the record to the reproducing apparatus all the sounds of an orchestra at the same time. And for that matter, the mere fact that we hear many different tones at one time proves that our eardrums must be able to vibrate in many different ways at the same time. Practically every instrument used in music produces a tone which is the result of a complex vibration caused by a body vibrating not simply in its fundamental form, but also, at the same time, in its two-segment form, its three-segment form, and so on. Simple harmonic motion is so rare in the actual world of music as to be practically nonexistent. Because of this fact—that bodies may vibrate, and usually do vibrate, at the same time as a whole and also in parts (complex vibration)—many or all of the tones in the harmonic series belonging to a certain fundamental may be made to sound simultaneously by setting the body into vibration. It is hard for us to imagine how a single piano string, for example, can vibrate simultaneously in a whole series of more or less interfering forms, producing a whole series of "thoroughly mixed" harmonic partials. And yet careful attention to its sound will reveal the presence of one after the other of these partials, particularly if the finger be placed at a point on the wire which would be a *node,* or point of rest, for the tone being listened for. The fact that the upper partials are already present in the total complex tone is demonstrated by the fact that they may be elicited by placing the finger on a node *after* the string has been struck. The tone immediately "jumps" to the corresponding harmonic.

If the key for the lowest tone of the series: , be depressed silently on the piano and held down, and the fourth, fifth, and sixth partials, forming the triad: , be struck sharply and then released, these same three tones will be heard to sound from the low fundamental string, which has been made to subdivide through "sympathetic resonance" so as to produce these tones as partials. As soon as the low C key is released, the chord ceases to sound. The experiment will not work if the key on either side of C is held down, since these tones would not correspond in frequency to the fundamental of the tones in the C major triad.

Inharmonics

Many vibrating bodies have upper partials whose frequencies are not an integer number (whole number) of times the frequency of the fundamental, and which therefore do not coincide with the partials of the harmonic series. For example, if an upper partial has a frequency greater than five times the fundamental frequency but less than six times, it would fall somewhere between the fifth and sixth harmonic partials, and would be called an *inharmonic partial,* or *inharmonic.* These give a characteristic, more or less unmusical, quality to tones. A good example is the jarring, clanging tone when a cymbal is struck, or the initial high ringing sound when a tuning fork is struck by metal. These will be discussed in Chapter 3, section C.

Vibration Form and Tone Quality

Tones produced by musical instruments vary in three ways. They may differ in pitch, in loudness, or in tone quality. We have already seen that pitch depends on frequency, and loudness on amplitude of vibration. Tone quality depends largely on the *degree of complexity* of the vibration. In other words, differences in tone quality result from the number of partials present, and their relative intensities to each other. For example, a tone produced by a harmonic series with a strong fundamental and weak overtones will have a different quality than one produced by a weak fundamental with strong third and fourth partials, or any other of countless combinations. It is this attribute of tones that makes it possible to distinguish the sound of two different instruments, even though they are playing the same pitch at the same loudness. Generally speaking, an oboe tone contains a larger number of overtones than a violin tone, which itself contains a larger number than a flute. And what is more, the particular relationship of the *relative strengths* of the overtones, in other words the *vibration form,* is fairly characteristic of various instruments.

Since the possibilities for variation in the vibration form are practically infinite, especially when a large series of partials, harmonic and inharmonic, are available, the possibilities for various kinds of tone qualities are also infinite. Many possible tone qualities have not yet been used. New ones are being discovered through new instruments which synthesize tones by electrical means. Our present orchestral instruments, with the single exception of the flute, have not been subjected to the rigorous scientific development which Theobald Böhm expended on that instrument. Like Topsy, they just grew, our ability to perform on them running far ahead of our understanding of the physics or physiology of their operation. The composer of the present day and of the future, however, will have many more tone colors at his disposal than the composer of the past, although it may take considerable time to outgrow prejudices based on "classical tradition."

It should be clear that the type of vibration of the fundamental, or of any other *single* partial of a complex vibration, is *simple harmonic motion*. It is only when two or more simple forms exist together that we have complex vibration. An instructive experiment may be performed with a set of ten or more tuning forks, mounted on resonator boxes, and comprising a fundamental tone and its harmonic partials. If the fundamental be sounded alone, a sweet but dull sound will result. Then if one after the other of the partials are added, the tone will become more and more full, rich, sonorous, and "living." And yet the blending is so perfect that we do not realize there is more than one source sounding. If the forks are then silenced one by one from the highest downward, the tone becomes less rich and finally, when the fundamental alone is left, the tone is again dull and uninteresting. Thus a *pure* tone is frequently a *poor* tone for the purposes of music, unless used in combination with other tones. We demand a certain amount of the "brightness" produced by overtones. In the pipe organ, whose tones on the whole are deficient in upper partials, "mixture stops" are used, which for every key depressed will cause *several* pipes to sound, tuned to certain of the harmonic partials of the tone. The same effect is occasionally used by orchestral composers, who call for the doubling of melody tones, frequently by softer instruments, at such intervals as perfect twelfths, major tenths and seventeenths, and so on, not primarily as chords per se, but for enriching the timbre of fundamentals. The familiar *Bolero* of Ravel is one example.

All of this indicates that the upper partials, though difficult to "pick out" of a complex tone as partials, are nevertheless heard by the ear in the composite effect of the tone, and are the cause of the infinite number of possible variations in timbre. The more upper partials present, or the stronger they are, the more the tone quality becomes rich, brilliant, cutting, or even strident.

Such complex tones "cut through" an orchestral or choral mass better than simple tones. This is why an organist will add brighter stops if his choir is flatting. Complex tones with many strong overtones tend to be heard as higher. Sometimes musicians even make a mistake of an octave in judging their pitch. The tones produced by whistling (which are fairly pure) are often judged to be one or two octaves below their true pitch.

A good illustration of the fact that tone quality depends on the number and the relative strengths of the overtones is to be found in the way that a piano soundboard can imitate different instruments. If the dampers be lifted, and a clarinet, for example, blown strongly toward the soundboard, the sympathetic resonance of the strings, resounding to whatever partials are present in the clarinet tone, will "re-echo" a sound which, though weaker, will be similar in color. A strongly sung "ah" or "ee" will return a similar vowel, in the same manner. Even a cough will cause a response, though the initial explosive part of the imitation is masked by the original sound.

Tone quality differs not only among instruments, but varies also on any one instrument with changes in loudness and pitch, often changing markedly with changes of only two or three tones in pitch. Speaking genèrally, the louder the tone the more complex it is; and the lower the tone the more complex it is. In the lowest range of the piano, the tones are largely carried by the harmonics, the fundamental becoming very weak.

Certain types of tone quality are sometimes described by adjectives from other sense departments, such as "white," "dark" (from sight); "rough," "smooth" (from touch); "sour," "mellow" (from taste); and so on. Analogies with various simple and complex sensations are seen in such words as "thin," "dry," "liquid," "covered," "open," "metallic," "pinched," "pushed," and so on, when applied to tones.

Too great a complexity (especially if caused by inharmonic partials), or too great an irregularity of vibration form from wave to wave, produces noise. Thus, in the case of a gong or other percussion instrument, the complex vibrations have no constant form but are continually changing, since the different modes of vibration are *inharmonic,* their frequencies bearing no simple numerical relation to each other. Such a complex thing as traffic noise shows vibrations of even greater wave-to-wave irregularity, usually so great, in fact, that no periodicity can be seen. Naturally, there is no clear line of demarcation between musical tone and noise. The quality of even a musical tone must be considered usually as a complex of both harmonic and inharmonic components, if we include the noises of tone production on the various instruments, such as the thud of the piano hammer, the embouchure hiss in wind instruments, the scraping of the bow in stringed instruments, and so on. (See Chapter 3.)

A rough classification of sounds in terms of increasing complexity is as follows. The classes of course have no sharp dividing lines, but merge into each other:

Relatively simple. . . ("Hooty," smooth, dark, dull at low pitches)	Tuning forks Falsetto "oo" Blown bottles Wide, stopped, organ flue-pipes Female and boy soprano voices Flutes
Moderate complexities. . . (Richer, normally most pleasant)	Female mezzo or alto voices Open organ flue-pipes Soft horns Soft male voices Pianos Strings
Greater complexities. . . (Rich, bright, brilliant, cutting, blaring, or even strident)	Wood-winds except flutes Organ reed-pipes Loud male voices Loud brass Chimes and bells Ensembles Noise

Harmonic and Formant Theories of Tone Quality

There are two theories of tone quality, both of which are necessary to explain the tone qualities of musical instruments.

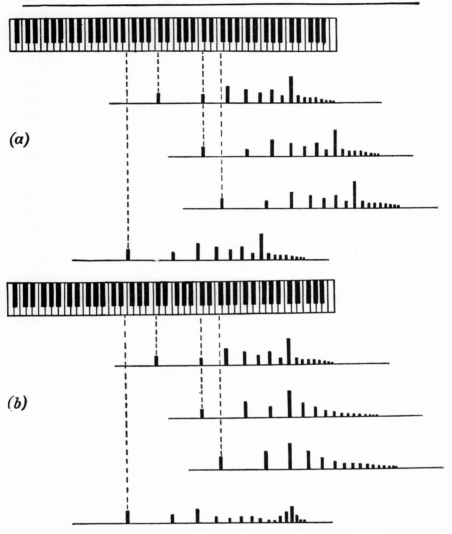

Fig. 4—Harmonic and formant theories of tone quality.

Neither one tells the whole story alone. The *harmonic theory* states that the characteristic tone quality of an instrument is due entirely to the relationship among fundamental and upper partials, which relationship is supposed to remain unchanged no matter what the fundamental is. Thus, if an instrument produces for, say, Middle C, the first "spectrum" shown in Figure 4a, where the vertical lines represent the relative strengths of the first sixteen partials (fundamental plus fifteen overtones), the harmonic theory would require it to produce exactly that same spectrum on any other tone taken as fundamental, as shown for example on the three tones, C_{52}, F_{57}, and E_{32}, respectively.

The *formant theory* states that the characteristic tone quality of an instrument is due to the relative strengthening of whatever partial lies within a *fixed or relatively fixed region* of the musical scale. This region is called a *formant* of the tone. Thus, in the spectrum on Middle C, it will be noticed that the eighth partial is quite prominent, corresponding to a frequency of 2093 cycles. This region could be a "formant region" of the tone, and then the formant theory would require whatever partial comes nearest to this region to be strengthened. It is obvious that this will change the appearance of the spectrum. Thus in Figure 4b, when the fundamental is an octave above Middle C, it is not the eighth partial but the *fourth* that is strong. Similarly, when the fundamental is raised again, to F_{57}, it is the *third* partial that is strong. When the fundamental is lowered to E_{32}, the nearest partials to the formant region are the twelfth, thirteenth, and fourteenth, and they are all strengthened.

The difference between the theories may easily be seen if one notices that any particular partial, the fourth, for example, has the same strength in each spectrum of Figure 4a, but usually varies markedly in the spectra of Figure 4b. Thus, according to the harmonic theory, if the instrument plays a different pitch, the vibration form will still be similar, since, although the particular harmonic series will be shifted, its members will still retain the same intensity relation to each other. But according to the formant theory, whatever partial lies within or close to the *formant range* will be strengthened. If the pitch of the fundamental changes, so that some other partial comes into the formant range, this other partial will be strengthened. Thus, although the formant range is fixed, the vibration form will change as the fundamental changes.

As an additional illustration of the formant theory, we may consider the previously described series of tuning forks, tuned to a harmonic series, representing a complex tone with partials. If all of the forks are caused to vibrate at a uniform loudness, and the series be brought close to an air column tuned to the frequency of one of the forks, the tone sounded by this fork will be picked out by resonance, and strengthened over all the others. The tone quality of the mixture will of course be changed. In a series of forks based on another fundamental, it would be another partial which would be reinforced.

The strengthening in the formant range usually occurs through resonance of a certain part of the instrument, or of an enclosed body of air in the instrument, either of which has a natural period at the formant range. Thus it will be seen that the formant need not be at a harmonic point. Under certain circumstances, a resonant part of the instrument or an enclosed body of air, even though inharmonic to the fundamental, may be set into vibration at its own natural frequency.

It is of course true that the tone quality is affected not only by the range of the formant, but by the relative intensity within that range, compared with the intensity of the fundamental and other partials.

The formant theory was first applied in the explanation of vowel differences. Fletcher, generalizing from the work of several investigators, has reported that two concentrations of overtone energy, around points near to 400 and 800 vibrations per second, respectively, will color a fundamental with the sound of the vowel-quality "oo." This will take place regardless of whether the formants are produced by harmonic or inharmonic sources, and regardless of the fundamental pitch, so long as it is not higher than 400, of course. Other pairs of formants produce other vowels. When we whisper "ee-ah-aw-oh-oo" we hear a lowering of a formant pitch. According to Hermann-Goldap, the oboe, in the fundamental range from F_{45} to F_{57}, shows the presence of a formant in the region from $G\sharp_{72}$ to $B\flat_{74}$, due to some peculiarity of its construction. It is thought that the quality of the fine old Italian violins may be due in part to formants at certain frequency regions. Recent work at the Peabody Conservatory has shown that the fine male voice, particularly in good tone production, has among others a strong formant in the region of around 2600 to 3100 vibrations per second, probably caused by the resonating of the laryngeal chamber in a certain way.

The formant theory can explain the fact that the quality of an instrument tends to simplify as the fundamental pitch rises, because, when the fundamental reaches any formant pitch, that formant drops out of the complex tone, leaving it that much simpler. As has been said, however, both the harmonic and the formant theories, and indeed other considerations as well, such as the duration of the tone, the vibrato, and the effects of pitch and loudness changes in most instruments, are necessary to explain the manifold differences between tone qualities, differences so great that they go a long way in themselves toward giving music its manifold power of emotional expression.

Tonal Attributes Summarized

Thus all vibrations have the three physical attributes: *frequency, amplitude,* and *vibration form,* which give rise in the mind of the hearer to the three psychological attributes, or *tonal attributes,* as they are called: *pitch, loudness,* and *tone quality.* The correspondences between these sets of phenomena are listed in the table on page 20.

Clear distinctions must always be drawn between the physical terms and their psychological counterparts. Physical phenomena can be accurately measured, at least in theory; psychological phenomena, being but sensations in the brain, are not subject to physical laws, can be only very roughly measured, if at all, and often vary in very complex ways as the physical stimuli are varied in simple manner. For example, we say that loudness depends

PSYCHOLOGICAL TERMS (Sensations)	PHYSICAL TERMS
1. Pitch *depends on*	fundamental or predominating frequency.
High tones [4] *caused by*	high frequencies. Usually produced by small bodies.
Low tones *caused by*	low frequencies. Usually produced by large bodies.
2. Loudness *depends on*	amplitude, or physical "intensity."
Loud tones *caused by*	vibrations of considerable force and extent.
Soft tones *caused by*	vibrations of small force and extent.
3. Tone quality *depends on*	vibration form (the number of overtones and the way the energy is distributed among them).
Musical tones *caused by*	relatively regular and periodic vibration.
Pure tones *caused by*	simple vibration form.
Richer tones *caused by*	more complex vibration forms.
Brilliant tones *caused by*	very complex vibration forms.
Noise *caused by*	relatively irregular and nonperiodic vibration, often with inharmonic overtones present.

on amplitude. However, the way that it varies as the amplitude changes is not in a simple proportion. Similarly, we say that pitch depends on frequency, but recent experimental work in various laboratories indicates that this classical definition must now be modified. The psychological experience—pitch—does not vary directly with frequency except in the mid-range of hearing. At the upper extreme, frequencies must be *more* than

---

[4] The word *tone* is correctly limited here to mean a sound of definite pitch. The word *note,* often used for this same meaning, is usually limited in this book to its proper meaning, of the printed symbol on the staff.

doubled to produce a rise of an octave, and at the lower extreme *less* than halved to produce a drop of an octave. These effects increase the nearer the frequencies are to the limits of hearing, and vary with individuals. This is a reason why piano tuners often sharp the upper tones and flat the lower ones. Furthermore, pitch is somewhat influenced also by the other physical attributes, intensity and vibration form. For example, Fletcher has found that if a pure tone at, say, 200 cycles is greatly increased in strength, it will no longer appear to have the same pitch. A tone of 200 cycles at an intensity level of 40 units sounded the same pitch as a tone of 222 at 100 units. A tone of 400 at 40 units gave the same pitch as one of 421 at 100 units. The 200 and the 400, at 40 units, sound an octave, both successively and simultaneously. The tones of 222 and 421, at 100 units, are judged an octave apart when sounded successively, but do not blend into a consonant interval when sounded together at this intensity. It has been reported that at a loudness level of 120 units, if a pure tone with a frequency of 200 increases its frequency to 400, its *perceived* pitch increases from 158 to 368, a change of considerably more than an octave.

Pitch is also influenced by the relative speed of source and listener, as is discussed on pages 82 and 83.

Furthermore, the other sensations, loudness and tone quality, are not dependent just on the intensity and the vibration form, respectively, but each one is influenced by all three of the physical variables, as has been described by Fletcher, as well as by the characteristics of their cyclic variation with time in the case of vibrato effects. The dependence of tone quality on other elements than the vibration form has also been discussed by Ortmann. Even the apparent duration of sounds is found by Lifshitz to vary with their loudness.

Vibrato

This other determinant of tone quality must now be mentioned, and it is one whose important influence is seldom fully realized. In the human voice, under conditions of good usage, and increasing slightly with the emotional content of the passage, there appears an involuntary effect called the *vibrato*. It is a periodic and fairly even variation of the tone, occurring normally about six or seven times a second, and usually involving the

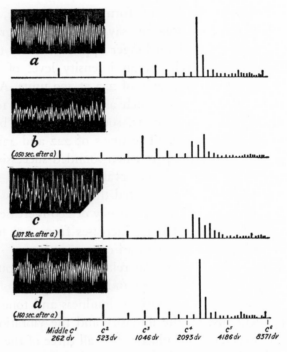

Fig. 5—Four instants during one cycle of a voice vibrato.

frequency, the amplitude, and the vibration form. In other words, these three attributes go through a cycle of variation six or seven times a second. The frequency may vary as much as through a band a semitone wide, and at times more, while the amplitude of the vibration may vary quite appreciably. The vibration form may vary to an astonishing degree. For example, Figure 5 shows the analyses at four different instants during one vibrato cycle in a good-quality baritone voice, singing "ah" loudly on Middle C. (The small graphs at the left are the actual wave forms recorded by an oscillograph, and will be more fully described in the next chapter.) The change in harmonic content is very evident in the spectra. It is seen in this case to consist largely of an interchange of energy between the region above 2093 and the region below 2093. At *d*, one cycle has been completed, and the vibration form has returned to the same form as at *a*, to begin the next cycle. As a matter of fact, the images on the two parts of the original film at *a* and *d* can be superposed quite closely, so that when one looks through the two thicknesses of film there seems to be but one wave image. For this reason the wave at *d* has not been given a separate harmonic analysis, the spectrum here being a copy of that at *a*. The complete cycle from which these instants have been selected took a little less than one sixth of a second, and similar variations take place in all fine voices, the cycles repeating themselves regularly at this same speed of between six and seven a second, on an average.

However, the amount of variation that tones undergo during the vibrato cycle is not at all sensed by the ear, probably because of their rapid alternations back and forth through the central point from twelve to fourteen times a second. Particularly are the amounts of pitch change and tone quality change unsuspected or denied, even by musicians, although both are pronounced enough to be heard easily if the tones did not vary so fast. The loudness change may appear more marked than it is, however. The proof of these statements is easily demonstrated by slowing down any phonograph record of a fine singer to about half-speed. The pitch will of course drop an octave, but the elements of the vibrato will be made very prominent. These variations, when again brought up to their normal rapidity by playing the record at normal speed, are no longer heard in themselves. However, they impart to the total complex tone a certain "liveness" or richness, which we are inclined to attribute to overtones unless we learn to direct attention to its true source. Some single intermediate pitch is "heard," but with an added richness.[5]

The importance of an even vibrato to the satisfying quality of a voice appears to be considerably greater than formerly realized. Tone qualities which are quite disagreeable when sustained without a perceptible, even, vibrato can be made passable if given artificially a proper amount of an even variation at proper vibrato speed. And, according to Kock, tones which without a vibrato are slightly off-pitch to an accompaniment, can be heard as correct if given a pitch vibrato which includes the correct pitch, because of the ear's ability to accent subjectively whatever pitch it concentrates on.

The fact that the true voice vibrato is rarely under even partial conscious control, and often is completely involuntary, indicates that its frequency, usually from six to seven or slightly more per second, is determined by some natural physiological cause, such as a neural or a muscular period of some sort. Westerman has given a good explanation of the physiology involved. Whatever the cause, the vibrato has the effect of resting the voice mechanism by changing the "set." Its intimate connection with the nervous system is shown by its reflection of

---

[5] It can be proven mathematically that the variation of a tone in intensity or in pitch actually introduces physically a series of other tones on either side of the central pitch. These, although not overtones, give a factual basis to the experience of "added richness." The ear hears only the central pitch, however.

In the case of simultaneous and sustained pitches from various sources, the ear possesses a similar ability. If two tones of almost the same frequency and amplitude sound together we know the ear hears a central pitch with beats. (See Chapter 2.) And if a number of tones of nearly the same frequency and amplitude are sounding together, the resulting tone will be judged by the ear as having a pitch which is an approximate mean of the two extremes. The hum of a swarm of bees is an illustration. As the number of sources increases, the beating between the various tones becomes very complex. Thus, whereas only one beat tone is present with two sources, with three sources three are possible, with four sources six, with five ten, and so on. The result is a multitudinous beating which no longer is objectionable or even audible as a beating. The peculiar charm of a large pipe organ ensemble is partly due to this "pitch fringe." The same is true of a large orchestra. The ear hears the central pitch, but with considerably more satisfaction than when nothing is present save one dead-level frequency. Choirs and orchestras owe much to this ability of the ear, because of the physical impossibility of ten or fifteen individuals performing exactly in unison, even if no vibratos were used, and even if there were no differences of opinion as to the proper intonation of all of the tones of the passage.

emotional intensity by variations of different sorts, and, according to Professor Scripture, by the singular fact of its complete absence in the speech of epileptics.

Many performers and builders of other instruments have devised means of producing or imitating with varying success the vibrato effect. The vibrato on string instruments is a good example. Another example is the organ *tremulant* stop, which, however, produces primarily a variation of the loudness of the tone rather than of its pitch. With regard to this type of vibrato there is some evidence that its ideal speed is slower than in the case of the type of vibrato which involves pitch. Thus, on the pipe organ, tremulant speeds are frequently lower than six, or even than five per second, while the beating speed of *celestes,* also primarily an intensity vibrato (see page 60), may be as low as even two per second. Sometimes celestes are arranged to beat, for instance, at three per second in the lower range, and to increase to six in the top octave. The ponderousness of the instrument, its "tradition," the large reverberation of cathedrals, and the particular quality of the tones used for celestes, all may have an influence in lowering in this way the ideal vibrato speed. However, in the vibrato as found in a well-produced voice, must be found the primary aesthetic appeal of vibratos in all other instruments. The human voice far antedates all other instruments, and far surpasses them in flexibility and variety of tone quality and emotional portrayal. We find more pleasure in a violin tone with vibrato than in one without. Does not the reason for this lie in the fact that the string vibrato is a more or less satisfactory imitation of the vibrato in the voice, to which humanity has for ages reacted pleasantly? And the reason the voice with a proper vibrato was much easier to listen to through all the centuries than the one without was because it was a better produced voice, and aroused no sympathetic strain on our throats or our ears as we listened. Thus was the aesthetic value of the vibrato first established, and when we now hear a tone, instrumental or vocal, with a free, even, vibrato, we feel that it is produced in a free and "relaxed" manner. The time seems almost to have come when instrumentalists who are unable to produce a satisfactory vibrato on their instrument, either intentionally or unconsciously, even including all of the wind instruments as well as the strings, will not be considered to have technical mastery of their instruments. Possibly devices will be invented, or teaching methods improved, so as to make more easy the production of this most important aspect of good quality.

The vocal *tremolo* [6] is not unrelated to the vibrato, but is caused by incoordinated muscular tension, and expresses itself as an inartistic extreme of one or more of the three variables, or by a departure from the evenness of their variation. Also, it is often faster than seven per second. Professor Seashore has suggested that we scrap the term *tremolo,* since it has so many varied meanings, and use instead only the generic term *vibrato,* defining in specific terms the particular type of fault which makes the vibrato objectionable.[7]

---

[6] This is not to be confused with the use of the term *tremolo* in string instruments, where it implies a rapid alternation of up-bow and down-bow strokes, resulting in little if any change in pitch, but principally a series of changes in loudness, since at the instant of changing the direction of the bow little or no sound is being produced.

[7] Considerable work has been done on various aspects of the voice vibrato by Seashore and his associates at the University of Iowa, and by Stanley and other investigators. The violin vibrato has been investigated by Cheslock at the Peabody Conservatory of Music.

2

Sound Waves and Their Characteristics

Resonance

WITH this preliminary survey of the relationships between vibrations and music in mind, let us return to a more detailed consideration of the nature and effects of vibration, beginning with the phenomena of resonance, and leading from this into the characteristics of wave motion. A vibrating body can set another body into "sympathetic vibration" provided it has the same, or nearly the same, frequency as the second body, or provided it has an overtone partial of the same or nearly the same frequency. We have all noticed this in the way a vase or other object will rattle when a certain tone is produced. This phenomenon is called *free resonance,* or simply *resonance.* Thus a flute may be made to sound softly without blowing it if a vibrating tuning fork is held close to its opening while at the same time the fork tone is fingered on the flute. If another pitch is fingered, the effect is absent. When the natural periods are quite accurately in tune with each other, a very marked vibration may be set up in the second body, because, though each individual vibration of the first body possesses only a very small amount of energy, each one of them is timed exactly right to continue and increase the amplitude of the second body. This principle is illustrated in the way that two children may set a heavy swing into considerable motion by standing facing each other, on either side of the swing, and properly timing their pushes.

The same principle is responsible for the fact that troops are ordered to break step when crossing a bridge, to prevent vibration and possible breaking of the bridge if its natural frequency coincided with that of the regular tread of marching. Similarly, in electrical or mechanical machinery, "critical" or "resonant" speeds may induce large forces which if unbalanced may cause serious damage to the machinery. Two pianos in tune with each other may softly "play each other" if the dampers are lifted. The air waves from one tuning fork may set another of exactly the same pitch into vibration, even at some distance away, if mounted on resonator boxes. The effect can even be secured with an obstacle between the forks, since sound waves bend around obstacles. This becomes more striking when we remember that steel is some six thousand times as heavy as air. However, it must be remembered that resonance does not create new energy. The first tuning fork will expend its energy much faster in the presence of a resonator such as a resonance box or a second fork, so that the louder the resonant sound is, the shorter the time it will continue audible.

A vibrating body can also set another body into a certain amount of vibration when the natural periods are different, as when a tuning fork sets a table top into vibration. This is called *forced resonance*, but the broader term *resonance* is loosely applied here also. Many instruments make use of forced resonance, as will be discussed later in the book, under the section on Reinforcement.

Transverse Wave Motion

The way in which resonance can set a body into vibration at a distance from the vibrating source shows us that the vibrations are carried through the air in some way. This, however, can be better understood by performing the experiment of jiggling a little block of wood up and down at a regular rate in a pond. The series of waves generated thereby will travel across the pond, and if they meet a similar block floating on the surface will make it bob up and down at the same frequency as the source. We shall find that many of the properties of sound are made clear by studying the action of water waves. When a stone is dropped into water, it displaces the water immediately under it, as in Figure 6, and starts the first of a short series of ever-widening waves. The number of these waves to pass a given point in a second would be their frequency. The vertical distance from the top of

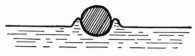

Fig. 6—Formation of circular water wave.

a crest of a wave to the bottom of its trough would be the amplitude of the wave.

Let it be emphasized that the actual motion of the water is not at all the same as its apparent motion. Taylor has described the process: "When we say that the waves advance horizontally, we mean, not that the masses of water of which they at any given instant consist, advance, but that these masses, by virtue of the separate vertical motions of their individual drops, *successively arrange themselves in the same relative positions,* so that the curved shapes of the surface, which we call waves, are transmitted *without their materials sharing in the progress."* If a light chain be held suspended from one hand and a quick motion imparted to it by suddenly moving the hand, a wave may be seen to run down it, but the chain itself has not traveled downward, and will presently become quiet again in its original position. Similarly, in "cracking the whip." Another example is furnished by moving a cane under a tablecloth. A "wave" is seen to travel across the cloth, but it is evident that the particles of the cloth have moved only up and down, as the cane moved under the cloth.

Water waves, although actually very complex, may be regarded for our purposes as examples of *transverse waves,* waves in which the displacement (up and down) is at right angles to the direction the wave is traveling (across the surface of the water).

Longitudinal, or Compressional, Wave Motion

In the case of the air, things are different, because there is no "surface" to the air. It is all around us, in every direction, since we live at the bottom of a sea of air. Let us imagine a tiny bomb no bigger than a pinhead. When it explodes, it pushes back the surrounding air in *every* direction, crowding the air particles together, so that a *sphere* of *compression* is started outwards, followed by a sphere of relative *rarefaction,* where the particles are farther apart than normally. These spheres increase in size in all directions similarly to the manner in which the circular crests and troughs widen in but two dimensions on the surface of the water. The movements of *any* vibrating body give rise to wave motion in a similar way to the explosion of the little bomb. The air particles which are adjacent to the disturbance are pushed into motion first, and these push on more distant particles, and so on. Due to the inertia of air (its "stay-as-it-is-ness"), it is not set into motion as a whole. The particles farther away do not respond as soon as the first ones. Consequently, the air is crowded together or compressed immediately around the source. This compressed condition—followed, of course, by a rarefaction (and by other compressions and rarefactions, caused by repeated vibrations)—advances outward through the elastic atmosphere with a definite speed which may be taken roughly as 1100 feet per second, or 750 miles per hour. The air as a whole does not move, any more than the whole body of water moves when a wave passes through it, but the individual air particles at any point move slightly backward and forward as the compressions and rarefactions pass along through the air. The phenomenon is similar to the way in which a locomotive's push is transmitted through a standing train of loosely coupled cars, or the way in which the individual stalks of grain sway back and forth when a gust of wind sends a wave across a wheat-field, although more difficult to comprehend because the air particles are invisible to our sight. If a hundred boys stand in a row, join hands, and "crack the whip," we have an illustration of transverse wave motion.   But if they stand in a line, each with his hands on the shoulders of the boy in front, and the end boy be given a push, the heads at that end will be pushed closer together, and a "wave" of "closer-together-ness" or compression will travel through the line.   Each head, however, will partake

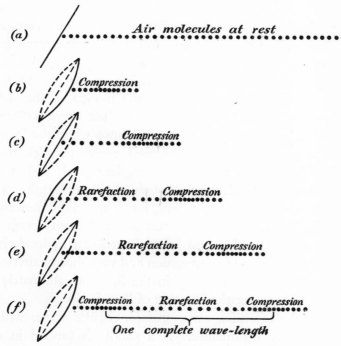

(a) .... Air molecules at rest ....

(b) .Compression

(c) Compression

(d) Rarefaction   Compression

(e) Rarefaction   Compression

(f) Compression   Rarefaction   Compression

One complete wave-length

Fig. 7—Formation of air wave by vibrating string.*

of only a small back and forth movement. If, in Figure 7, we represent the push as produced by a vibrating string, for example, and instead of the line of boys we have a row of air molecules, we have the same phenomenon on a smaller, but more rapid, scale. When the string swings to the right, as in *b* (the amplitude has been magnified in the drawing), the adjoining molecules are pushed together to make a compression, and the

* Adapted by permission from Loomis, A., and Schwartz, H. W., *How Music Is Made.* Elkhart, Ind.: C. G. Conn, Ltd., 1927.

same push which made the compression also starts it traveling through the air, so that eventually all the molecules shown in *a,* and many more not shown, will be pushed together as it travels through them.

When the string swings back again on its return trip through its rest position, as at *c,* and on to the left, as at *d,* it leaves a space into which some of the compressed molecules rush. However, they are few and far apart immediately next to the string, and this region is called a rarefaction. When the string starts back on its second trip to the right, as at *e* and *f,* the molecules again pile up to produce another compression, to be followed by another rarefaction, and so on until the motion of the string dies out. Thus the individual molecules of air move constantly back and forth through only a short distance while the "wave" (the compressed-and-rarefied *condition*) passes through them. And while a molecule makes one complete (back and forth) vibration the "wave" advances through one wave-length. This may be seen if the reader will follow, for example, the movement of the air molecule immediately next to the string through the phases shown in *b, c, d, e,* and *f.* Any particular molecule is at one instant in a region of compression and very shortly afterward in a rarefaction, just as any boy in the line may alternately be in a region of "compression" or one of "rarefaction."

Now, in the case of a water surface, circular waves will be produced by *any* disturbance. If a paddle is pushed in one direction, a wave is started in that direction, but that wave soon spreads around so as to fill up a whole circumference of an expanding circle. Similarly, in the case of the air, *spherical* waves will be produced by any disturbance, whether it pushes back the air in every direction as did the little bomb, or whether it is produced by something which is vibrating in only one line of motion. This is because sound waves, as we shall see later under Diffraction, tend continually to spread in every direction. Thus the movements of *any* vibrating body give rise to *spherical* waves, and if we imagine the action illustrated by Figure 7 as taking place *outward in every direction* from the sounding body instead of just in one line, we can visualize the formation of these spherical sound waves. The actual distance that the air particles travel back and forth is extremely small. Thus sound waves pass readily through quiet smoke without imparting any visible motion to it.

We have already defined the terms *frequency, period,* and *amplitude,* when applied to the original vibrating source. These terms now may be given other definitions for use when con-sidering the passage of compressional waves through the air. *Frequency,* as applied to an air vibration, means the number of complete waves (each wave consisting of compression and rare-faction) to pass a given point in a second. *Period* means the time required for one complete wave to pass a given point; *amplitude,* the *amount of variation in air pressure* from com-pression to rarefaction. Thus, if the normal air pressure of, say, fifteen pounds per square inch be varied between 15.001 and 14.999, the maximum "pressure amplitude" is .002. (However, many writers prefer to define amplitude as the maximum varia-tion from the equilibrium situation, so that in this case the pressure amplitude would be .001 pound per square inch.)

"Air waves," no matter by what sort of vibration they are produced, are examples of *longitudinal,* or *compressional* waves: waves in which the displacement of the individual particles is back and forth in the *same* direction that the wave is traveling, as contrasted with *transverse* waves, in which the displacement of the particles takes place at *right angles* to the wave direction. Each sound wave consists of a pulse of compression and a pulse of rarefaction. However, a single wave by itself seldom, if ever, exists. Just as a single disturbance in a body of water gives rise to several waves before its effect disappears, so do air disturbances usually give rise to a series of waves, even in quite short sounds, although of course the first one may be much stronger than the succeeding ones. Thus, the shortest *staccato* sound ever heard in music consists of a number of waves.

If these compressional waves be prevented from spreading outwards in all directions, as when they are confined in a long, smooth-walled tube, they can travel for great distances without being appreciably weakened. Thus, the faintest whisper uttered at one end of a Paris conduit pipe could be heard distinctly at the other end, a distance of 3120 feet, and Koenig was able to set a fork into sympathetic vibration by another fork through a conduit over a mile long, by pointing the open ends of their resonating boxes toward each other.

Diffusion

Normally, however, sound spreads out in all directions. This spreading out of sound in spherical waves as it leaves the source is called *diffusion*. Since the spheres of compression and rarefaction get larger and larger, the energy of the sound is more and more widely distributed. Thus, in an open space where there is no reflection of sound by walls, the sound heard diminishes in strength very rapidly (inversely as the square of the distance). The sound energy intercepted by an envelope held up fifty feet from a band is four times that intercepted at a hundred feet, and sixteen times that at two hundred feet. Music heard in the open air is frequently unsatisfactory because the subtler nuances are lost. In addition to this effect, sound in air is further weakened in other ways. Uniform diffusion through air could exist only in an entirely open space away from the earth, with uniform density and temperature, no reflections, and freedom from winds. Such an ideal case is never met, however, and sound is weakened by friction with the earth's surface, by the viscous resistance of the air caused by friction of the air particles themselves, by atmospheric absorption, changes in density and temperature of the air, air currents, multiple reflections, and so on. In these processes, which eventually dissipate the energy of the sound waves, the components above 1000 in frequency usually lose out more than those below this point. Band music heard from a distance has lost many of the high-pitched instruments, and thunder heard from a distance is only a rumble, having lost the higher frequencies that produce the crack and crash. The effect was simulated by Weber in the "Bauernwalzer," of *Der Freischütz,* where as the musicians depart only the basses are finally to be heard. When the human voice is heard from a considerable distance all that remains are some of the vowels, whose components have lower frequencies and greater energies than the consonants. And on a still night we can hear prominent higher tones in the complex sound emitted by an airplane or a distant band, whereas in the daytime these will often be lost because of the disturbance of the atmosphere by the rising of currents of sun-warmed air. Dirigibles have been seen to be wafted upward a bit as they passed through each layer of hot air rising from the streets of a hot city, alternately sinking a bit between each street. This indicates the lack of homogeneity in the daytime atmosphere. And even inside of an auditorium—where, as we shall see later, sound is reflected back and forth many times from walls, ceiling, and floor before it dies out—there is a loss of brilliance because the long paths traveled by the waves in their many reflections give time for atmospheric absorption to get in its work. These effects, however, may be modified or even reversed if the higher-pitched components of a complex sound are actually being produced at much greater intensities than the lower ones. Furthermore, the ear loses its sensitivity as the frequency drops below its most sensitive range. This range lies from 1000 to 5000 (the resonance of the ear-canal lying at about 2800-2900), so that, as frequency drops below 1000, the ear loses its sensitivity rapidly. And if a low pitch and a medium pitch (for instance, C_{28} and A_{49}) sound equally loud at a certain distance from their source, at a greater distance it will be found that the low one has lost more in loudness than the medium one. Thus as the distance is changed the relative loudness of sounds changes. This may help to explain the differing opinions as to quality by listeners at different points, even when no reflection phenomena are considered.

It would appear, therefore, that the medium frequencies are the ones which will persist the longest as the distance from the source is increased, since the higher ones are lowered below the zero level of loudness by atmospheric absorption, while the lower ones are lost because of the lowered sensitivity of the hearing mechanism. And even the medium frequencies are normally weakened for a listener at least as rapidly as the inverse square law.

This is an appropriate place to discuss the alleged "carrying power" frequently attributed, sometimes rather mystically, to some types of tone production. Some singers, for example, are supposed to be able to make their lightest whisper carry throughout a large auditorium. If a tone quality which is produced by a certain amount of sound energy spread fairly equally over a large number of partials be changed into one in which the same amount of energy is concentrated in one or at most a few partials, it is clear that these stronger partials can travel to a greater distance than the weaker partials of the first sound before being weakened to a point below audibility. For example, there is evidence to indicate that the good male voice tends to concentrate its energy into two or three regions to a greater degree than the throaty voice. This is a possible explanation of "carrying power." A better explanation, perhaps, is to be found, as pointed out by Drew,[1] in the fact that when a performer softens his tone to a *pianissimo* his audience frequently becomes less fidgety and therefore less noisy, permitting a softer tone to be heard than was possible before. "The better and more interesting—or even the more famous and expensive—the artist is, the more likely is it that this kind of silence on the part of the audience will occur. So arises the idea that some artists are endowed with the power of outlawing themselves from the realm of acoustics for their own purposes."

---

[1] Drew, W. S., *Singing, the Art and the Craft*, page 134. New York: Oxford University Press, 1937.

Reinforcement

Since sound usually weakens rapidly as it travels away from its source, it is necessary to reinforce the primary tone of musical instruments. Anything that will cause a larger body of air to be set into vibration will accomplish this. Thus, horns, enclosed bodies of air, soundboards of large area, and other types of resonators are fitted to the vibrating body. We do not always realize that the sounds we hear from a piano or a violin come to our ears not from the vibrating strings, which in themselves are poor sound radiators, but from the vibrations of the soundboard or enclosed air. This is why the body of a good violin is costly, not the strings. A damaged violin may still be valuable if its belly is still able to reinforce tones fairly evenly throughout the scale. The piano, the violin, and the harp would have very poor and weak tones if it were not for their soundboards (and in the case of the violin and harp, the resonance of their enclosed bodies of air), because the strings by themselves would merely cut through the air, back and forth, without generating much sound. "Practice fiddles" are sometimes made without the soundboard body, for quietness. The tone is not only quieter, but less pleasing. In the case of such an instrument as the violoncello, which rests on the floor, the stage floor should be capable of vibrating as a giant soundboard.

It should be borne in mind that the setting of a larger body of air into vibration takes added work. Thus, for example, a piano wire will cease vibrating sooner when made to vibrate a soundboard than when not made to do this extra work.

Reinforcement is thus an application of the principle of resonance, the terms being somewhat synonymous, and all musical instruments have resonators of one sort or another. Thus, the clarinet reed would give a poor tone if this were not strengthened by the column of air inside the tube. In the organ, every tone has its own tuned resonator in the column of air in each pipe.

The manner of reinforcement often has a marked influence

not only on the power, but on the tone quality. In such an
"instrument" as the jew's-harp, the entire variation is caused by
differences in the natural frequency of the body of air in the
mouth (possibly aided by the cupped hands), which reinforces
the tone. The characteristic quality of a violin is due in part to
the way in which the wooden parts vibrate in reinforcing the
string tone, strengthening some frequencies and weakening
others.

The Helmholtz resonator furnishes a good illustration of the
principle of reinforcement by resonance. It is a spherical shell
of metal or glass enclosing a body of air tuned to a certain pitch,
and having an aperture for the sound to enter, and another
smaller aperture in a protuberance which fits into the ear. When
placed to the ear, it can be heard to respond quite strongly if
its particular pitch is present in the surrounding air, and very
weakly, if at all, to other pitches. The "sound" of a sea shell
or an empty bottle, when placed to the ear, is an example of this
principle.

The natural pitch of such an air cavity depends on its volume
and on the size of the aperture. When a Helmholtz resonator
is vibrating, the enclosed air is being alternately compressed by
some additional air being forced through the opening, and then
rarefied by some of the enclosed air being emptied out through
the opening. The air at the opening is therefore acting like a little piston, alternately compressing and rarefying the enclosed air.
If we increase the volume of the resonator, the natural pitch will
be lowered, and, on the contrary, if we decrease the volume, the
natural pitch will be raised. The rise in the pitch of the sounds
made when a jar is filled at a spigot is due to the decreasing
volume of air remaining in the jar. If we decrease the size of
the aperture, the pitch will be lowered, since the smaller this
aperture is the more is the piston action slowed down by air
friction. When the aperture is enlarged, the air may pass in
and out more readily, and the pitch is raised.

Helmholtz used a series of these resonators tuned to the

various tones of the harmonic series of a certain fundamental, in order to tell in a rough way which overtones of the sound were prominent, and which ones weak or absent.

The principle of reinforcement by resonance affects the acoustic properties of auditoriums. Rooms may act as resonators of low pitches in the same manner that Helmholtz resonators do, particularly if they have hard walls. Such pitches may often be found by humming up and down the scale, especially in a small room or alcove. When a resonant point is reached, the whole room seems to be sounding. Wooden walls or paneling may have resonant action at certain frequencies. Church pews, floors, paneling, or chandeliers sometimes vibrate sympathetically, or are forced into vibration, when low organ pedal tones are played. The effects of such resonant frequencies are known to organ tuners. When an organ is in its final position, the pipes must be "voiced" to give the correct intensity for the hearers, and this entails making some of them actually softer or louder at the source, in order to compensate for resonance and reflection effects. Thus one man listens from the auditorium, calling his directions to the man at the pipes.

Velocity of Sound in Air

Whether a sound is reinforced by some means or not reinforced, whether it is a strong or a weak sound, of high or low pitch, or of complex or simple nature, it is always produced by a series of expanding spherical compressions and rarefactions of corresponding nature, traveling outward from its source. And as these spheres of alternate compression and rarefaction expand through the air (or for that matter through any medium), we find that their velocity along any particular line from the source is constant, and *nearly independent of the pitch*. Thus if we are listening to music from a distant band, the tones from the high-pitched instruments do not travel toward us any faster than those from the low-pitched ones, but all pitches travel at the same speed, roughly 1100 feet per second, or 750 miles per hour.

The velocity of sound in air is also nearly independent of its loudness, at least for all ordinary sounds, the loud tones of the band arriving at the same instant as the soft ones if produced at the same instant. However, in the case of very powerful vibrations, as in explosions, the velocity near the source may be considerably greater than normal. Thus the order to fire a cannon has been known to arrive at a listener's ear *after* the sound of the explosion has been heard. Generally speaking, however, the louder the sound, the *farther* it will travel, not the faster.

The velocity of sound in air is also nearly independent of the tone quality, complex tones traveling just as fast as simple tones.

The velocity of sound in air varies somewhat with the atmospheric conditions, increasing slightly with an increase in temperature. Thus the figure of 1100 feet per second is only strictly true for a temperature slightly over 40° Fahrenheit. For colder temperatures it is less (about 1088 at the freezing point), and for warmer temperatures more. The increase is a little over a foot per second for each degree Fahrenheit. Thus the pitch of wind instruments, which depends on the speed of sound waves up and down the air column, varies with the temperature of the enclosed air. At ordinary room temperatures sound travels about 1130 feet per second. The velocity of sound also increases slightly with an increase in moisture content.

What we often fail to realize is that, although the speed of sound is a rapid speed, it is by no means so rapid that it may be considered instantaneous, and be neglected. Light waves are so rapid that for our purposes they may be considered to be instantaneous, but sound waves are about 900,000 times slower. If a long procession is marching behind a band, and every man puts his foot down when he hears the drumbeat, they will not be in step with each other, since each rank farther back hears the sound a little later than those ahead. Bragg suggests that by watching the bobbing of the heads an actual "ripple" can be seen to run down the line at each step, traveling of course at the speed of sound. In a hall 226 feet long, sound would take a fifth of a second (the interval of time between two watch-ticks) to travel the length of it. Thus a man watching an orchestra from the rear of a large hall will be disturbed by the apparent constant lagging of the instruments behind the conductor's baton. Even the conductor himself, as well as the individual players, as Redfield points out, are troubled by this phenomenon if the group is very large, as in the "massed chorus," or even more so in the massed band or orchestra playing in lively tempo, where precision is perhaps more essential than in most choral singing. Redfield points out further that many band leaders believe lagging tubas to be due to the time required for tone to travel through the unusually long tube from the mouthpiece to the bell. Such an explanation would reveal a misunderstanding of the form of vibration of brass-wind instruments. Even so, such a short time would often not be as long as the time taken for the sound to travel from the bell to the director's ear. The lag may be caused instead by the players imagining that the production of sound is simultaneous with the (preliminary) setting of the lips.

Still another example of the relatively slow speed of sound compared with light is to be seen in a very large motion-picture theatre. When the sound is synchronized with the action on the screen for observers in the front of the hall, it lags appreciably for those sitting in the rear, unless small auxiliary loud-speakers are introduced farther back in the hall in addition to those behind the screen. Practically, it should be adjusted for a midway position, although observers in the front will then hear the sound a tiny bit before they see the corresponding action, and observers in the rear a tiny bit later.

Under exceptional atmospheric conditions, sound may travel to unexpected distances. Even the noise from such a tiny source as the sound-producing organ of the cricket has, according to Darwin, been heard at night across the distance of a mile. If we imagine a spherical shell with a radius of a mile, we get some idea of the great mass of matter, from five to ten million tons, thrown into sonorous motion by such a tiny insect, weighing only a small fraction of an ounce. The human voice has been heard across an air distance of eight miles.

Bragg has reported hearing the strokes of an axe across a distance so great that when the sounds finally arrived at his ear the woodcutter had straightened himself and begun to move away. It is easy to see how a man could be shot from a distance by a rapidly moving rifle bullet before he heard the report of firing. The story is told of a ship's crew in the South Atlantic hearing strange bells which later information proved to have been sounding in a festival at Rio de Janeiro, over 120 miles away. At this distance a musical selection nearly ten minutes long could have been completed and in transit before the first tone arrived at the ship! The report of the explosion of the meteor of 1783 was heard at Windsor Castle ten minutes after its disappearance, which would mean that it was about 125 miles away. Of course, the louder the original sound, the farther it will travel. Thus cannonading has been heard 200 miles away from the scene of battle, as when the battle between the English and the Dutch, in 1672, was heard in Wales. Sounds from the terrific eruption of Tamboro, in Sumbawa, Dutch East Indies, were heard more than 900 miles distant. At the usual speed of sound in air, they would have taken well over an hour to travel such a distance. Such sounds are transmitted readily through the earth, also.

The most remarkable instance on record of distance traveled is that of the eruption of Krakatoa in 1883, which shot up a column of debris seventeen miles high. Sounds from this eruption were heard over a vast area, especially towards the west. They were noticed at Rodriguez, nearly 3000 miles away, at Bangkok (1413 miles), in the Philippines (about 1450 miles), in Ceylon (2058 miles), and in West and South Australia (from 1300 to 2250 miles). And though we do not have any record of actual sounds being heard farther than these distances, this eruption caused a world-wide disturbance of the atmosphere, made evident by the change in barometric pressure recorded at various stations. This gigantic "sound wave" (for such it really could be called, being an atmospheric pressure variation traveling at a speed comparable with the ordinary velocity of sound), traveled outwards from the volcano as a center until it became a great circle enveloping the earth, then on to the other side, diminishing in size until it contracted to a point on the earth diametrically opposite from Krakatoa. This passage around the earth took about 18 hours. The wave was then reflected so that it traveled backward to the volcano, from which it was again sent out in its original direction. In an article in the Eleventh Edition of the *Encyclopedia Britannica*, Sir R. Strachey says: "In this manner its repetition was observed not fewer than seven times at many of the stations, four passages having been those of the wave traveling from Krakatoa, and three those of the wave traveling from its antipodes, subsequently to which its traces were lost." Thus this gigantic sound wave traveled for at least 127 hours. Tremendous water waves were also generated by this eruption, which caused the loss of over 36,000 lives. Some of these waves traveled as far as 8000 miles, or more.

Wave-Length

The distance in the air, at a certain instant, from a point on one air wave to the corresponding point on the next (for example, from maximum compression to maximum compression) is called the *wave-length*. This is illustrated in Figure 7f, although it must be remembered that the waves go out spherically in every direction. Suppose some material body is vibrating at a frequency of one vibration per second, although of course this is too slow to be heard as a tone by the human ear. Each spherical wave (compression-rarefaction) that it gives off travels at the rate of 1100 feet per second, the speed of sound. At the end of the first second, the "front" of the first wave will have traveled 1100 feet (in every direction), and the second wave will be just starting to be formed. Thus in a given direction the disturbance for a single wave takes up the whole 1100 feet, and its wave-length is said to be 1100 feet. If the body were vibrating with a frequency of two vibrations per second, there would be two waves in the 1100 feet (since the speed of sound waves is constant). In this case their wave-length would be one half of 1100, or 550 feet. If the frequency were three per second, there would be three waves distributed along the 1100 feet, and the wave-length would be 1100 divided by 3, or 367 feet. Thus, if we know the velocity of sound and the frequency, we can find the wave-length by dividing the velocity by the frequency. Naturally, then, the higher the pitch, the shorter the wave-length. Some approximate wave-lengths are given here, based on the now commonly used pitch of A-440. In calculating them the velocity of sound was taken more accurately at 1129 feet per second, which is close to the actual conditions under which music is heard in concert halls:

	Frequency	*Wave-length*
Lowest C	16.4	69 feet
Lowest C on piano (C_4)	32.7	34½ feet
Middle C (C_{40})	261.6	4⅓ feet
Violin A (A_{49})	440.	2½ feet
C four octaves above Middle C (C_{88}) ...	4,186.	3¼ inches
Highest audible tone (roughly)	20,000.	0.68 inches

Thus, when the orchestra tunes to the oboe at 440, the predominant length of the air waves in the hall is 2½ feet—2½ feet between successive compressions, or 1¼ feet between compressions and adjacent rarefactions.

Sound Waves in Other Media

Sound waves (that is, compressions and rarefactions expanding spherically) can pass through solid, liquid, or gaseous substances, but not through a vacuum. They travel faster in most liquids and solids than in air, because the former, though denser, are yet in proportion very much more elastic.[2] Sound waves travel through water at between four and five times the speed they travel through air, and through steel at about fifteen times their air speed. If one is standing by a telegraph pole, and a pole some distance away be struck with a hammer, a faint noise of the blow will be heard, apparently coming from the near-by pole, an appreciable instant *before* the actual air-transmitted sound arrives. This is because the sound traveled faster through the metal wires to the near-by pole, and thence to the ear, than when it traversed the air for the whole distance. In many instru-

---

[2] The proper scientific usage of the word "elastic" is implied here. Ganot's Physics defines the force of elasticity as that force "with which the displaced particles tend to revert to their original position, and this force is equivalent to that which has brought about the change." This differs from the customary popular use of the term, in which, for example, rubber is considered highly elastic because it undergoes considerable change of form on the application of a small force. Liquids and solids, in the true meaning of the term, are highly elastic because they require a very large force to compress or otherwise distort them, and then tend to restore themselves to their former shape or position with an equally strong force.

ments it is essential for sound waves to pass through solid substances, which they do with ease. An example is the bridge and
the sound post of a violin. Even our sense of hearing is dependent on the conduction of the vibrations through the bones of the
middle ear, and when the normal hearing mechanism of the
middle ear is damaged the vibrations may be conducted directly
to the cochlea (inner ear) through the bone of the head. Persons
who are deaf to air-borne sounds may still hear if the vibrating
body is placed in contact with the teeth or the bony skull. The
same is true if an electrically amplified reproduction of the air-
borne sound be impressed on the bony skull, as in the case of the
"bone-conduction" type of hearing aid. (See Chapter 5.)

An example of the ease with which sound passes through solid
substances is afforded by a wooden rod. The ticking of a watch
is usually inaudible at a distance of twenty-five feet. However,
if one end of a long wooden rod be placed against the watch,
and the other end over the entrance to the ear, the ticking will be
heard very plainly. The grain of the wood aids the passage of
the sound. Through such a long wooden rod, music has been
transmitted from the soundboard of a piano several floors away,
and with the aid of another soundboard, such as the body of a
violin, placed in contact with the end of the rod, the music was
made audible to a roomful of listeners. The passage of sound
through or along the walls of a building is another illustration
of the ease with which these waves pass through solid substances.
Sound travels readily through the earth, and more readily in the
direction of the geologic strata than across them. The sounds
of horse hoofs can sometimes be heard from considerable distances if the ear be placed against the ground. With the aid of
under-water microphones, the water-borne sound waves from
explosions many miles distant may be detected.

Sound waves in the air are almost totally reflected when they
strike a much denser material, as, for example, a water surface.
Thus, a submerged swimmer cannot always hear a pistol shot in
the air above him. If, however, a vibration be produced *in* the

water, sound can travel great distances through it, because water is quite homogeneous as compared with air. Ships carrying under-water microphones can detect icebergs as much as three miles distant by loud, deep, characteristic sounds believed to be due to the cracking of the ice under water. It should be remembered that this is due to the passage *through* the water of enlarging spherical compressions and rarefactions. The *surface* waves on a body of water, although useful in illustrating certain facts of wave motion, are something quite different and much slower, being examples of transverse wave motion.

Sound cannot travel through a vacuum. If an electric bell be suspended in a jar, and the air pumped out of the jar, its sound will grow weaker and finally become inaudible, even though it can still be seen to be ringing. If the air be then permitted to flow back into the jar, the bell becomes audible again.

Graphic Recording of Sound Waves

The rapidity of sound waves and the extremely small energy they normally possess make it difficult for us to believe that they exist, since we like to *see* what we experience. However, the existence of these compressional waves may be made evident by raising the palm of the hand while facing an explosion. In watching skyrockets, for example, especially if one is fairly close, at the moment that the sound is heard, a faint pulse of air may actually be felt on the hand or fingers. No air has come to the listener from the explosion, but a *compressed condition* of the air has traveled through it. It is occasionally even possible, because of the unequal refraction of light by air of differing density, to *see* the initial wave produced by a powerful explosion. Thus a rapidly flying shadow has been seen to sweep across the sky and over clouds during cannonading.

Usually, however, sound waves are too small and rapid to be seen by the naked eye. In addition, as we have seen, they are usually quite complex. Since it is often necessary to be able to study them, in order to analyze the tone and learn what overtones are present, it is essential to be able to record them in some permanent, and preferably magnified, form. A graph of the motion of a pendulum may be secured, as has already been described (see Figure 1), by causing it to trace its path on a strip of paper which is moving at right angles to the pendulum's motion. Similarly, if we could get something to vibrate in response to the air waves (as in forced resonance through the air), and could then get that vibration to trace itself in some way, we would have our record. The air waves are not strong enough to set a heavy pendulum into vibration, but they can set a small sensitive diaphragm into motion. The early phonograph records were made by collecting and concentrating the sound waves with a horn, letting them set into vibration a diaphragm stretched across the small end of the horn. The resulting movement of this diaphragm, by a system of levers, was then caused to scratch a wavy line on a revolving wax cylinder or disc.[3] A more modern method is to have the recording diaphragm part of a microphone. The effects of its movement can then be greatly amplified electrically. The resulting pulsations of the current are made to cause a beam of light to swing back and forth in sympathy with the sound. If this beam of light be focused on a strip of photographic film moving at right angles to the movement of the light, that is, *across* the vibration direction, a permanent "picture" of the sound wave is secured. This is called the *microphone and oscillograph* method.

Since these methods all use a diaphragm moved more or less accurately by variations in *air pressure* (except "velocity" microphones), the wavy "transverse" curve they produce becomes merely a graph of how the air pressure varied when the train of waves struck the diaphragm, and not at all a picture of how the air particles move. The air particles do not pass along in wavy "transverse" curves, but move back and forth in very short

---

[3] The human ear has a somewhat analogous construction. A "horn," now rudimentary (the outer ear), a diaphragm (the drum), and a lever system (the ossicles) are present. (See Chapter 5.)

straight lines as the "wave" passes along. In Figure 8*a*, the heavy black circles represent diagrammatically the regions of greatest compression in the expanding sound waves produced by a simple form of vibration. The largest circle represents the first wave that was formed. Four additional, later, waves have been produced and the compression part of the fifth is being formed at the source. The individual air particles move backward and forward in the directions indicated by the small arrowhead lines, as the waves pass outward. The *graph* of the variation in air pressure produced by these waves as they pass a given point is

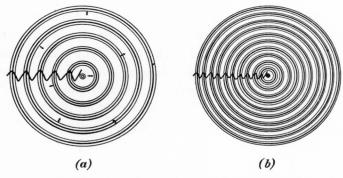

(*a*)   (*b*)

Fig. 8—Simple sound waves with graphs of pressure variation.

indicated by the wavy line, and this latter is the type of record secured from recording devices such as the oscillograph. A similar diagram is shown in *b*, representing a vibration of double the frequency (the octave), but of less amplitude (softer tone).

Figure 9 illustrates the formation of complex waves. At *a*, let us imagine a reed vibrating in complex vibration, starting at dotted-line position 1, traveling to 2, back to 3, then to 4, and then to 1 to start the next cycle. When it swings from 1 to 2 it produces a strong compression. When it swings back to 3, a rarefied region results. When it swings to 4 another compression is formed, though a weaker one than the compression formed when it traveled as far as position 2. When it swings back to 1, another rarefaction is produced, but this time a more marked rarefaction than when it traveled only to position 3. These variations in air pressure are translated into corresponding differences in the height of the line produced by a recording instrument, as shown in the wavy curve. Three waves have been produced in the diagram, the secondary compression of the third wave having just been completed and pushed away by the reed's traveling to position 4 (full line). Such a curve as this, having one auxiliary hump in each fundamental cycle, is produced by a complex vibration which contains in addition to the fundamental a vibration at double the frequency of the fundamental, and shows therefore the presence of the octave in the original tone.

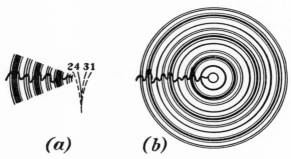

Fig. 9—Complex sound waves with graphs of pressure variation.

In *b,* another complex wave is shown. Here the fundamental frequency is the same as in *a,* since the distance between the points of maximum compression is the same, but instead of the second partial being marked, it is here the third partial, since *three* approximately equidistant humps mav be counted in each fundamental cycle.

Figure 10 shows actual oscillograph records of fourteen tones of the same pitch, A-440. The first illustration is that of a tuning fork, which vibrates practically in S.H.M., giving rise to a practically pure tone. The graph is seen to be a sine curve. No other record is even approximately pure, although if the various instruments were played at higher and higher pitches, the wave forms would simplify more and more, as has already been mentioned. Various degrees of complexity in the wave forms of Figure 10 reflect corresponding variations in the air pressure of the original wave, these relative compressions and rarefactions

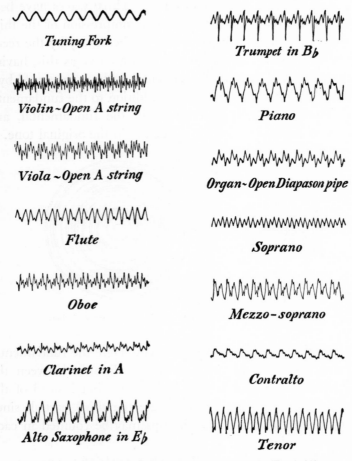

Tuning Fork

Trumpet in B♭

Violin~Open A string

Piano

Viola ~Open A string

Organ~Open Diapason pipe

Flute

Soprano

Oboe

Mezzo–soprano

Clarinet in A

Contralto

Alto Saxophone in E♭

Tenor

Fig. 10—Oscillograms of different instruments sounding A-440.

having been produced by similar complexities in the original vibration form of the sounding instrument. And when this vibration form is undergoing a change, a corresponding change in the recorded picture is produced, as in the wave forms in Figure 5, page 22, which show the variations in a baritone voice on Middle C, during the vibrato cycle, each cut containing about four complete waves.

It is difficult to visualize the ease with which the air particles follow such complex changes in the pressure they are under, but we have many proofs that they do. And it is easy to recall how an extremely complex mixture of several wave motions on a water surface affects in a correspondingly complex fashion any floating chip. We know that if a large number of simple vibration forms of different frequencies are present at the same time in some vibrating body (such as in most musical instruments), its resultant motion (the motion that it actually undergoes in its attempt to satisfy the demands of all of its many components), is an extremely complex motion, and far from anything approaching S.H.M. In the case of tones containing inharmonic elements, the complexity is even greater. And yet, no matter how complexly such bodies vibrate, they give rise to trains of air waves which exactly parallel every changing movement of the source. Every movement or partial movement of the sounding body which is toward the hearer, no matter how small, causes a tiny compression to start toward him; every movement or partial movement in the opposite direction causes a corresponding rarefaction to follow the compression. These complex air waves, when they reach a receiver, such as the diaphragm of a recording microphone, set it into vibration which is a more or less faithful copy of their own movement. Through electrical magnification (as explained on page 47), we can secure these oscillograph "pictures" of the manner in which the air pressure varied, or in other words, of how many subordinate "peaks" (compressions) there were to each principal one. And that will be the key to the manner in which the vibration took place originally in the sounding body. Thus we see that in the open diapason pipe record in Figure 10, the tone contains, among others, a strong third partial; while the mezzo-soprano record reveals the presence, among others, of strong second and seventh partials.

The curves of Figure 10, however, should not be considered

as necessarily typical of these instruments. Variations between instruments, or between several players on the same instrument, are responsible for many, and frequently large, variations in the tone quality. And if the records had been made at different pitches or at different intensities, they would differ greatly. For example, Figure 11 illustrates the differences produced in the tone of an oboe as the pitch rises by whole-tone steps from its low Bb (Bb₃₈) to high D and then F (F₆₉), the highest tone of the oboe. The progressive simplification of the vibration form is evident. A somewhat similar simplification occurs if we produce a series of tones from loudest to softest on any single pitch.

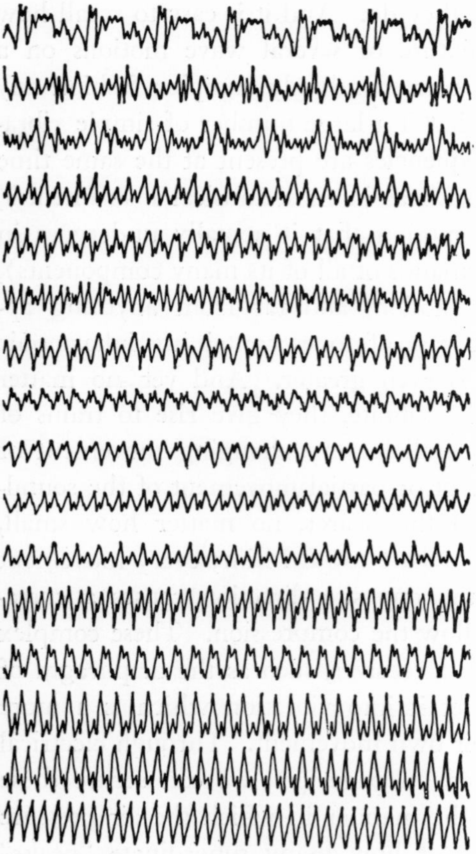

Fig. 11—Change of tone quality in the oboe with increasing pitch.

If such a curve as any of those in Figures 10 or 11 is impressed with reduced amplitude in some more permanent material, as is done, for example, in the making of a phonograph record, where the edge of the groove is a miniature replica of the graph of the entire sound wave; and if some sort of a stylus or needle is made to trace the path of the wave, a reproduction of the original sound occurs. Compressions and rarefactions are produced by the vibration of the needle in just the pattern that they originally formed when the record was made by the original sound.

Usually they are strengthened by the resonance of a horn, or by electrical amplification. This will be further discussed in Chapter 6.

Fig. 12—Analysis of complex wave into two partials.

Harmonic Analysis

The process of determining what overtones are present in a complex sound is termed *harmonic analysis*. It may be done in a very rough way by examining the oscillograph curves visually, or by the use of Helmholtz resonators as previously described. It should be done, however, with much greater accuracy —for instance, by tracing the curve with a delicate machine called the Henrici analyzer, or by various electrical methods. Figure 12 shows a curve and its analysis into two partials, the fundamental and the octave. If the vibrations represented by the last two curves could be simultaneously produced by two pure sources, such as tuning forks at the proper frequency and amplitude, the vibration form represented by the top curve would be reproduced in the air, and we would hear a copy of the original complex tone. It is easy to see what a useful tool harmonic analysis can be in the case of much more complex sounds. Thus, Figure 13 shows one com-

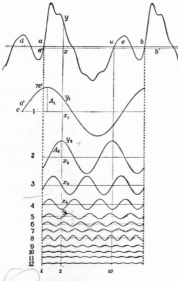

Fig. 13—Analysis of complex wave from organ pipe into twelve partials.*

---

*From Miller, Dayton C., *The Science of Musical Sounds*, page 125. New York, The Macmillan Company, 1916.

plete wave of the graph of an organ pipe tone of a certain quality, followed by its analysis to the twelfth partial (fundamental and first eleven overtones). It is seen that these partials do not have to start "in phase", with each other—in other words, the curves do not need to cross the zero line at the same time.[4]

Having analyzed the tone into its components, we may again synthesize it from its components. If we produce sounds from twelve different pure sources having the frequencies 1, 2, 3, 4, etc., times the fundamental frequency (in other words, lying in a harmonic series), and adjust their amplitudes to match those shown in the analysis, their tones will fuse into what we would hear as an organ pipe tone of that particular quality. And if in addition we were able to produce them in the particular phase relation shown in the analysis, the graph of their summation would reproduce the top curve.

Principle of Superposition

It should be clear by now that vibrating substances (including the air) have no difficulty in responding to more than one vibration form at the same time. Furthermore, the various vibration forms do not even have to be in a harmonic series relation, nor do they have to be produced by a single source. Thus in the experiment already mentioned, in which music was transmitted through a long wooden rod from the soundboard of a piano several floors away, the rod carried a multitude of vibrations from the piano wires and soundboard at the same time, without destructive interference. This was proved by the fact that when another soundboard, such as the back of a violin, was rested on

---

[4] Thus, in Figure 13, at the instant chosen for the beginning of the complex wave, the fundamental (first partial) is seen to be near its crest, representing a compression phase, at the same time that the octave (second partial) is in a rarefaction phase (below the line). The fourth, fifth, sixth, and seventh partials are seen to be almost at the zero line at this instant, while the third and eighth are in rarefaction phases. Many experiments have shown that changes in these phase relations of the partials do not change the quality of the tone as heard by the human ear, provided the relative strengths of the partials remain unchanged. Thus, wave forms which would appear different to the eye may produce tones indistinguishable to the ear. There is, however, some experimental evidence indicating that the phase relation does affect the quality.

top of the end of the rod, the music became audible throughout the room, and was easily recognized as being produced by a piano. If a chord of six tones, for example, was heard and recognized in the lecture room, the only inference is that a wooden rod can simultaneously respond to vibrations of at least six different types, since this many fundamentals were present. And since *piano quality* was recognized, many overtones must also have been transmitted. The fact that a phonograph needle, or a radio loud-speaker, can transmit the many tones of an orchestral ensemble simultaneously, proves that they are capable of responding to many vibration forms simultaneously, just as the air may have a large number of vibratory motions existing in it at the same time.

All of these are examples of the *principle of superposition,* which we define as follows: Two or more different wave trains (series of enlarging spheres of compression and rarefaction), from one or many different instruments, voices, or other sources, may exist in the air (or in any other medium), at the same time. These series of pulses will travel through each other without destroying each other, in a similar manner to that of circular waves on water. The actual position of any particular air particle at any instant will be the resultant of the forces acting on it from the various series of waves. But the wave trains will not be destroyed. As Bragg says, any number of sounds can use the air at the same time. Suppose that when a sound was traveling across a certain air space no other sound could travel in that same space, or at least could not travel without the sounds seriously affecting each other. What confusion would result, which even our ears, marvelous as they are, could not disentangle! Thus it is both remarkable and fortunate for us that however many sound wave trains are already present in a certain space, and in however many directions they are traveling, a new wave train can find its way across that space just as easily as if no other sound were there. Of course, as Bragg emphasizes, this does not mean that the ear, or rather the brain, already trying to analyze a mixture of sounds, will be as sensitive to the new sound as if there had been silence until the new one came.

The principle of superposition enables us to pay attention to one sound in the presence of others. It is hard to understand how these waves can go through each other without being destroyed, unless we remember that water waves do the same thing. Light waves go through each other with ease also, or else we could not see clearly one object in a room through all the waves crossing and recrossing from all the other objects.

Interference

If two superposed wave trains are from sources having the *same* frequency, there will be points where the atmospheric disturbance due to one of them is always met by an equal and opposite force from the other. Thus, when a compression is arriving at such a point from one wave train, a rarefaction is arriving from the other, and vice versa. At these exact points there will theoretically be silence. At other points, the compressions will arrive together and the rarefactions together, making the sound louder than that due to either single source. These regions of comparative silence and unusual loudness make up what is called an *interference field,* though the term is a misnomer when we consider the wave trains as a whole, for if they are not of too great amplitudes they pass through each other without being destroyed, "interfering" with each other only to the extent of strengthening each other at some points and neutralizing each other at others. The energy which vanishes at one point always reappears at some other point, and, as Colby says, even though the distribution is modified, the total amount of the outward flow of energy is equal to the sum of the outputs of the two sources. We seldom experience the sensation of complete silence in proximity to sounding bodies, because if one ear does happen to be at a silent point the probability is that the other ear will not be, and will therefore hear the sound. The "dead spots" in an auditorium may be due to an interference field set up by a source and its reflected echoes. If, for a certain pitch, the sound waves reaching the ear of a hearer directly from the stage are exactly one half wave-length "out of phase" with those reaching him through reflection from a near-by wall, that particular pitch will be greatly weakened, although not completely silenced, since the amplitude of the reflected wave is always somewhat less than the direct one. For a hearer in another position that pitch is likely to be strengthened and another one weakened. However, the "dead spots" are usually produced by the uneven distribution of the sound by curved walls or domed ceilings, as explained on page 66, and in this case are not limited to certain pitches.

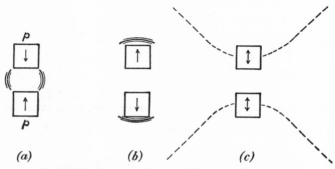

(a)   (b)   (c)

Fig. 14—Interference of waves from tuning fork prongs.

The phenomenon of interference is illustrated by the tuning fork. When a tuning fork is held free in the hand, its sound is extremely feeble, due largely to its lack of a resonance box, but also in part to the fact that the prongs always vibrate in opposite directions. One prong is often producing for a certain listener a compression while the other is producing a rarefaction, resulting in more or less weakening or destroying of the sound. If the fork be slowly rotated about its axis near one ear, four silent points will be noticed, caused by interference between the wave trains coming from the two prongs, since at certain points the waves from one prong neutralize those from the other.

This can be better understood from Figure 14, looking at the ends of the prongs. In *a,* at the instant that the prongs are approaching each other, compressions are being "squeezed out" from between them, but at this same instant, rarefactions are being formed in the wake of the prongs (at points *p*). A half period later, Figure 14*b*, while the receding prongs are "stretching" the air between them into a rarefaction, compressions are being formed in front of the prongs, as indicated. The result of the interference of these two series of waves is that, in the directions indicated by the dotted lines in *c*, no sound is heard. However, in this case, by simply passing a pasteboard tube over one of the prongs, the waves from this prong are in part intercepted, the interference is lessened, and an augmentation of the sound results. More sound is then heard from one prong than formerly from two.

Beats

A special case of the principle of interference occurs when two tones sound at the same time but at slightly different frequencies, the resulting pulsations of tone being called *beats*. This may be understood by imagining two persons clapping hands, one at the rate of three claps a second, the other at the rate of four. Their claps will coincide once a second, and when they do they will sound doubly loud. Beats result from the alternate coinciding and interfering of two wave trains, for when a pulse of compression coincides with another pulse of compression, and rarefaction with rarefaction, the sound is strengthened; but when a pulse of compression coincides with one of rarefaction the sound is weakened. Imagine two tones, vibrating 100 times and 101 times a second. If they start out together, in the same "phase," at the end of half a second the one will have made 50 vibrations while the other has made 50½ vibrations. Thus a compression in the first will be opposing a rarefaction in the second, and the resulting sound will be weakened or even perhaps destroyed completely for an instant. At the end of the hundredth vibration of the first, the second will have made a hundred and one, they will be in step again, and the resulting sound will be louder than that from either one separately.

Thus, when two sources are fairly close in pitch, the ear usually hears neither pitch separately, but an intermediate pitch, which undergoes variations in loudness, called beats. Sometimes the intermediate pitch may seem to be undergoing a pitch vibrato, also. The interval between two beats is the time taken by one tone to gain a complete vibration on the other, so that the number of beats per second will be the difference in frequency between the two tones. For example, if two tones of frequencies 110 and 125 are sounded simultaneously, they would produce 125 minus 110, or 15 beats per second.

Figure 15 is an oscillograph record illustrating the production of beats. The recording film was here moved very slowly so

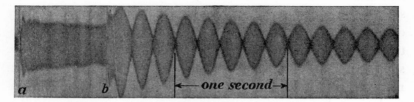

Fig. 15—Beats from two tuning forks.

that the individual vibrations are not discernible. At *a* a 440 tuning fork was struck. The very wide and sudden initial amplitude is the result of the noise of the blow. It vanishes immediately, but is succeeded by the almost instantaneous increase in the amplitude of the fork and its resonating box to a maximum, from which the amplitude begins to decrease slowly. This decrease, from *a* to *b,* illustrates the slow weakening in the loudness as the tone begins to die away. At *b* a 435 fork was struck, both forks being on the same resonator box. Beats were immediately produced, at the rate of five per second, and the alternate strengthening and weakening of the resulting tone is clearly seen. Any five consecutive beats cover a second of time.

Naturally, the nearer the generating tones approach each other, the slower the beats become, so that two tones can be tuned to unison very accurately by tuning them free of beats. And since most tones contain at least the first overtone (the octave), it is possible to tune octaves very accurately by eliminating the beats between the overtone octave and the played octave. Violin players "true up" double-stopped octaves and other intervals in this way. An excellent way to observe beats is to try to hum the same tone while blowing a mouth-organ tone. The effect will also occur with overtones, either of the mouth-organ tone or of the voice.

Beats have at least one artistic usage. Such organ stops as "voix celeste" or "unda maris" consist of two ranks of pipes, one tuned slightly sharper or flatter than the other. Occasionally such a stop will even have three ranks, one at normal pitch, one sharper, and one flatter. In other words, every key on an organ with such a stop drawn will blow at least *two* pipes tuned slightly differently. The resulting waviness, caused by slow beating between them, gives the characteristic pseudo-vibrato effect of these stops. The uncertainty in the pitch is a definite advantage in many types of music, "softening the edges," as it were, and introducing elements of tenderness, vagueness, or mystery. Perhaps the development of such stops is another example of an attempt, not always successful, to secure a satisfactory imitation of the voice vibrato. And, as has been mentioned on page 25, for some reason such a vibrato, which involves primarily only the intensity instead of the pitch, seems most effective at slower speeds than are desirable for the vibrato which does involve pitch, as in the violin or voice. Perhaps, however, the reason lies in the particular types of tone quality involved.

Care must be taken not to point the speaking mouths of the pipes toward each other, or else to have them a sufficient distance apart. If this is not done, the two pipes of each pair will "couple" together, pull each other into unison, and greatly weaken in strength or even cease to sound altogether. This is due to the fact that the air is simply streaming back and forth from one into the other without transmitting sound energy to the surrounding air. A similar effect is to be noticed with adjacent large and therefore low-pitched pipes which are even a semitone or whole tone apart. If they are placed too closely to each other, when one is sounded the other is sometimes affected also, by resonance, and tuning is rendered very difficult or impossible, because each affects the pitch of the other. If the speaking mouths are turned away from each other or sufficiently separated, the "coupling" is negligible, and the pipes have little or no effect on each other. In the case of a properly laid out stop of voix celeste pipes, neither pipe of any pair will pull the other pipe-tone into unison with it, but the beating will continue, unless they are tuned extremely close, when they may pull into unison.

Even a single pipe may be made to beat and sound out of tune with itself! If two tuning forks which are sufficiently out of tune to produce beats are brought close to an organ pipe tuned close to them in pitch, the pipe will reinforce the sounds of both of them. In other words, the column of air in the pipe is responding at the same time to two different driving frequencies from two distinct systems, and each series of vibrations, even though they are brought quite near to coincidence, continues to affect the other. The result is that the pipe appears to be beating at an average pitch, as if it were producing two tones itself, instead of striking a balance and resonating without beats to an average pitch.

Difference Tones

As the generating tones are separated more and more, it becomes increasingly difficult to hear them as fused into a single, average, beating tone. We tend instead to hear the separate generating tones with their accompanying dissonance. As this occurs, the number of beats increases beyond the point where they can be separately distinguished. When beats from strong sources follow each other at the rate of about 20 or more per second, and particularly when they are produced by two loud tones on the same instrument, instead of by two different instruments, they produce a tone called *beat tone* or *difference tone,* with a frequency equal to the difference between the generating frequencies. The violinist Tartini was among the earliest observers to call attention to difference tones. They usually have a "subjective" character, as if they were sounding inside our heads, and not reaching us from the air outside our ears. As a matter of fact, they are produced by an *asymmetrical* response of some vibrating part when caused to vibrate at large amplitudes, and this vibrating part, though sometimes a part of the instrument or its contained air, is frequently the drum or ossicle-chain of the middle ear itself, or even some structure in the inner ear. Whenever such a vibrating body fails to respond with movements proportional in both directions to the forces applied to it, as when the elasticity is defective, extraneous frequencies are introduced. And when a body is forced to respond to two frequencies at once, unless they are very soft tones, extraneous frequencies appear, the most prominent of which is that of the difference between the generating frequencies. The two-toned toy whistle produces a clearly audible low difference tone. With either side sounding alone we hear but one tone; with both sides sounding we can distinguish three tones. The effect is often to be noticed with two high soprano voices, or in a soprano and flute duet.

Since any two tones separated by at least 20 vibrations may produce a difference tone, the number of possible difference tones in an orchestral ensemble becomes very large. Because of the complexity of the result when several difference tones are combined with their generators and with each other, their contribution to the total effect is largely as noise. However, since they are so much softer than their generating tones, this contribution is of minor importance, and seldom sensed.

Difference tones are sometimes employed in organ construction. The lowest pedal pipes, since they are so large, become quite expensive to construct. Also, they frequently need to be longer than the space available for them. The tones of these pipes are sometimes imitated by producing difference tones between higher (smaller) pipes, although this is frequently an unsatisfactory substitute. For example, the lowest C-pipe on a "32-foot" pedal stop vibrates about 16 times a second, and needs to be approximately 32 feet long, if an open pipe. If made of metal it would weigh close to a thousand pounds. The pitch of this pipe may be faked by sounding two pipes, one of approximately 16 feet and one of $10\frac{2}{3}$ feet (or, if stopped pipes, 8 feet and $5\frac{1}{3}$ feet), which vibrate 32 and 48 times a second, respectively, giving a difference tone of 16 vibrations. (The second and third partials of a fundamental of 16 would be 32 and 48.) If room for pipe height is the only consideration, such tricks are not necessary, however, since pipes may be mitered or doubled back on themselves with little or no loss in volume or quality. The difference-tone principle has even been used occasionally to secure "64-foot" tone, in which the lowest difference tone would have a frequency of 8 per second. The importance and value of such a "tone," with its fundamental lying so far below the usual lower pitch limit of audibility, is open to question.

Some theorists draw a sharp distinction between beat tones (beats above 20 per second) and difference tones, but for our purposes we may consider them as being closely related.[5]

Summation tones exist also, and have frequencies equal to the *sum* of the frequencies of the two tones which generate them. They are less easily heard than difference tones, and of little importance in music.

Reflection; Types of Echoes

Passing mention has already been made of the reflection of sound. We practically never hear any sound that has not been subjected to some reflection. Let us now consider this property of sound waves in more detail.

Reflection is the bouncing back of sound waves when they strike a surface, such as the walls, floor, or ceiling of a concert hall. In Figure 16a, three sound waves are indicated, traveling outward from the source at *s*. The first has reached a wall and is just beginning to be turned back. In *b*, it has been further reflected, with constantly increasing radius, while the second wave is just beginning its reflection. In *c*, all three waves have been reflected, and are continuing to expand as if coming from a source at *s'*, the same distance behind the wall that *s* is in front

---

[5] See Beatty's *Hearing in Man and Animals,* pp. 94-98, for further justification of this assumption. An elucidation of the differences between beat tones and difference tones may be found in physical treatises on sound.

of it. This "acoustic image" is quite similar to the mirror image in the case of light, which appears to be as far behind the mirror as the actual object is in front of it.

If for any reason we imagine sound to travel in lines or "rays," a single ray is reflected in a way similar to the bouncing of a ball, or the reflection of a ray of light, in both of which the angle of reflection equals the angle of incidence. Thus, in Figure

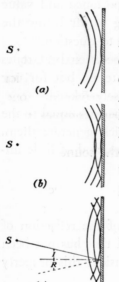

(a)

(b)

(c)

Fig. 16—Reflection of sound waves by plane wall.

16c, the portion of the sound energy that is traveling in the direction of the thin line is reflected, as shown in the dotted line, (at an equal angle with the perpendicular, the angle of incidence I equaling the angle of reflection R. It is seen that the new direction is in a line *away* from s'. It should be mentioned, however, that the reflection of sound is seldom if ever precisely limited to straight lines to the extent that the reflection of light appears to be. There is some spreading of energy to either side of the true angle of reflection. Common reflecting surfaces are not large enough in proportion to the wave-lengths of sound to prevent considerable scattering or spreading. This will be discussed under Diffraction. We must remember also that the idea of sound "rays," although useful in understanding reflection, is an abstraction, and that in sound we have always to deal with *spherical wave-fronts of increasing radius.*

If the reflecting surface is relatively large, sound striking it perpendicularly will be returned to its source as a *simple echo.* Sound striking it obliquely will be reflected (at an equal angle) to a distant point, also a simple reflection. Thus reflection may produce the effect of apparent change in direction of a sound, as when at a street corner the noise of an approaching car is reflected from an opposite wall. The reflection of sound is what enables a blind person to know how near he is to a wall, and the same principle is used in depth-sounding by vessels and in altitude measurements by airplanes.

Two or more reflecting surfaces will give rise to a *multiple echo*. Instances have been reported of places where as many as thirty or forty distinct and separate echoes can be heard.

Sometimes a reflecting surface is of such a nature as to return only some of the harmonic partials of a complex tone. For example, the edge of a woods will sometimes appear to return a tone as its octave, the fundamental having been filtered out, as it were. This is called a *harmonic echo*. The opposite condition prevails when certain types of wall construction reflect low tones better than high tones, and thus tend to purify complex tones by screening out their high partials. When there are a large number of reflections in such a room before the sound dies out, the sound thus becomes less brilliant.

A series of regularly spaced palings or steps will reflect echoes of a sharp, impulsive sound, which will arrive at the ear each a little later than the preceding one, and at regular intervals. Since a rapid series of impulses reaching the ear at regular intervals gives the sensation of pitch, these echoes are perceived by the ear as a short, somewhat musical tone, whose pitch depends not on the original sound, but on the distance between the successive reflecting surfaces. A pistol shot echo will have a musical ring in such a case. This is called a *musical echo*. A good example is heard when the noise of the starting gun at a track meet is reflected from the opposite side of a nearly empty stadium. The phenomenon can frequently be noticed as a "ping" when walking beside a picket fence, especially in cold, dry weather, if the heels be scuffed on a hard surface or the hands sharply clapped. It is sometimes to be noticed in auditoriums where architects, unaware of the phenomenon, have called for ornamental grilles with equally spaced slats. Even the applause in such an auditorium takes on a curious pitch-aspect. If slats or beams or other reflecting surfaces in an auditorium are equally spaced but far enough apart so that the individual echoes do not occur at a great enough frequency to be heard as a pitch, a "flutter echo" is sometimes heard.

Uneven Distribution of Reflected Sound

An uneven reflection of sound is the explanation for the phenomena of "whispering galleries." Thus, in Figure 17a, sound

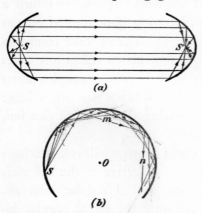

"rays" from a source at s are being reflected by the curved wall so that they travel approximately in a single direction, to the right, instead of spreading in all directions. This is similar to the focusing of light by curved mirrors. Persons inside the beam hear well, those outside, poorly. If such a beam meets another similar curved wall, the rays are made to converge again to a

Fig. 17—Reflection of sound waves by curved walls.

point s', where the sound is still stronger. However, as has been said already, the reflection of sound does not follow these rules as precisely as does the reflection of light waves. In order to secure precise focusing of a sound by curved reflectors the dimensions of the reflectors need to be many times the wave-length of the sound. The same principle is applicable to sound screens if large sound shadows are required, as is discussed later under Diffraction.

Another type of uneven distribution is illustrated in Figure 17b, where a sound generated at s tends to "hug" the circular wall through successive reflections, being heard louder along the wall than at points away from it.

Whispering galleries are effective for persons placed in certain positions, but are generally bad acoustically, because the sound is not evenly distributed so that all may hear. Since they are always associated with concavely curved walls or domed ceilings, these should be avoided in the designing of auditoriums, except possibly at the back, sides, and roof of the stage, where curves of large radius will aid in projecting the sound out towards the audience. Plane walls and a rectangular shape will prevent the focusing and concentration of sound at certain regions to the detriment of others.[6] If concavely curved surfaces are employed, they should be designed, as Sabine [7] says, so that the centers or axes of the curvatures do not fall either near the source of sound or near any portion of the audience. In halls where such curved surfaces already exist and cannot be reshaped, the offending surfaces should be coffered to break up the reflection, or covered with absorbing material. And since concavely curved surfaces tend to concentrate sound, convexly curved surfaces (such as wide cylindrical pillars) tend very effectively to *diffuse* it. Recently, several broadcasting studios and music halls have been designed with such cylindrical surfaces on walls and ceiling, in order to secure a thorough spreading of the sound energy throughout the room.

Reverberation and Absorption

The principles of acoustics, particularly those pertaining to reflection, are of great importance in the designing of rooms or auditoriums in which music is to be performed. A sound heard in the open air will change its character considerably if some surface be placed near by to reflect part of it back to the hearer. This is illustrated in the marked change in the noise of an auto-

[6] The effect of various shapes of auditoriums may be studied through geometrical methods, or by observing the action of water ripples in a ripple tank shaped like a section of the auditorium, or by actually photographing a sound pulse in a miniature auditorium by means of spark photography.

[7] Sabine, Paul E., *Acoustics and Architecture,* page 177. New York: McGraw-Hill Book Company, Inc., 1932.

mobile, noted by a passenger when the automobile passes from open road into a hedge-lined section of road. Similarly, the noise of a train varies greatly when it passes a building wall close to the track, or when in hilly country it alternately travels over fill-ins and between high banks. In these cases, the reflecting surfaces are so near to the source of the sound that the original sound merges with its reflection. In other words, no echo is heard, the word *echo* usually implying a return of the sound from a reflecting surface far enough away to permit an interval of relative silence between the original sound and its echo.

Similarly, speech when confined in a narrow corridor sounds quite different from its sound out-of-doors. Here again the difference is caused by the merging of reflections of the sounds with the original sounds, no distinct echoes being heard unless perhaps from a fairly distant wall at the end of the corridor. In an ordinary room, having moderately hard walls, there may be several hundred rapid, successive, overlapping reflections of a sound from walls, ceiling, floor, furniture, and so on, before it becomes inaudible. This will strengthen the sound for the hearers, and, if the reflecting surfaces are not concavely curved, will have the advantageous effect of distributing the sound energy fairly equally throughout every bit of the room. Instead of a listener hearing a single impulse from a certain direction, he will hear a roll of sound of decreasing loudness, caused by the summation of overlapping waves from every direction, appearing to fill the room more uniformly, and incapable of analysis into distinct reflections. (And, of course, in large halls there may even be a distinct, separated, echo—an effect which is always bad.) This phenomenon of a continuing roll of sound is called *reverberation*. It is really a multiple echo, but with the individual echoes so numerous and so close together as to overlap, as in an auditorium with hard walls. Another example is found in the two walls of a canyon, where the discharge of a gun is heard not as a single sound, but as a prolonged rumble like thunder. In fact, the rolling of thunder itself is caused in part by multiple reflection from many cloud and earth surfaces.[8]

The length of time that a sound continues to be heard in a room, through reflections, after its source has stopped sounding, is called the *reverberation time* of the room. An arbitrary definition has been given to the term by engineers—the time required for the residual sound (a pure tone of 512 cycles is usually used) to decrease to one millionth of its original intensity, or for the intensity level to decrease by 60 *decibels*. (See page 206.) The usual sensation level of speech or music in an auditorium is roughly in the neighborhood of 60 decibels, one million times the minimum audible intensity.

A certain amount of reverberation is useful in increasing the sound energy in the room. Thus, soft music might not be heard in the open, where there were no walls to confine it. As Mills [9] says, "A string quartette or a vocal soloist is at a disadvantage when there is no reverberation. On the other hand, whether by tradition or otherwise, a band seems more mellow in the open air where its (loud) sounds are quickly dissipated and only the direct sound reaches the listener." In a hall, the intensity may be increased severalfold over that which would be heard coming directly from the source in open air. What this means, however, is that each sound, instead of dying out quickly, keeps on sounding and interferes more or less with the sounds coming after it. As Watson has said, if music be played in a room with too long a reverberation time the effect is similar to a piano being played with the damper pedal kept down, and the result is not only louder, but badly blurred. The reverberant sound in a hall may have a ratio as great as ten times that of the direct sound. If a

---

[8] Another cause is the fact that the zigzag lightning streak which gives rise to the initial clap may extend a long distance and have one end farther from us than the other. Since sound is being generated all along the streak, but takes longer to reach us the farther away it is generated, this will have the effect of "stretching out" the initial clap into a continuous roar or roll, although of uneven loudness because of the uneven direction of the streak line.

[9] Mills, J., *A Fugue in Cycles and Bels,* page 166. New York: D. Van Nostrand Company, Inc., 1935.

lecturer is speaking we have difficulty in understanding him, since several syllables are always sounding at the same time. Increasing the loudness of the source may make matters worse instead of better. On the other hand, if the reverberation time is too short, the room seems too "dead," and speech and especially music become too crisp and *staccato,* a condition popularly termed *non-resonant.* This has a bad psychological effect on listeners as well as performers. A reverberation time of from one to two seconds seems best for all purposes, although a longer time is acceptable in larger rooms, and a longer time is tolerable for music than for speech, since the components of speech are usually not sustained as long as those of music. The extremely long reverberation in large cathedrals has been at least partly responsible for the type of liturgical music which has developed, particularly in its slow tempi and monotone chanting. It may also be the explanation of the slowness of satisfactory organ tremolos in relation to the normal speed of the voice vibrato, as discussed on page 25.)

Absorption is the weakening of sound waves through incomplete reflection. Hard plaster reflects a large amount of sound, absorbing little. Felt absorbs a large amount and reflects little. The fraction of the sound energy which is reflected is called the *coefficient of reflection.* The fraction which is not reflected, either because of being lost in the material of the reflecting surface or being transmitted through it, is called the *coefficient of absorption.* Thus the material of the walls, ceiling, and floor is of great importance in determining the acoustic action of a room, because materials differ greatly in their ability to absorb or transmit sound. Hard substances with smooth surfaces, which allow no entrance of portions of the sound waves into tiny openings where their energy can be destroyed through friction, will reflect sound with very little weakening. A room with hard, smooth walls will react on sound similarly to the way a room lined with mirrors will react on light. On the other hand, air passages which are very small in cross section cause considerable resistance to the oscillating movement of air particles in vibration. This friction transforms part of the energy of a sound wave into heat, dissipating and absorbing it. Thus, if sound enters a small crack in a thick wall it may be completely absorbed (dissipated into heat) before it can be reflected or can emerge on the other side. This is the reason why the channels and interstices in felt, carpets, and other porous materials are effective in acoustic correction in over-reverberant auditoriums. If one is accustomed to the sound effect in a living room with a large rug, it is easy to know when the rug has been rolled up, even though entering the room in the dark, by the change in reverberation, the room sounding quite differently to us without the rug than we are used to with it.

A few examples of the differences between materials in their ability to absorb sound, as calculated for a pitch of 256 cycles by the Riverbank Laboratories, are as follows:

Material	*Percentage of sound striking it which it absorbs (approx.)*
Hard plaster	3%
Cotton draperies hung against wall ...	8%
Velour draperies 4 inches from wall..	33%
Perforated metal enclosing 1½ inch thickness of mineral wool	74%
Open window (theoretically)	100%

Thus if an auditorium has a reverberation time of, say, four seconds, which means that sounds travel nearly a mile, through many reflections, before becoming inaudible, it may be corrected by covering part of the walls, floor, or ceiling with some material with a high absorption coefficient, such as heavy curtains, rugs, hair-felt, or some one of the many commercial products available for this purpose. The upholstery of chairs will cut down reverberation time greatly. Thus, in a certain opera house, when empty, the seats themselves supply well over 50% of the sound absorption. The human body is a good absorber of sound. Consequently, in auditoriums, the reverberation time is much less when completely filled than when empty or only half filled, and almost any auditorium is satisfactory with a full audience. The difference in reverberation between full and empty halls can, however, be minimized by using heavily upholstered chairs.

It makes not a great difference in what part of the room the absorbing material is placed, since sounds which are reflected many times must hit every part of the room, and run into the material sooner or later. As a general rule, however, the stage should be "live," and backed with a hard wall, to aid in projecting the sound through reflection out to the audience, and to give a desirable psychological reassurance to the performer or speaker. As Jeans [10] has said, since the loudness of a tone as heard in a room is proportional to the length of the period of reverberation, "a long period naturally induces an exhilarating feeling of effortless power, not to mention a welcome slurring over of roughnesses and inequalities of force and tempo, while a short period produces the despair of ineffectual struggle, the music has only had time to show its blemishes in all their nakedness, and is already dead." Even so, the rear walls of the auditorium should be relatively absorbent to prevent undesirable echoes and overreverberation around the listeners. And naturally, since it takes more sound energy to fill a large hall than a small one, the greater the intensity of the sound, other things equal, the larger the hall should be, and vice versa. Chamber music is normally not effective in an orchestral hall, nor a symphony in a small hall.

Insulation

When light strikes a surface it may be either: (1) *reflected,* as in the case of a bright shiny metal surface; (2) *absorbed,* as in the case of a thick black curtain; or (3) *transmitted,* as in the case of a light porous curtain. These same three effects also occur in the case of sound, frequently existing simultaneously.

---

[10] Jeans, Sir James, *Science and Music,* page 212. New York: The Macmillan Company, 1937.

The first two we have discussed. Often it is just as necessary to lessen the transmission of sound from one room to another as it is to lower the reverberation time within the rooms. There is an increasing demand for "sound insulation" in hospitals, studios, offices, apartments, airplane cabins, and so on, to prevent outside sounds from entering and inside sounds from passing out. Many concert audiences are annoyed by traffic noises from the outside. Walls which are not sufficiently rigid vibrate as a whole like a large diaphragm, passing sound readily into the next room, although damping the high frequencies much more than the low. One of the most effective ways of lessening sound transmission between rooms is to build the structure as rigidly as possible, and to construct the wall as a composite of materials differing greatly in density. This is because sound is partially reflected at every change in the density of the medium through which it passes. A thin film of water or of any substance of great density compared with air, can prevent the transmission of as much sound as a much larger thickness of highly absorbent hair-felt, the channels of which contain air. Stewart suggests an easy way of verifying this, by putting cotton in the ears, then noting the great difference caused by the additional use of a thin film of vaseline or soapy water at the opening. Similarly, the ticking of a watch is readily heard through a piece of cloth held between it and the ear, just as the sounds of a motion picture are transmitted from the loud-speaker through the porous screen. But if the cloth or the screen is wet, so as to fill with water the little openings between threads, the sound heard is greatly weakened.

Thus, walls which are to prevent sound transmission are built to contain alternate layers of greatly varying density. For example, in the Preparatory Department building of the Peabody Conservatory, the wall construction from each studio through the wall to the adjoining studio is as follows: plaster, hollow tile, a dead-air space, a blanket of hair-felt, another dead-air space, a sheet of metal, another dead-air space, hair-felt blanket, dead-air space, hollow tile and plaster. Transmission from one floor to another is lessened by "floating" the finish flooring on a layer of hair-felt or other absorbing material, so as to lessen the solid connection with the ceiling structure of the next lower room. This principle is easily understood by noting the enormous softening of the sound when a piece of spongy rubber is interposed between the base of a tuning fork and its resonator box, or the deadening effect of resting the peg of a 'cello or the legs of a piano on a very thick pad.

In soundproofing buildings, care must also be given to the proper mounting of machinery, and particularly to the proper design of ventilating ducts.

"Good Acoustics"

The word *auditorium* derives from the Latin word for "hearing." Too often, auditoriums have been designed with solicitude for every aspect except that of how well the auditors can hear. The term *good acoustics,* when used to describe any room, large or small, in which one must hear, should imply: (1) a size of room fitted to the music or speech to be performed; (2) an even distribution of sound (no curved walls or ceilings with foci near source or audience unless treated with absorbent material, except possibly around the stage); (3) an "optimum reverberation time" throughout the frequency range (not too much nor too little absorption of sound at any frequency, and of course no separate echoes); and (4) freedom from transmitted noise from other rooms or outdoors (secured by rigid construction, and using materials differing greatly in density).

Mention has already been made, under the topic of Reinforcement, of the effect of the resonant properties of rooms, alcoves, walls, floors, paneling, and so on, on the acoustics of auditoriums. In these cases it is usually the low tones which are favored. Aside from the resonant action of alcoves, these may act, and so also other deep recesses such as certain types of domes, as virtual absorbers of sound, since the sound is reflected around within them until it is greatly weakened before being reflected out from them again.

The stringing of wires or cords across an auditorium was formerly thought to be of value in improving its acoustics. This idea has little or no scientific basis, although it still persists in the minds of some. Sound waves flow around such wires as readily as water waves flow around narrow stakes. Of course, if a very large number of cords of some soft material like cotton were stretched quite close together, there would be some damping action. It would be easier, however, and probably more effective, to stretch strips of cheesecloth or sheeting, than to trouble with individual threads.

It should be borne in mind, furthermore, that in this matter of the acoustics of an auditorium, as in so many other matters where art is concerned, the aesthetic aspect must not be neglected. Thus, what may be an improvement mechanically, physically, or even physiologically, in the production of tone or in its reception by the hearer, may often be undesirable because it violates some psychological or aesthetic aspect. And even if the aesthetic aspect has no more important *raison d'être* than that of tradition, tradition may not be ignored in the world of art in the way that science may, and sometimes must, ignore it. For example, it might be thought that if any one type of music more than another should have the advantage of being performed and heard in a non-reverberant hall, this type of music is that of the pipe organ, with its typical sluggishness of speech, both in starting and stopping the tone, its definitely sustained character, and its lack of any percussion such as the piano has at the beginning of each tone. And yet most organists desire to perform in halls or churches which, by accepted standards of measurement, are too reverberant. Perhaps the reverberation, in strengthening the tone, gives an element of "percussiveness" and of relief from a dead-level sustaining of it. Perhaps reverberation is welcomed for its power of covering up the organ's sluggish response with a far greater sluggishness of build-up and cut-off of tone. But at least part of the desire for reverberation is to be explained by the fact that the organ has always in the past been associated with extremely reverberant cathedrals, and this "organ tradition" must be considered as well as the matter of blurring of sound. And when the tradition is an honored one, it becomes a desired end in itself. Sir Walter Parratt is credited with saying that even a sneeze would sound musical in St. Paul's Cathedral. And, as a matter of fact, even the literature which was composed for organ and choir has tended somewhat to be such as would be adapted to such halls.

Until recently there have not been in this country many great, resonant, cathedrals as found in Europe. This fact undoubtedly has had its effect on such matters as the tonal design of American organs, as pointed out by Mr. Donald Harrison, and on the taste of the public for liveness or deadness in a hall. In Bayreuth, as Mills points out, Wagnerian music is produced in a highly reverberant theatre. Italian opera, on the other hand, has usually been produced in smaller halls, with tiers and balconies, and therefore with less reverberation. The "Wagnerian tradition" cannot help but be influenced by the acoustics of Bayreuth, nor Italian opera by the acoustics of Italian opera houses. Such influences even affect later composers. The chamber music tradition, for example, has had its effect on composers. Chamber music has usually been performed in small halls with little audible reverberation, although it might be thought that such small tones would profit by any enlargement they might receive from a reverberant room.

There is evidence of a trend toward shorter reverberation times than in the past, particularly as more absorbent building materials become available, as well as means for amplifying sound without undue distortion. However, many mistakes have been made by over-treating music studios or other auditoriums where music is performed, through considering only the utilitarian aspect—speech intelligibility—without the equally important or even more important aspect, for music, of aesthetic fitness. A music studio, church, or any auditorium where music is to be appreciated, should not be too absorbent.

Diffraction

The Dutch astronomer Huyghens has described how *any* point on a wave front may become the origin of a secondary series of waves, which diverge in spheres. This important principle is in reality the explanation of the reflection of sound waves, discussed earlier. Furthermore, it helps us to understand the phenomena of *diffraction,* which means a change in the direction of sound waves caused by the introduction of obstacles around which the waves bend. When sound waves diffract around a barrier, they tend to fill up the "shadow" space behind it. When an advancing wave front reaches a barrier with a small opening, a new wave-center is produced at the

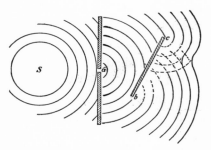

Fig. 18—Diffraction of sound waves.

opening. Figure 18 shows this in a rough and somewhat idealized form. The portions of the waves advancing from the source at *s,* which get through the narrow opening at *a,* begin at once to spread out in semicircular waves from *a* as a center, in the same way, as Bragg says, that a great ocean-wave surge through the narrow opening into a harbor will start a disturbance which spreads all over the harbor. And the portions of the new series of waves which get past the corners of the barrier at *b* and *c* begin at once to spread around into the space behind, somewhat as if they were originating from *b* and *c* as centers, although the actual situation is considerably more complicated. (Reflected portions of waves are omitted from this diagram in the interest of simplicity.)

Thus, diffraction, this spreading effect of waves, enables us to "hear sounds around corners." We do not have to be able to see the source of sound to be able to hear it. We do not have to be in a direct line of vision of an instrument to enjoy its sound. A sound entering an open window does not go just in a straight line across to the opposite wall, as sunlight would do, but immediately spreads out and fills the whole room, as if the open window were the source of the sound. Of course, the loudness of the sound heard depends on how high the window is opened, that is, on how much of the area of the original sound waves is permitted to enter.

"Sound shadows" are therefore practically nonexistent, or at most much smaller than corresponding light shadows, and are vaguely defined *unless the obstacle is many wave-lengths large in its dimensions*. Thus, the lower the pitch, the less defined is the sound shadow. In a busy street we hear the roar of traffic, but if we go even a short way down a side street, the sound is soon muffled. Only the lower tones tend to persist, because the houses obstruct more effectively the sounds of higher pitch. If we hold our hand straight out to the right from our shoulder, in an open place where there is no reflection from walls, and rub the thumb on the first finger, we produce a high-pitched sound which is heard by the right ear. If we then cover this ear the sound is no longer heard, since its wave-length is small enough to be prevented from diffracting around the head to the other ear. Sounds of lower pitch, however, easily spread around the head and are heard by the other ear. This varying effect of diffraction on sounds of different pitch can be further illustrated if one walks behind some large object like a billboard while listening to a band concert. The low tones (long wave-lengths) bend around the obstacle and are heard, while the high pitches are enfeebled because of the greater sound shadow cast by obstacles which are large in relation to the wave-length. The distortion in the quality may be heard in the loss of brilliance. Deeply recessed side-boxes in a concert hall may be similarly affected, particularly if lined with curtains which minimize the aid of reflections.

Thus diffraction lessens as frequency increases. With very high frequencies, high enough that the wave-length is small with respect to the size of an opening or a reflecting surface, sound waves may be directed so that a large part of their energy travels in a certain direction with relatively little divergent spreading. When driving past a succession of fence posts, the sound reflected to the driver is of the nature of a whisper or hiss (which contain only high frequencies), the lower frequencies having been lost by diffraction, having passed around and beyond the fence posts.

Refraction

We have seen how sound waves may be changed in direction through reflection, or through diffraction. Let us now discuss a third way. *Refraction* is the bending of a wave front, due to a change in the density of the material through which it is passing, or to a wind effect. The apparent distortion of a pencil in a glass of water is an illustration of the refraction of light waves when they pass from water to the much less dense air. Similar effects occur with sound waves. For example, sound is better heard at a distance on a clear, cool evening than at noon on a hot day. In the first case, the wave fronts are bent down toward the earth because of the higher velocity of sound in the

(a) evening   (b) noon

Fig. 19—Refraction of sound waves by temperature gradient.

upper air, which is less dense because of being warmer than the air immediately next to the cooling earth. In the second case, the opposite condition holds, and the wave front is bent upward away from the earth. Differences of temperature of this sort are called "temperature gradients." Thus, in Figure 19a, since the air becomes warmer for some distance the farther away it is from the earth, and since the speed of sound increases the warmer the air is, the sound waves are distorted in the manner shown, and along the arrowheaded paths indicated, sound is being bent back toward the earth. In *b,* where the speed is greatest immediately next to the hot earth, the distortion is reversed, and even the portions of the waves which start out to travel along the earth's surface tend to be bent upward, though here, too, diffraction modifies the effect.

Refraction may also occur through a bending of the wave fronts by winds, since winds usually blow faster farther away from the earth's surface. Differences in wind velocity of this sort are called *wind gradients.* When the wind is blowing in

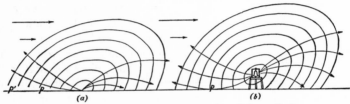

Fig. 20—Refraction of sound waves by wind gradient.

the same direction as the sound is traveling, the wave front is bent down, and sound can be heard farther, unless it be destroyed by friction with the earth's surface. When the wind is blowing in the direction opposite to the sound, the bending is such as to tend to lift the sound-wave front away from the surface of the earth. Thus, in Figure 20*a,* with the wind blowing from left to right, the sound waves tend to be lifted off the ground to windward, and bent down toward the ground to leeward. If we walk into the wind, away from the sound, until it becomes inaudible, as at *p,* we can then hear it again if we climb a ladder. At a still farther distance, *p',* a higher ladder is necessary. Aside from the sense of smell, this is the reason the hunter has the advantage over the bird sitting on the ground when he approaches upwind, as Wood [11] points out, because the sounds of

---

[11] Wood, Alexander, *Sound Waves and Their Uses,* page 26. London: Blackie & Son, Ltd., 1930.

his approach are refracted upward and pass over the prey weakened or unheard. When he approaches downwind, the sounds are refracted downward and are well heard on the ground.

Refraction away from the earth can be lessened by elevating the source, as in Figure 20*b*. Here the curvature is the same, but some of the sound from the bell sweeps downward at points distant from the source, as at *p,* before it continues its curving flight upward.

It should be emphasized that sound waves have always a speed considerably greater than that of the wind, and in addition spread out in *all* directions from the source. An electric fan illustrates these differences between sound waves and air currents. The fan produces an air current in one direction, an actual movement of the air as a whole. But we can hear the hum of the fan in all directions, since the sound waves go out nearly equally well in all directions, being, as they are, the movement of a *condition* through a *medium* and not a movement of the medium as a whole from one place to another. The air stream produced by the fan is relatively much slower in speed than the sound waves radiating from it.

Since the speed of sound in water is considerably greater than in air, when an air wave strikes the surface of a body of water, the refraction effect is such as to lessen the angle of penetration. If the angle at which it strikes the water surface is less than a certain "critical angle," the sound wave may not enter the water at all, but may be completely reflected. If, then, an air-temperature gradient exists such that the upper layers of atmosphere are warmer than those near the water, or if the wind is blowing with the sound and faster above the water than on its surface, then the sound will be refracted (bent) down again toward the water, and will be again reflected. Thus sound can skip along the water similarly to the way a stone may be skipped—as in Figure 21, which shows the direction taken by one "ray." [12]

Guns, and the barking of a dog, have been heard across eight

---

[12] Humphreys points out that if this occurs on a river bordered by high cliffs, a still further confinement of the sound occurs. The river is then one surface of a gigantic "speaking tube," and sound may travel to a surprising distance.

miles of water, and the paddles of a steamer across fifteen miles. Herschel has reported the instance of a conversation being held between two men across the harbor of Port Bowen in the Arctic regions, a distance of a mile and a quarter. Possibly refraction was aiding here.

"Silent zones" near explosions are probably to be explained by refraction of the sound away from the earth, and a later reversal of refraction direction to bring it down again at a point farther

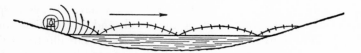

Fig. 21—Successive refraction and reflection over water.

on. Or, it may be made audible at this farther point by the natural spreading in of sound by diffraction from another direction.

Refractive effects are of little importance in music (except possibly the music of the carillon), but of considerable importance where sound must be heard over long distances, as in fog-signaling. Also, because of the spreading effect of sound, refractive effects are frequently not complete, but only tendencies.

Doppler Effect

For completeness, one other aspect of sound waves should be mentioned, though it does not have any importance for music as ordinarily heard. If a person is anchored in a small boat in a body of water, a certain number of waves will pass his boat in a unit of time. If he then rows into the waves, he will meet more of them in the same unit of time, but if he rows with the waves, in the same direction, fewer of them will reach him in the same unit of time. A similar effect occurs with sound waves, although because of their much greater speed, a correspondingly greater speed of motion of the observer relative to them must occur, before the effect is noted. Walking speeds are insufficient. Thus, if an observer approaches a source of sound fairly rapidly (say in an automobile traveling thirty miles an hour), he will encounter enough more sound waves per second to produce an apparent small rise in pitch over that observed when he is stationary. Similarly, if the source approaches him, a higher pitch will be heard. If source and observer approach each other, the effect is increased, and a still higher pitch is heard. The observer's sense of pitch depends on the *number* of pulses which reach him per second, and if this number is artificially increased over the number actually produced per second, he will hear a higher tone. If the source recedes from the observer, or the observer from the source, or both from each other, the pitch will appear to be lowered. This is known as the *Doppler effect*. The amount of rise or drop in pitch over that heard normally will naturally depend *only* on the speeds of source and observer and not at all on the distance between them.

A common misunderstanding of this phenomenon by students is shown on examination papers by the statement, "The nearer you get to the sound, the higher it is, and the farther away, the lower it is." This is false. The nearer one gets to the sound, the *louder* it sounds, of course, but the amount of *pitch* distortion is constant so long as the speed is constant. If one could stand alongside a track and listen to a train come from a distance at a constant speed while continually blowing its whistle, the whistle would first become audible at a certain higher-than-normal pitch, and remain at this pitch, growing louder and louder until the moment of passing. It would then *suddenly* drop to a lower-than-normal pitch and remain at this pitch as the train got farther and farther away, the tone getting softer and softer until no longer audible.

The Doppler effect is quite noticeable in this day of high-speed transportation, when vehicles pass each other. Differences of half and whole tones and minor thirds may be heard by passengers in automobile traffic, differences of major thirds in railway travel, while much greater differences can be heard with airplanes. The principle can be illustrated in various other ways.

For example, if two sources are mistuned sufficiently to produce beats at a certain rate, and one of the sources is then placed in motion toward or away from the hearer, the number of beats per second will change. Furthermore, extending this principle to inanimate "observers," if we imagine two tuning forks in unison, one vibrating and the other not, the vibrating one will not arouse sympathetic vibration in the other (the "observer"), unless they maintain the same spatial distance from *each other*. They may be in motion in space, as long as they have no relative motion to each other.

3

Vibratory Sources of Sounds
Used in Music

A. STRETCHED STRINGS [1]

IF a string be stretched between two supports, its elasticity is revealed. Thus, if it be displaced, it will tend to return to its former position, and because of its momentum it will overshoot this point more or less. These are the conditions which make vibration possible. Perhaps the beginning of all stringed instruments is to be found in the twang of the bowstring that discharged the primitive arrow, although Egyptian mythology attributes it to the dried tendons of a dead tortoise, stretched over its shell.

Traveling Waves

If a long rope, loosely stretched between two supports, be given a sudden sharp impact, a pair of waves can be seen to travel away in opposite directions from the impact-point toward the ends, be there reflected, and approach each other again, but reversed in position. That is, if the original pulses were crests on top of the rope, the reflected ones will return on the bottom, looking like troughs. In Figure 22, *a* shows, quite diagrammatically, such a pair of *traveling waves,* produced by an impact at the midpoint. When they are reflected at the ends they will

---

[1] The term *stretched strings* is understood to include stretched filaments of any material, as, for example, metal wires.

look like the dotted-line troughs. If the impact be less sudden, the waves will be longer, as in *b*. If the impact were still slower, and took place near the end of the string instead of at the middle, the result would approximate that shown in *c*, the familiar type of motion when a string is said to be vibrating in its fundamental mode. Traveling waves occur also, although too fast to be seen,

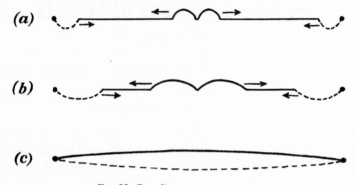

Fig. 22—Traveling waves on a rope.

in strings stretched tightly enough to give audible sounds when struck or otherwise displaced, as in the various musical stringed instruments.

Transverse Standing Waves, Loops, Nodes

When such strings are periodically displaced as in regular vibration, and when the tension and the speed of vibration are carefully adjusted, the reflected waves are superposed on the on-coming ones, the two sets augmenting each other at certain points and neutralizing each other at others, thereby producing *transverse standing waves*. Thus the superposition of two sets of waves traveling in opposite directions gives the familiar picture of standing waves, with their characteristic *loops* (points of movement), and *nodes* (points of relative rest). In the special case of the string vibrating in its fundamental form, there are only two nodes (at the ends) and one loop. In the case of a string producing its octave, there are three nodes and two loops, and so on. Figure 23 shows five successive phases of one complete vibration of this latter type.

There are three methods of displacing the strings used in music: (1) *plucking,* as, for example, in the harp, or in a violin *pizzicato;* (2) *bowing,* as in the instruments of the violin family; and (3) *striking,* as in the piano. Neither plucking, bowing, nor striking permits the string to vibrate in S.H.M., because all three give a more or less angular or unsymmetrical move-

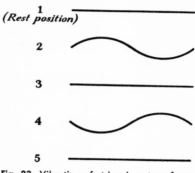

Fig. 23—Vibration of string in octave form.

ment to the string, especially when the displacement point is not at the center of the string—and it rarely is.

Plucking

If a string be plucked to one side by some thin, hard-pointed object at *A,* Figure 24, for example, and then let go, a pair of waves will travel away from this point, causing the string to pass through a cycle of forms of which nine are shown here, representing one half of a complete to-and-fro vibration. Number 9 is the reverse of number 1. The arrows indicate the directions in which the waves travel away from the original displacement point to meet again in a new displacement point on the other side of the string (number 9). The string will then return through the same forms to the original form, completing one whole vibration, as indicated by the numbers 10 to 17. (The arrows would have to be reversed to indicate this second half of the vibration.) Number 17, the same form as number 1, will then start a new cycle. The action is fundamentally different from the curved lines of S.H.M., being characterized by sharp corners instead of curves. A kinked "curve" of this sort, if analyzed, will be found to contain numerous high partials, which give a metallic timbre to its tone. If the string be plucked with the finger it will show a vibration form with less-sharp corners, because the finger is softer, larger, and more rounded. This will result in a tone which contains fewer of the high partials, and is therefore more mellow.

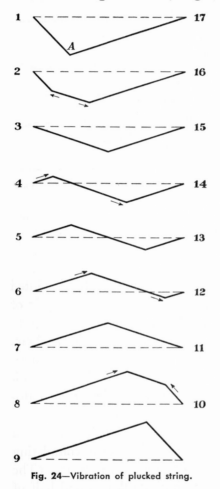

Fig. 24—Vibration of plucked string.

Bowing

The case of the bowed string has been investigated by Helmholtz and others. When the bow is in action, its resinous surface engages the string by friction, pushing or pulling it to one side. When the elastic tension of the string increases sufficiently, the bow friction can no longer hold it, and once released from the bow it skids back over the bow hairs even though the bow is still moving forward, overshooting its mid-position until its tension in the opposite direction brings it to rest. Then the bow engages it again, carrying it forward for the next vibration. Thus the to-and-fro motion of the string is maintained by a one-way motion of the bow. This type of motion will naturally result in a complex vibration form since the pressure of the bow to one side will tend to give an angular displacement. This pressure of the bow to one side will also tend to twist the string slightly, so that the movement will contain not only transverse vibration but *torsional vibration,* in which the displacements are neither transverse nor longitudinal, but in a twisting direction. Still other irregularities will be introduced by the fact that the velocity of the string is quite suddenly reversed at the moment when it ceases to adhere to the bow, and its movement backward is faster than its movement in the bow direction.

Thus we might suppose that an oscillograph record of the wave form would be similar to that in Figure 25.

Fig. 25—Graph of vibration of a point on a bowed string.

This sort of vibration, with its marked discontinuities at the angles, would give rise to a tone with many high partials. Actually, Helmholtz observed a form similar to this by watching a point on the string through his vibration microscope. In practice, however, the wave form of a bowed instrument as heard through the air is much modified from this form by the characteristics of the bridge, belly, and other reinforcing materials. Figure 10, page 50, shows an oscillograph record of the tone of the A-string of a violin as heard through the air.

Striking

The case of the struck string is similar to that of the plucked, in that a hard, sharply pointed hammer produces a more kinked wave form and thus a more brilliant or metallic tone, while a softer, more rounded hammer produces a less kinked wave form and a mellower tone. Photographs have shown, according to Richardson,[2] that in a piano the hammer may not remain in contact with the wire for even as long a time as one complete vibration before it rebounds. This means that the struck point is displaced in advance of other parts of the string which may still be in their position of rest. The string as a whole is not permitted to adjust itself to the displacement before being released, as in the plucked string.

---

[2] Richardson, E. G., *The Acoustics of Orchestral Instruments and of the Organ,* page 113. London: Edward Arnold & Co., 1929.

It is a little realized fact that after a piano hammer has once struck, the pianist has no longer any control over the tone quality except through pedal effects. For that matter, the hammer travels as a free body during the latter part of its stroke, swinging on its pivot but not in contact with the key mechanism, so that actually all the performer can do is to give it a certain velocity by depressing the key with a certain strength, after which he has no further key control over the tone. Thus, wiggling the finger, rolling the forearm, or continuing to press on the key after the tone has sounded, have absolutely no effect on the tone quality, although they may produce a valuable physiologic relaxation or a valuable psychologic effect on performer or hearer. Give the hammer a certain velocity and it will always strike in the same manner. Thus the possibilities of "touch" are more limited on the piano than commonly realized. The violinist has a much more intimate control of his quality. On the piano, all possible effects are explained by the variables: hammer velocity, impact and action noises, and pedal effects, although the possibilities here are manifold. All else is illusory, though sometimes of psychologic or aesthetic value. Ortmann has discussed these matters, especially in his book, *The Physical Basis of Piano Touch and Tone*. The article by Hart, Fuller, and Lusby, listed in the bibliography, gives a further discussion.

Since plucking, bowing, and striking all give more or less angular or unsymmetrical movements to the string, they therefore produce complex vibration forms, which, however, can be shown by analysis to consist of several simple forms superposed on each other. These of course produce complex tones containing partials in the harmonic series.

Harmonics

A particular partial tone may be isolated from its fellows by lightly touching the vibrating string at a point which would be a node for that partial. It then sounds forth by itself as a fairly pure tone called a *harmonic*.[3] Conversely, by causing the string to be displaced at certain points, the partials which would have nodes at these points are greatly weakened or eliminated. Thus if a string be displaced at or near its midpoint, the octave and all the other even-numbered partials are automatically eliminated or at least diminished, because they all require the midpoint to be a node. This was actually the case in the *cembal d'amore,* a rare instrument of the clavichord family. If a stretched string be plucked at one seventh its length from one end, the dissonant seventh partial in the harmonic series may be practically eliminated. The hammers in a piano are made to strike at about one seventh to one ninth the length of the string, except in the case of the highest strings. These are struck still nearer the end in order to compensate somewhat for the loss of higher partials through the increasing stiffness of such short wires.[4] A violin bow engages the string *usually* at about one ninth to one twelfth the length of the open violin string (a greater distance in *piano* playing and less in *forte*), thereby weakening these partials but permitting all those below them to be present. If it were bowed at its midpoint, all the even-numbered partials would be weakened, and in addition the amplitude of the fundamental would be lessened. In the fundamental form of vibration, the excursions of the string are nowhere else as large as at the midpoint, and if this point is restricted by the bow hairs to a narrow amplitude of vibration, the fundamental is weakened. Bowing the string near the end produces a richer tone as well as a stronger fundamental. (See pages 97-98.) The squeakiness heard from an unskillful violin player is frequently due to uncontrolled harmonics, or to the very high tones caused by

---

[3] *Natural harmonics* imply those produced on an unstopped string; *artificial,* those produced on a stopped string.

[4] However, an investigation by Kaufmann indicates that the principal advantage of having the striking point at one seventh to one ninth of the length may not be the elimination of these partials after all, but the fact that the fundamental has its maximum amplitude when the hammer strikes at about this distance. (See also the small print on pages 97 and 98.)

longitudinal vibrations of the string generated by a sliding of the bow along the length of the string during its stroke.

The formation of harmonics may be observed by fastening one end of a cotton thread to a support and the other to a prong of an electrically driven tuning fork, or the clapper of an electric bell held in the hand. With a little practice the thread may be tensed just the right amount to cause it to swing in its fundamental form of one loop. In order to secure the two-loop form, since the driving frequency cannot change, it is necessary to *loosen* the tension until a point is reached where this frequency corresponds to the octave of a new lower fundamental. When this is done, the vibration form can be seen to become unstable and suddenly jump into a standing-wave form having two loops. Further loosening will show sudden jumps into higher-loop forms, which can be demonstrated by placing paper riders at various points. Those at nodal points remain on the string, while those at other points are knocked off when the string (or an adjacent string tuned to the same pitch) is set into segmental vibration. In Figure 26, the first three cuts show the fundamental, the three-segment, and the five-segment standing-wave forms produced in this way. Forms with as many as eight or ten segments may be secured if thin enough threads be used.

When the tension of the string is constant, the fundamental is unchanged, and the higher-loop forms correspond to members of the harmonic series. Thus Paganini, by using violin strings made especially thin, and touching the string lightly at a nodal point, was able to produce the twelfth harmonic partial. The higher harmonics tend to sharpen slightly, however, because of the increasing stiffness of the wire when forced to divide into many short segments. (See page 95.) Most violin literature does not call for more than the third or fourth harmonic.

In instruments such as are used in music—where the vibration is produced by plucking, bowing, or striking—such simple

(a)

(b)

(c)

(d)

Fig. 26—Simple and complex forms of string vibration.

93

forms, containing but a single mode of vibration at a time, rarely exist, if ever. The situation is rather as shown in Figure 26d, where several forms are superposed on each other, to produce a tone containing various overtones in strengths corresponding to the relative strengths of the vibration forms producing them. Furthermore, it almost never happens that the vibrations of a string actually lie in one plane. Most commonly they consist of rotations more or less complicated, and in addition, except perhaps in the piano, a certain amount of torsional (twisting) vibration.

Pitch

The fundamental pitch of a stretched string, determined by the frequency, depends on its length, its tension, and its weight.

As a string or wire is shortened, its frequency rises proportionally. Stated mathematically, the frequency is inversely proportional to the length. Thus the strings of a harp are lifted a half tone or a whole tone by shortening their vibrating lengths by a device operated from the pedals. The strings of a violin have their vibrating lengths shortened by stopping them with the fingers. (The fact that the frequency rise is proportional explains why the actual spacings for stopping any interval, such as whole tones, for example, must constantly decrease, the higher the positions played.) The alteration of pitch secured by causing a string to sound a harmonic is really an illustration of this same effect of string length, since the vibrating lengths of the string have been shortened through segmentation.

As a string or wire is tightened, as for example by turning a peg of a violin or a tuning pin of a piano or harp, its frequency rises also, varying as the square root of its tension. The highest-pitched string of a violin, the E-string, bears on the bridge with the greatest tension (and is often made of metal instead of gut). Since heat expands metal and gut slightly, reducing the tension of a stretched string or wire, pianos, violins, and similar instruments are slightly flatted in hot weather and sharped in cold, unless compensating changes occur through expansion of the frames which hold the strings.

As a string or wire is made heavier—as for example in the piano, harp, and violin family—by making it thicker or by wrapping it with other wire, its frequency lowers. The G-string of a violin is thus thicker than all the other strings. Expressed mathematically, the frequency varies inversely as the square root of the mass.

These principles are all illustrated in the piano or violin. If the length, tension, and weight of the string are kept constant, the amplitude has little if any effect on the frequency. If it did have any marked effect, string music in its present form could not exist, for every variation in the loudness of a tone would vary its pitch as well, and its pitch would vary as it died away.

In addition to the above-mentioned determinants of frequency, a less important one should be mentioned. This is the stiffness of the wire or string, the effect of which is similar to adding a small tension. However, the amount of this effect varies with the frequency, so that the various members of the harmonic series, for example, are differently affected, and therefore distorted somewhat from their true positions. The "harmonic series" is rendered slightly inharmonic whenever the stiffness of strings is appreciable, as will occur with thick metal wires. In the wires used in musical instruments, however, the effect is very slight, the overtones lying extremely close to their true positions. Speaking generally, thin wires will be less stiff, and therefore able to subdivide easily into shorter vibrating segments corresponding to quite correct harmonics. Thick wires will be less able to overcome their stiffness and produce harmonics, and when they do, the "harmonics" will be distorted (sharped) from their true frequency.

Loudness

The loudness of the tone of a stringed instrument, determined by the amplitude of vibration, depends on the force used in plucking, bowing, or striking, and of course also on the manner of reinforcement of the sound, and on the strength of the materials to withstand the tensions and the displacing forces. The power of the modern piano, for example, is largely due to the improvements made during the last century in the tenacity and elasticity of steel wire, and the rigidity of steel frames which carry total tensions of upwards of thirty tons in the largest instruments.

The manner in which the sound is reinforced also has its effect on the total loudness. For example, the tone of a violin string or a 'cello string is augmented by the vibration of the body of the instrument. But the 'cello gets an additional re-inforcement from the vibration of the floor on which it rests, whereas the violin tone is somewhat absorbed in the shoulder, the instrument having no solid contact with the floor.

Softer tones may be procured in the instruments of the violin family by the use of the *mute,* a clamp of wood, metal, or other material, with several split prongs which enclose the wooden bridge when pushed onto it. By thus weighting and restricting the vibration of the bridge, the mute decreases the loudness of the sound, but changes its quality as well, since the high fre-quencies are reduced in greater proportion than the low fre-quencies. In the piano, softer tones may be procured by the use of a pedal which reduces the length of throw of the ham-mers (as in "uprights"), or else shifts them so that they strike only one or two of the two or three wires present for each pitch (as in the *una corda* in "grands").[5] These effects also, how-ever, cause quality changes as well. The so-called "loud pedal" adds loudness only by lifting the dampers from all of the wires and thereby permitting them to be set into sympathetic vibra-tion. The harp, having no dampers, has this effect constantly unless the performer damps the strings with his hands.

Tone Quality

The tone quality of a stringed instrument, determined by the manner of vibration, is dependent on such factors as the fol-lowing:

---

[5] The lowest tones of the piano are produced by single wires. Thus no softening of these tones is produced by the soft pedal in a grand.

a. Type of string displacement (whether plucked, bowed, or struck, and at what exact point)

b. Material and shape of the instrument used for plucking, bowing, or striking

c. Bow pressure, bow speed, piano-hammer speed, etc.

d. Tension, length, thickness, and elasticity of the string

e. Characteristics of reinforcing materials, such as the bridge, soundboard or belly, sound post, air resonators, etc. Use of mute, *una corda,* etc.

Mention has already been made of the different types of string vibration caused by plucking, bowing, and striking. The effect of the position of the point of displacement in any one of these cases has also been described. The nearer to its midpoint the string is displaced, the hollower its tone will be, and the nearer to an end, the brighter the tone, because of more and stronger harmonics. The player can make use of this fact to secure differences in quality, by plucking or bowing at various points along the string. Some of the modern harp effects used by Salzedo are explained in this way. The violinist secures his *sul ponticello* and *sul tasto* qualities in the same way, since, as the bow moves nearer the bridge, it does not lie over the nodes of any except the very high harmonics, so that moderately high harmonics are still strongly produced. Conversely, as it is moved away from the bridge, even the moderately high harmonics are weakened. Thus, whereas the average bowing point is at about one ninth to one twelfth the length of the open string, the performer sometimes bows as far as one fifth or as near as one twenty-fifth of the length.

A modifying exception to the above paragraph must, however, be noted. It is true that if bow speed be kept approximately constant, bowing nearer the end of the string will increase the strength of the higher harmonics at the expense of the fundamental. If, however, the bow speed and pressure are correspondingly increased as the bow is moved nearer the end of the string, the quality of the tone will not appreciably change. In fact, the fundamental will increase in strength until the bow comes very near the end, provided the bow speed and pressure can be sufficiently increased. This is because the portion of the string under the bow, although displaced, is definitely limited in its amplitude. Thus, if a string be vibrating in its fundamental form, it can attain a wider amplitude as the bow is moved away from the center. The string can nowhere vibrate as widely as at its center. If therefore the bow is at its center, vibration is limited. This limitation decreases as the bow moves away from the center toward an end, *provided bow speed and pressure can be increased sufficiently to maintain the fundamental form of vibration.* Similar reasoning applies to any partial, so that, as Saunders surmises, more tone of any particular partial will be produced the nearer the bow moves to one of its nodes (but not too near).

These opposing effects seem contradictory, and perhaps they tend to balance each other. Both Helmholtz and Jeans have pointed out that the vibration form of a violin string is tolerably independent of the point of bowing.

As we have seen, the softer or the more rounded the displacing instrument is, the less rich will the tone be in higher partials; and the harder, the narrower, or the sharper the instrument which displaces the string, the more prominent will the higher partials be. An example is in bowing *col legno* (with the wood of the bow). If there are too many of these high harmonic partials, their dissonance [6] causes the quality to become metallic, "tinpanny," like that of a worn-out piano. Such a piano may be improved by having its hammers tipped with soft new felt, or by pricking the old rutted felts with a needle to soften them and produce a mellower tone. A too dull piano should have its hammers filed to a sharper or harder point.

---

[6] Dissonant harmonics must be carefully distinguished from inharmonic partials. Dissonant harmonics are those higher partials in the harmonic series which lie within a whole tone or less of each other, and therefore are dissonant with each other, and frequently with the fundamental. However, they may still be truly harmonic, and just as natural as any of the lower ones, if their frequency is an exact multiple of the fundamental frequency. They are formed by the subdivision of a string or air column into a whole number of segments. Inharmonic partials, on the other hand, bear no simple frequency relation to the fundamental, and thus do not coincide with tones in the harmonic series. *All* inharmonic partials are likely to be dissonant, not only with themselves, but with the fundamental as well, and for this reason tones which contain them in any strength are of little musical value except in percussion instruments.

A certain relation must obtain between bow speed and bow pressure in the instruments of the violin family. Too great a pressure for the speed "crushes" the tone. Too great a speed for the pressure gives the characteristic whistling of harmonics. Recent studies by Abbott and Saunders indicate that if bow speed and the point of bowing are kept constant, an increase of bow pressure, though possibly changing the tone quality, produces on the average no increase in the intensity of the tone. The extra energy must go into heating the string and bow by friction. And when the bow pressure is increased sufficiently the tone will break down (crushed tone) unless the bow speed be increased also.

Mention has already been made of the effect of piano-hammer speed as the principal determinant of piano quality.

The marked effect of string characteristics on quality is well known. Gut strings sound different from metal strings, thin strings from thick. For example, a thin metal violin E-string has a more brilliant tone than a thicker one would have. The thinner the string, other things equal, the stronger will be its high partials, because thick strings cannot divide into many vibrating segments as easily as can thin ones. When thick strings are forced to subdivide so as to produce a harmonic and lose the fundamental entirely, these "harmonics" tend to be distorted from their true positions, because of the stiffness factor, as has been described. On the other hand, when a uniformly bowed string is sounding its fundamental with overtones it tends to vibrate in a steady state only possible with truly harmonic overtones. The result of these two tendencies is therefore a compromise, in which the overtones of such a thick string when sounding its fundamental are truly harmonic but greatly weakened. A somewhat similar effect will be described under the subject of Air Columns. It is not always realized that the flute-like quality of violin harmonics is not limited to these tones, as pointed out by Giltay, but that almost the same quality appears with firm-stopped tones of the same pitch, *if made on the same string, and without vibrato.* The reason nearly all passages played in harmonics sound so differently from those not so played (aside from the lighter bow pressure and the frequent absence of vibrato), is that the harmonics are usually being produced on lower (thicker) strings and shorter vibrating lengths than those used for tones of the same pitch when firmly stopped, and this tends to weaken or eliminate the overtones lying above the desired harmonic, and purify its quality as compared with normal violin quality. For the same reason, if a tone of some pitch higher than the open E-string be played successively on, say, the E, A, and D strings in the natural, firm-stopped, manner, the lower the string used, the more mellow the tone will be, in the sense of having fewer and weaker overtones.

Large differences in tone quality and loudness may result from relatively small variations in the characteristics of the reinforcing materials, since the tone that reaches our ears comes largely from them. For example, the difference between the quality and volume of a grand piano tone and that of an upright lies partly in the increased soundboard area of the former (and also, of course, in its longer strings and greater tensions). In the case of the violin instruments, the shape and thickness of the bridge is important. The effect of mutes of various materials and weights has been mentioned. Small differences in the graining of the wood of the belly may affect the tone considerably. Saunders feels that the ease of response of a good violin may perhaps be the result of a breaking down, through years of vibration, of the cell walls in the summer growth of the spruce in the belly, thereby making the wood more flexible. The size, thickness, and curvature of soundboards are factors in determining the tone quality. The harp, for example, has an elongated pyramidal shaped soundboard which rests on the shoulder and encloses a body of air. The piano has a soundboard which is almost flat. The rigidity with which the glue binds at the edges of a violin top, or even in its "purfling," may affect its stiffness and therefore its type of vibration. Saunders feels that the rawness of a new violin may be partly explained in this way, and that when it is older and the glue has begun to crack a bit the plates may vibrate more freely. Instruments made of thick wood (and therefore stiffer), emphasize the higher frequencies, those with thin, the lower frequencies. The varnish itself seems, according to recent scientific investigation, to have but little effect on the tone quality. However, since the inside surfaces of a violin are usually not varnished they are able to absorb moisture, which changes the weight and elasticity of the wood. Saunders has pointed out that since the human body loses moisture to the air rapidly, a dry instrument brought near to the player could change its characteristics somewhat through absorption of this moisture by gut strings or wood surfaces. This condition perhaps explains the value of "playing in" instruments that have been out of use for a time.

The sound post, which stands between the front and back panels of the violin body, held by their pressure, needs to be of a certain material and a certain length, and placed accurately in a certain position. The sound post transmits the motion of the bridge and belly to the back, enabling sound energy to be radiated from the back, particularly for low frequencies, and enables the belly to bear the pressure of the stretched strings without being distorted. If the sound post be removed, the lower frequencies are greatly weakened, destroying the mellowness. Too thick a sound post will destroy the brilliancy of the tone. Similarly, the placing of the sound post too far from the bridge will destroy brilliancy. Its proper position is slightly behind the right foot of the bridge, although high-built instruments require it nearer the bridge than normal.

The characteristics of the bass-bar, which spreads the vibrations over the belly while at the same time reinforcing the belly, are important. The bass-bar has strengthened since the day of Stradivarius, due to the increased string tension caused by the rising of the pitch standard and the lengthening of the finger board. Such a change has altered the weight and elasticity of the belly. Since all or nearly all of the fine old instruments have been altered by the substitution of a longer finger board or by some other repair, such as a stronger bass-bar, it is doubtful if any of them sound today as they did originally.

Occasionally a tone played on a violin or other stringed instrument will coincide in pitch with a natural frequency of some part of the wood or enclosed air of the body of the instrument. If this resonance is too strong, an undesirable "wolf note" results, often occurring about a perfect fourth above the lowest tone of the instrument, in which the violin or other instrument takes up so much energy, as Richardson [7] says, that the control of the tone seems to pass out of the player's hands. The bow refuses to "bite," and a satisfactory tone is unobtainable. If the bow pressure is increased, the resulting tone is often unsteady and of variable intensity. Often, on the other hand, one can kill the wolf note entirely by using enough energy to ride over it. They are most likely to occur when one is playing softly. Ordinarily, the wood of a violin has a complex but small vibration amplitude, but during a wolf note its motion is of simple form and large amplitude.

The size and shape of the "*f*-holes" has an effect on quality, also. The size of these openings determines the natural frequency of the resonant air enclosed in the body. This frequency is normally about that of Middle C or D. The shape and position of the *f*-holes appear to be important in determining the degree of flexibility of the belly, as Giltay points out. The shape and position of the holes has been determined empirically. When either is changed, as has been repeatedly tried, the flexibility of the belly and its nodal divisions are altered. The accepted form seems best.

---

[7] Richardson, E. G., *The Acoustics of Orchestral Instruments and of the Organ*, page 125. London: Edward Arnold & Co., 1929.

Duration

The duration of the tone of stringed instruments depends on the elasticity of the string, the original amplitude of displacement, friction, and the manner of maintaining tone. In the case of the piano, the highest tones are produced by wires which must be stretched very tightly, and are quite short as well. The resulting stiffness causes their vibration to die out very much sooner after being struck than in the case of the lower-pitched wires. This is why the highest keys of the piano are not provided with dampers.

Instruments

The instruments in which stretched strings (or wires) are used are:

Struck strings:	*Plucked strings:*
Piano	Harp
Bowed strings:	Mandolin
Violin	Guitar
Viola	Banjo, etc.
Violoncello	Also *pizzicato* in instru-
Double bass	ments of violin family

B. AIR COLUMNS

A body of air is an elastic substance in the sense that if it be compressed it tends to expand again to its normal density. However, it "overshoots" the normal point, expanding until it becomes less dense than normal, or relatively rarefied. Then it tends to "shrink" again and become more compressed, but again overshoots and becomes more compressed than normal, and so on. Thus, since air is elastic it can vibrate, and we find that a column of air when enclosed by wood, metal, or some other rigid material, has some parallelism to a stretched string in its vibration, although there are marked differences also.

Traveling Waves

In the case of the stretched string, the waves which travel along it and are reflected at the ends to superpose on each other and produce standing waves, are *transverse waves.* In other words they are caused by displacements of the string at *right angles* to the direction the wave is traveling. In the case of a column of air, these traveling waves are *longitudinal waves,* waves of relative compression and rarefaction—in other words *sound waves*—and therefore are produced by displacements of the air particles back and forth in the same line of travel that the waves themselves follow.

Compressional Standing Waves, Loops, Nodes

If the frequency of these waves be constant and properly adjusted with relation to the length of the air column, their reflections from the ends of the column of air will be superposed on the unreflected waves, producing "standing waves," which greatly reinforce the original vibration. These standing waves are similar in principle to the standing waves on stretched strings (which were set up when the frequency of forced vibration was properly adjusted with relation to the length of the string), except that their displacements are longitudinal instead of transverse.

Since the "standing waves" in an air column are compressional, if we could see them they would not look at all like those on a stretched string, with the familiar loops and nodes. However, we still keep these same words to describe the points of *greatest motion* and of *little or no motion,* respectively. Thus, if the end of an air column be stopped by a piece of wood or metal, the back-and-forth motion of the air particles adjoining it is prevented, and thus the stopped end of a pipe will always be a *node* (point of no motion), while there will always be a *"loop"* (point of greatest motion) at, or close to, the open end.

The compressional type of vibration in an air column may

be visualized if we imagine the air to be replaced by a long, coiled spring. A sudden push at one end would travel as a "compression wave" to the other end and be there reflected. In a series of regularly spaced compressions and rarefactions, produced by regular pushes, the effect of the superposition of direct and reflected waves is to produce apparent standing waves, with the coils moving slightly back and forth at "loop" points and remaining quiet (although undergoing pressure variations) at nodes.

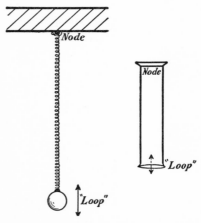

Let us consider in detail, following the description by Bragg, the simplest form of vibration of such a spring— that in which a long, weak spring is hung as in Figure 27 from a rigid support, such as the ceiling. When the ball at the end slowly oscillates up and down, the action of the spring simulates the more

Fig. 27—Longitudinal vibration of a spring.

rapid action of the air in the inverted jar or pipe when set into vibration. At the opening (the "loop"), the air rushes back and forth, while at the surface of the upper, closed end (the node), there is of course alternate compression and rarefaction, but no movement. If, when the ball is at rest, we give a very sudden pull on it, displacing it downward, and stretching the portion of the spring immediately above it, the ball will tend to stay in this new position a very short instant, during which the stretched region travels up the spring as a "wave of stretch" to the ceiling, is there reflected, and comes down the spring again. When this stretched region again reaches the ball, it acts to pull the ball up again, because of the elasticity of the spring. As the ball suddenly flies up, its momentum carries it beyond its normal rest position, and it compresses a section of the spring immediately above it. This compressed region then travels up the spring to the ceiling as a "wave of compression," is there reflected, and returns to the ball. The compressed region then acts, because of its elastic pressure, to thrust the ball downward again, and the whole process is repeated. In the case of the inverted pipe the action is similar, except that the column of air takes the place of the elastic weighted spring, and the movement at the mouth is not so abrupt as we have described for the ball. And, as in the case of the spring, compressions are reflected back as *rarefactions,* and rarefactions as *compressions,* at free (open) ends, *but are reflected without change at rigid (stopped) ends.*

Wave-Length

Therefore, whenever a compression arrives at the end of the pipe open to the atmosphere (whether the instrument be a flute, oboe, trumpet, organ pipe, or some other type of air-column instrument), part of its energy continues outward in the form of a compression wave in the atmosphere, while the remaining energy is reflected back as a rarefaction. Similarly, when the rarefaction arrives at the open end, part of its energy is reflected back as a compression, but the remainder has been passed outward in its original form to complete one wave-length in the outer air.

If we count the number of complete vibrations of the ball at the end of the spring in a certain time we find it is the same no matter whether the vibrations are started by a gentle up-and-down pulsation or by a sudden sharp tweak. As Bragg points out, all kinds of pulses, sharp or slow, single or double, any kind at all, travel through the spring at the same rate, and the time of vibration depends on this rate, which is determined by the elasticity of the spring. Between an instant when the spring is most extended, and the next instant when it is again most extended, the original stretch or rarefaction pulse has run up and down the spring, and then up and down again as a compression, and all of this to produce one complete vibration of the ball. Similarly, in organ pipes closed at one end, for example, while one complete vibration is being passed into the air, that is, one compression and one rarefaction, a pulse is traversing the length of the pipe four times. The pulse speed in the pipe is the same as that in the air outside of the pipe, about 1130 feet per second for ordinary room temperatures. Thus the wave-length of the tone may be roughly determined by multiplying the length of the stopped pipe by 4.

A more accurate result will be obtained if we can determine the exact distance from a node to the next loop, and multiply that by 4, since the loop is usually not precisely at the open end.

Furthermore, if we know the frequency of the tone, and the distance from node to loop, we can determine the speed of sound in the medium. In fact, this is one of the precision methods of measuring accurately the speed of sound in various liquids and gases other than air. Standing waves are set up by a known frequency in a tube filled with the liquid or gas, and the wave-length is measured by various methods. The wave-length multiplied by the frequency will give the velocity of sound in the medium.

Furthermore, knowing the velocity of sound, we may calculate roughly the length of certain types of pipes to produce a certain pitch. Suppose we want to know the approximate length of a stopped pipe necessary to produce the highest C in an "8-foot" stop in the organ, which has a frequency of 2093. We divide the speed of sound by the frequency to secure the wave-length, and the wave-length by 4 to give the stopped-pipe length, which gives about 1.62 inches as an answer. Organ pipes vary from more than 32 feet in length down to small pipes with speaking lengths of only ⅜ of an inch.

Edge Tones

There are two methods of setting into vibration the air columns used in music: (1) by *edges,* which produce *edge tones,* and (2) by *reeds.*

If a stick be held vertically in a smoothly flowing stream of water (or if it be pushed steadily through still water), little whirlpools or eddies will be passed off alternately from each side of the stick. These are illustrated roughly in Figure 28. (Richards has obtained beautiful photographs of the phenomenon by making the motion of the water visible by mixing into it small drops of milk and alcohol.) Figure 28 shows how regularly the eddies fall into an "avenue" at a short distance behind the stick. These eddies, being formed alternately on each side of the stick, will tend to push it to and fro, setting it into a periodic vibration at right angles, *across* the direction of stream flow. This can easily be felt by the arm holding the stick. The same effect can be noticed if, while standing in water up to the chest,

Fig. 28—Eddies formed in water flowing past an obstacle.

one pulls one's arm rapidly forward through the water. The arm, which is itself the obstacle here, tends to tremble or vibrate, actually traveling a somewhat sinuous path through the water.

Similar eddies are formed by moving air when it passes around a pole or wire. The fluttering of a flag in a breeze is an example. When the eddies are produced at a fast enough rate, they give rise to what are called *Aeolian tones*. If the frequency of the eddies happens to correspond to one of the natural frequencies of the wire, the wire can be set into considerable vibration. The Aeolian harp is an ancient instrument built on this principle. Other illustrations of Aeolian tones are found in the whistling of tall grasses or the singing of telegraph wires in a stiff breeze, and in the howling of the wind around a corner.

This same general principle is responsible for the production of *edge tones* in a flute or in organ flue-pipes. It is true that

edge tones may be heard quite independently of any pipe. However, if the edge be fashioned on one of the sides of a pipe, as in
Figure 29, which shows a section of one form of organ flue-pipe,
a reinforcement of the sound may take place. There is much to
be learned yet about the behavior of such air columns, but it
seems certain that eddy formation has something to do with
it. We can imagine the whirls that swing toward
or into the pipe causing waves of air compression to
travel up through the air column. When they reach
the end they will be reflected downward again, in
the way which has been described, and if the frequency of the edge tone be properly adjusted with
relation to the length of the air column (by varying
wind pressure or distance of edge from mouth), a
standing-wave condition will be set up, as has also
been described. Thus the column of air may be
considered as a resonator to reinforce through its
standing waves the feeble edge tone. When we
produce a tone by blowing across the mouth of a
bottle, it is *generated* at the edge and *resonated* by
the air column. However, the air column and the
edge tone need to be only in approximate agreement,
since the effect of the air column is so strong that it
will force its natural frequency on the weak edge

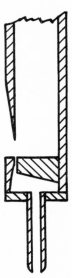

Fig. 29—Cross-
section of or-
gan flue-pipe.

tone while being very little affected itself by the natural frequency
of the edge tone.

Perhaps the primitive beginning of all air-column instruments is to be found in the hollow bone of a captured animal
or a slain enemy. It was pierced with one or more holes, originally for the purpose of hanging it up as a trophy or ornament,
or for decoration. By accident, perhaps from the blowing of the
wind, it was discovered to give tones when blown in a certain
way. Or perhaps the principle was discovered when the wind
produced a tone when blowing across a broken hollow stem of
some plant.

Reeds

Columns of air may also be set into vibration by *reeds,* as in clarinets, oboes, and so on, and in organ reed-pipes. A reed is a tongue, flap, or cushion, which by its vibration alternately opens and closes more or less completely the entrance to the pipe. Thus the stream of air is periodically interrupted at the frequency of the reed. If the natural period of the air column be adjusted to this same frequency, the air column will reinforce the tone strongly. In orchestral instruments and organ reed-pipes, however, where the air column has hard walls and is of definite length, its influence on the reed is so strong that the air column usually tends to impress its own natural frequency on the reed, forcing the reed to vibrate in resonance with the air column, if at all. When the reed occasionally escapes from the constraint of the air column with which it is coupled, as happens sometimes even in the hands of a skilled orchestral player, the result is a break in the tone, a distressing "quack," as Richardson [8] calls it. In the case of the human voice, on the other hand, the reverse situation exists. The vocal cords, which act as modified reeds, impress their frequency on the air column, because this air column is poorly defined, irregular in shape, soft-walled, more or less wide open at the mouth, and therefore unable to dominate the cords. Furthermore, the cords themselves are not of fixed shape or size as are wood or metal reeds, but capable of considerable variation and adjustment as occasion arises.

Reeds may actually hit the edges of the aperture (striking reeds), or may vibrate freely within the aperture (free reeds) with more or less complete interruption of the air flow. They may be single or double, and of wood, cane, metal, or almost any material. Even the player's lips may act as reeds, as in the brass-wind instruments. In the case of organ reed-pipes, the tone is improved and rendered less cutting by giving the tongue

[8] Richardson, E. G., *Sound,* page 184. London: Edward Arnold & Co., 1929.

a very slight curvature so that it *rolls down* over the opening instead of striking it. This causes the air stream to be shut off less abruptly. Consequently, the curving of the reed must be carefully and accurately done by the voicer, since a flat spot can be responsible for a blatant quality.

Some organ pipes are used as resonators for free reeds. Free reeds made of metal may even be used as sources of sound without the reinforcing effect of air columns, as in the harmonica, accordion, harmonium, and reed organ.

The type of sound producers known as *diaphones* really come under the classification of striking reeds.

Open and Stopped Pipes Contrasted

Tones may be produced by pipes that are open at only one end, or open at both ends. The former are called *stopped pipes* and the latter *open pipes*. A stopped pipe will have a loop at or near the open end and a node at the stopped end. An open pipe will have loops at both ends and therefore a node in the middle.[9]

The air column in the open pipe may be likened to a steel bar clamped at its midpoint and vibrating longitudinally, as in Figure 35c, page 132. Compressions and rarefactions travel inward from the ends, meet, and are reflected at the central node. As a result of the superposition of direct and reflected waves, the two ends are alternately slightly shortened and lengthened. The air column of a stopped pipe may be likened to a similar bar clamped at one end, or to the spring in Figure 27. Compressions and rarefactions travel from the free end to the clamped end and are there reflected. As a result of the superposition of direct and reflected waves the free end is slightly shortened and lengthened. Since an open pipe will have a node in the center, the distance from a loop to a node (which is one quarter of the

_____

[9] It will be remembered that stretched strings, when vibrating in their fundamental form, have exactly the opposite condition—nodes at both ends and a loop in the middle. The vibration of strings, however, is transverse instead of longitudinal.

wave-length), will be only half as long in the open pipe as in the stopped one, as shown in Figure 30*a*. Consequently, the entire wave-length will be only half as long in the open pipe as in the stopped one, which means that the open pipe produces a tone an octave higher than a stopped pipe of the same length. To get the same pitch, an open pipe would have to be twice as long as a stopped one. The pipes in Figure 30*b* will sound the same pitch, an octave higher than the pitch of the stopped pipe in *a*. An open pipe consists virtually

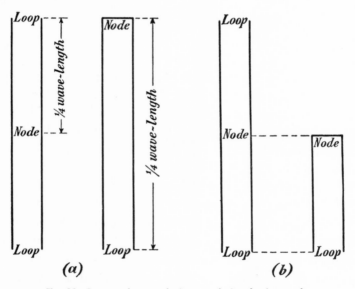

Fig. 30—Open and stopped pipes producing fundamentals.

of two stopped ones, with the central nodal surface as their common base.

Furthermore, because of the fact that a stopped pipe always has a node at the stopped end, its tone theoretically cannot contain any even-numbered partials. This is due to the impossibility of dividing up its length properly. For example, if the octave were to be produced, since the stopped end is always a node, there would have to be a loop at the middle in order to halve the wave-length. This would mean that there ought to be a node at the open end, but that end is always a loop. The same sort of difficulty is present for any even-numbered partial. Therefore a stopped pipe produces, at least theoretically, a tone containing only odd-numbered partials, with a correspondingly "hollow" quality. In Figure 31, *a* shows an open pipe when producing its second partial, the octave; *b* shows a stopped pipe when producing its third partial (the first overtone it can produce). The stopped pipe is here really equivalent to three stopped pipes, each one third the length of the whole pipe, with their open ends at the loops, and their stopped ends at the nodes. It is evident that a stopped pipe must always divide up in a manner unsymmetrical around its midpoint, in order to preserve a node at its stopped end and a loop at its open end. This will always produce an odd-numbered partial. The limitation may be gotten

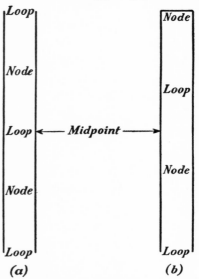

Fig. 31—Open and stopped pipes producing harmonics by overblowing.

around, however, by making the tube conical, as in the oboe, which will introduce the full harmonic series. The cylindrical stopped pipe is similar in vibration form to the stretched string displaced at its center, in that no even-numbered partials are markedly present. However, the positions of the nodes and loops are quite different in the case of the string, and its vibration is transverse instead of compressional (longitudinal) as in the air column of the pipe.

The open pipe, whether it be conical or cylindrical, can produce a tone containing even- and odd-numbered partials.

In considering the differences in quality between open and

stopped pipes, it is interesting to note, as emphasized by Buck,[10] that no even-numbered partial introduces any note into the harmonic series that is not already represented in a lower octave; while every odd-numbered partial does introduce a new note.

Thus the harmonic series is illustrated in the vibration of air columns in a way similar in principle to the way that stretched strings vibrate in many forms at once, giving rise to complex tones composed of different amounts of various harmonic partials. However, it is even more difficult to visualize a whole series of different vibrational forms existing together, in and through each other, all in the same enclosed body of invisible air, than it was in the case of the string, where at least the hazy outline of the complexly vibrating string may be visible.

Overblowing, Harmonics

Each pipe of an organ is intended to produce only a single tone, although, of course, the tone may be a complex of many partials in the harmonic series. Orchestral wind instruments, however, are designed to produce a series of tones. This is made possible by finger holes and by *overblowing*. If a pipe, such as one of the wood winds of the orchestra, for example, or even an organ pipe, be blown harder or with a different lip and tongue setting, it usually happens that one of the harmonic partials becomes so prominent as to dominate the fundamental, which seems to drop out completely. This frequently happens quite suddenly, in the same way that the segmental vibration of a string may suddenly subdivide into twice as many segments, and we say that the fundamental jumps to the harmonic. The shape of pipe helps to determine what partials can be produced and how easily. The narrower the tube the more difficult is the speaking of the fundamental and the easier that of the higher partials. Through practice, the wind-instrument player learns just how hard to overblow and how to shape his lips to secure

---

[10] Buck, P. C., *Acoustics for Musicians,* page 83. New York: Oxford University Press, 1918.

a certain harmonic. Overblowing permits an extension of the pitch range without altering the length of the tube. An open pipe, such as the flute, overblows first at the octave. A stopped pipe, such as the clarinet, for example, closed by the lips and stiff cane reed, overblows first at the twelfth, unless it be conical like the oboe, when it will give the octave, since the tone of a conical tube can contain any partial in the harmonic series. The saxophone may be regarded as a conical metal clarinet, combining characteristics of the oboe and the clarinet, and capable of producing the full harmonic series.[11]

Wood Winds and Brass Winds Contrasted

In the wood-wind group of instruments (which includes saxophones, even though they are usually made of brass), most of the pitch variation is obtained by a complicated valve mechanism for opening or closing side holes to shorten or lengthen the air column, unless all the holes can be reached by the fingers, as in simple fifes and recorders. In the wood-wind group of instruments only a very few overtones are used for overblowing, the double octave, number four in the series, being the highest one. However, a larger number of overtones are available in the brass-wind group of instruments (in which the lips are used as reeds). In these instruments practically all the tones used are overtones of the fundamental of the particular pipe length in use at the time. In fact, because of the small "scale" (ratio of width to length) in most brass winds, it is difficult and often impossible to produce the real fundamental. The "pedal notes" of a trombone are fundamentals. Partials from the second up at least as high as the eighth (triple octave) may be blown with comparative ease, however, and music scores sometimes call for still higher ones. The French horn can produce with comparative

---

[11] It should be mentioned that the clarinet is not strictly a stopped pipe. Redfield and Ghosh have shown that the chink between the reed and the mouthpiece never shuts completely, and that the vibration of the reed is responsible for the feeble presence of low even harmonics. These are, however, too weak to dominate the pitch when the instrument is overblown.

ease partials at least as high as the twelfth, and number sixteen of the series is quite possible.

However, even when using these higher partials, the chromatic scale is far from complete. Thus the bugle's tones are confined to members of one harmonic series. The gaps between the harmonics could theoretically be filled in by the use of side holes as in the wood winds. However, it has been found that the tone quality of brass-wind instruments is impaired unless every tone sounds through the bell-mouth. Thus, the use of side holes has been abandoned for these instruments, and the gaps between the harmonics have been filled in by the use of crooks, valves, or slides. These throw into operation additional lengths of tubing, which can lower the natural fundamental of the tube through several semitones, and hence, of course, lower the whole harmonic series as well, while permitting every tone to sound through the bell-mouth. Thus, a chromatic scale on a brass instrument with valves is made up from partials derived from several harmonic series. In addition, tones may be lowered by partially shading or closing the bell by the hand, thus slowing down somewhat the speed of vibration and lowering the frequency a corresponding amount. However, this materially alters the tone quality as well.[12]

Pitch

The fundamental pitch of an air column, determined by the frequency, depends principally on its length, and to a slight extent on the wind pressure, the temperature, and the thickness of the air column. In the case of wood pipes, the dimensions, and therefore the pitch, may be slightly altered by humidity.

The length of the air column may be altered by opening or closing holes in the side, as in the wood-wind instruments of the orchestra. And since the rise in pitch is proportional to the shortening of the air column, the actual spacings between such

---

[12] Under some circumstances, when the hand is completely inserted into the bell of the instrument, the pitch may be raised. But here also the tone quality is altered.

holes must decrease the higher any interval is played, in a manner similar to the way violin spacings diminish the higher the
position.

The fundamental frequency of an air column may also be
altered by any other means which lessens or increases the effective length of the column, as in the slide trombone, for example,
or in the additional lengths of pipe brought into use by means
of crooks, valves, or slides, as has been explained. And, of
course, the extension of the pitch range by blowing so as to produce higher partials, as in both brass winds and wood winds,
really amounts to shortening the effective length of the column,
by breaking it up into segments. Even certain organ pipes are
"harmonic," designed so as to blow an overtone, although of
course they cannot blow the fundamental at the will of the
player, who has no control over the embouchure or the wind
pressure. In harmonic flue pipes a small hole is frequently bored
at such a point as to aid in the formation of a "loop" of the
proper partial, and to discourage the sounding of the fundamental, as in, for example, the "harmonic flute" of the organ,
which is so voiced and blown as to produce principally its natural octave. The "zauberflöte," a harmonic-stopped flue pipe,
produces the natural twelfth (third partial) of the pipe length.
In Figure 33, page 125, showing a group of pipes all tuned to
Middle C, the next to the last pipe on the right is a harmonic
reed pipe, the "harmonic tuba." Naturally, it is twice as long
as the other pipes, since it must resonate in its *octave* form to
the same frequency as the others do in their fundamental form.

Practically all wind instruments have some means of altering the length slightly, for purposes of tuning. In many instruments this takes the form of a tuning slide, similar on a small
scale to the sliding parts of a trombone, which can increase or
decrease by slight amounts the length of the column. Since it
is difficult to alter the fundamental pitch of oboes without altering the tone quality, in Handel's time the custom grew up of
tuning all other instruments to the oboe. Clarinets, however,

which were not in the orchestra then, are even more difficult to tune. Stopped organ pipes are tuned by adjusting the stopper at the top, and open pipes by adjusting a sleeve over the end, or by slightly rolling or unrolling a metal tongue at or near the top. In organ reed pipes, the vibrating length of the reed must first be adjusted, and then the length of the pipe adjusted to resonance with the reed.

A very precise method of tuning two air columns an octave apart, applicable for that matter to stringed instruments as well as to wind, as already mentioned, is to adjust the lengths so as to tune them free of beats. The lower tone will usually be accompanied by enough of its second partial (octave) to produce audible beats with the higher fundamental tone unless the tuning is exact. This method is also applicable to other intervals, as has been mentioned before, provided only that the necessary overtones are present in sufficient strength to produce audible beats when the interval is mistuned in either direction.

The fundamental frequency of an air column is slightly raised by an increase in the wind pressure. However, as has been described, if the pressure is increased past a certain point, the pitch will suddenly jump to an overtone.

It might be argued that the passage of the performer's breath through an orchestral instrument while playing it might alter the standing-wave condition, and thereby the frequency. (Somewhat similar misconceptions are frequently met in voice texts which enlarge on the idea of the tone being "vocalized breath.") But the breath speed is in any case so very slow, in relation to the speed of sound waves, as to have a negligible effect. Very little air actually passes. With most instruments, and with the voice, a lighted candle in front of the mouth of the instrument will be only very slightly affected, if at all, whereas, if an appreciable amount of air were passing at any appreciable speed, the flame would flicker.

Since the tone from an air column is caused by sound waves traveling up and down the pipe, and since the speed of sound waves depends on the temperature of the air, the frequency of all wind instruments is raised when they are warmed. Because of this, cold instruments will be flat, and the players should breathe through them before playing in order to get them to a constant temperature and pitch, tuning them only when warmed. If tuned when cold, they will be too sharp after they have gotten warm. For the same reason, organs should only be tuned when the church is warmed to the temperature at which the instrument is to be heard, usually 70° here in America. If an organ is tuned to A-440 at 70°, it will sound approximately A-435 at 60°. One reason for the acceptance of concert pitches of A-440 or higher in this country some years ago may have been the fact that oboes and clarinets, made in France to sound A-435 in their usually rather cool concert rooms, were used in this country, where in our warmer halls they rose to approximately A-440. Organists are familiar with the frequent out-of-tuneness of reed pipes and chimes in extremes of heat or cold, but not all are aware that in such cases it is really the rest of the organ that is out of tune with the reeds or chimes. These latter, in which the tone is generated by the vibration of a metal part, are much less affected by temperature changes than are the flue pipes, which depend principally on the vibration of an air column and therefore on the speed of sound waves up and down the column. Since this speed increases with increase in temperature, the reeds and chimes will sound flat in relation to the rest of the organ in summer, since the pipes have gone sharp while the reeds and chimes have remained at the same pitch or have even slightly flatted due to the lengthening of their vibrating portions through expansion. Conversely, when churches are underheated in winter the reeds and chimes, having kept their pitch, will sound sharp to the rest of the organ, which will then have lowered. Modern organ reeds, however, as Barnes points out, stay in tune much better than formerly. The use of thicker tongues, thicker tuning wires, and increased air pressures all contribute to greater stability of tuning, particularly in such pipes as trumpets, for example, where full-length resonators are used. The pitch of such reed pipes is consequently apt to remain fairly well in tune with the flue pipes even though the temperature varies markedly. It is advisable to have the various sections of an organ on one level, since the upper levels in an auditorium are frequently warmer than the lower ones, and heat up more quickly when the building is warmed by sun or by a heating system. Pipes in higher positions would then be sharp. Unless the tuning is done under exactly the same set of circumstances as will maintain when the organ is used, it will sound out of tune. This difficulty is largely overcome if all sections of the organ pipework are on one level.

Mention was made in Chapter 1 of the fact that there seems to be a tendency for pitch standards to rise, in order to secure greater brilliancy, until they become so high that they must be brought down, whence they start to rise again. It is possible that another cause contributing to this rise in pitch standards is the fact that orchestral instruments are not always blown through sufficiently to warm them before a concert is begun. Some instruments, such as wood flutes, could perhaps continue to rise throughout a whole concert. Also, the temperature of concert halls usually rises during a concert, due to the presence of the audience. The performers and the audience would tend to become used to the higher pitches heard as the concert progressed. At the beginning of another concert, then, there might be a tendency to set up the beginning pitches a bit, and these would rise still more as this concert progressed.[13]

The fundamental frequency of the air column in a wood pipe will be affected by the humidity, since dampness causes wood to swell. Thus the wood pipes of an organ will usually need to be tuned after a prolonged damp spell or dry spell, since their dimensions and thus their pitches have actually changed.

---

[13] Still another possible contributing cause, operative both with wind and strings, lies in the fact that when several pitches are heard simultaneously, it is the highest one which has the greatest attentional importance. Even musically trained listeners frequently attend only to the top tone of a chord. Thus, in the process of tuning an orchestra there would be a tendency to adjust upward.

The pitch nomenclature used in the organ should be mentioned here. Since the foundation of the organ tone is in its open pipes, and the lowest open pipe of the manuals, two octaves below Middle C, is roughly 8 feet long (as it should be to produce C-65½), the term *8-foot tone* is used in organ terminology to mean the *normal* pitch. Naturally, therefore, *4-foot tone* would mean an octave higher, so that if the Middle-C key is played, C-523.2 will sound instead of C-261.6. *Two-foot tone* will imply two octaves higher than normal, *16-foot tone* an octave lower than normal, and so on. The system is even applied to the harmonic tones other than octaves, which are used to build up various tone-qualities on a large organ. Thus, *1⅗-foot tone* means that any key played will sound a tone two octaves and a major third higher (the fifth partial).

In the above paragraph, and in other places where the length of pipes has been mentioned, the length given has often been qualified by such adjectives as *roughly* or *approximately*. Sometimes the term *effective length* is used. This is because the assumption that the position of a "loop" is precisely at an open end is actually not correct, due to the influence of the walls of a pipe. This influence is such that the actual point where the air pressure undergoes no variation and is equal to atmospheric pressure (which point is consequently the "loop" of greatest motion), is found to lie at some short distance out from the open end. For a cylindrical pipe this distance is about three tenths of the diameter of the pipe. Thus, the actual wave-lengths produced by pipes are somewhat longer, and the pitches somewhat lower, than the pipe length itself would justify, the "end correction" increasing with the width of the pipe. Figure 32 shows three pipes, all of which produce the same pitch when under the same wind pressure. The influence of the end correction is quite apparent in their relative dimensions, and also in the relative dimensions of the open flue pipes shown in Figure 33, all of which produce the pitch of Middle C. As the width of a pipe decreases toward zero, the end correction decreases also.

The end correction might be thought to have no effect on the tone except in lowering the fundamental pitch. However, it also has an important effect on the tone quality. In fact, it gives an explanation of the great influence that the "scale" of a pipe has on its overtone content. The reason for this is that the end correction *varies with the frequency.* Thus, for example, if the fundamental of a pipe is 100, its second partial, produced by overblowing, might be 201 since the end correction is different.

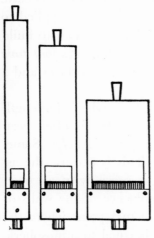

The third partial might be 303, the fourth 406, and the fifth 510, perhaps. The effect is to distort the harmonic series. And yet the pipe, when steadily blown at fundamental frequency, will attempt to vibrate in a steady-state condition only possible with harmonic overtones. Naturally, the result of this is a compromise. When blown at normal pressure the air column does vibrate in a steady state, with truly harmonic overtones, but these overtones are weakened in the complex tone in proportion as they depart from the true harmonic points when

Fig. 32—Effect of end correction on pipe length.*

produced separately by overblowing. Resonance decreases the farther away the frequencies are from true harmonic points. The influence of the pipe, which draws the fundamental edge tone into strong resonance with itself, will draw the octave into some resonance, the third partial into less, the fourth into still less, and so on. The wider the pipe in relation to its length, the more distorted and difficult of production is the overblown "harmonic" series (which of course is no longer harmonic), and consequently the truly harmonic overtones become rapidly weaker in the complex quality produced when blown normally. By making the pipe of

---

* From Audsley, G. A., *The Art of Organ Building,* Vol. 1. New York: Dodd, Mead & Company, Inc., 1905.

very wide scale, particularly with a stopped pipe, which already possesses no even-numbered partials, and especially if the mouth is "cut up high," with a blunt upper lip, practically a pure tone may be secured. In pipes of small diameter, where the end correction becomes insignificant, the high partials are prominent. Organ stops which demand considerable harmonic development are invariably of small scale, while flute-toned stops have wide scales. Brass-wind instruments, which require many available partials, are of very small scale; wood winds of larger scale.

It is interesting to note that the effective scale ratio is not constant in an instrument, but varies with the pitch. In such an instrument as the flute, for example, as the effective length of the air column is shortened for the production of higher pitches by opening finger holes, or by segmentation in the higher registers, the scale, which is the *ratio* between diameter and length, is *increased*. The diameter becomes more comparable with the length of the vibrating air column, and this tends to purify the tone more and more the higher the pitch produced.

Since at "loop" points the air particles move back and forth slightly, and there is no motion at nodes, a very deep dent in a small-scaled pipe (as in a brass-wind instrument, for example) might have the effect of slowing down (flatting) the pitch of whatever fundamentals have loops at that point, and not having this effect on those having nodes at the dent point. This naturally would also tend to distort the harmonic series of many or all of the tones producible, with corresponding variations in relative strength in the case of a steady-state vibration.

Loudness

The loudness of tones from an air column depends primarily on the force of blowing. However, such considerations as size, material, and manner of reinforcement have their effect also. For example, the pipes of a pipe organ must not be packed too closely together, nor too close to the walls of the organ chamber, if they are to be most effective in transmitting sound energy into the auditorium.

As mentioned before, the horn and trumpet may be muted by introducing the hand into the bell, which not only softens the tone but "veils" its quality and alters its pitch as well. Most of the brass-wind instruments and perhaps one or two of the wood winds may be muted by pear-shaped pieces of wood, metal, rubber, or other material, placed in the bell. Such mutes alter tone quality as well, however. They are not ordinarily used in wood winds, but composers are calling more and more for their use in the brass winds.

Generally speaking, with organ flue pipes, the louder tones are secured from pipes using greater volumes of air and greater air pressures.

Tone Quality

The tone quality of an air-column instrument is determined by the manner of vibration of the air column, which is in turn dependent on such factors as:

- *a.* Method of setting into vibration (by an edge tone or a reed)
- *b.* Size, shape, and material of mouthpiece, and of edge or reed producing the vibration
- *c.* Wind pressure, embouchure
- *d.* Whether stopped or open, or "half-stopped"
- *e.* Dimensions, material, thickness of walls
- *f.* "Scale" of pipe, taper of pipe, shape of bell, if any
- *g.* Size of openings, degree and suddenness of reed closure, use of mute
- *h.* Manner of additional reinforcement, if any.

Some of these factors affect the tone quality in complex, subtle, and unpredictable ways, and are but little understood as yet. The patient lifetime of work of Theobald Böhm, who was able to improve greatly the tone quality of the orchestral flute, as well as its intonation and fingering, illustrates the difficulties besetting the path of the investigator in this field. And the flute is a relatively simple instrument alongside reed instruments such as the clarinet and oboe. A thorough discussion of the ways that tone quality is varied by these factors is therefore beyond the scope of this text, where much must be omitted. Thus, for example, the many variations in design and dimensions of the lip, the mouth of the pipe, the languid, the wind slit, the nicking,

Fig. 33—A group of flue and reed pipes of various types and qualities, all tuned to Middle C.

the ears, the curvature of the reed, and the resonating pipes themselves, with which an organ builder secures quality differentiation, will not be discussed here, except to say that in flue pipes, in general, low-cut mouths and sharp lips tend to produce complex tones. Some idea of the extent of these variations can be gained from Figure 33, which shows a group of pipes all designed and tuned to sound Middle C. The last eight on the right are reed pipes, the reed being enclosed by the boot at

the bottom.   For a fuller discussion of these matters as they re-
late to organ pipes, the reader is referred to Barnes' book, *The
Contemporary American Organ.*

Generally speaking, the tone of a reed instrument is more
complex than that of one without a reed, and the tone from a
striking reed more complex than that from a curved rolling
reed or a free reed.

Wind pressure affects tone quality.   In general, the higher
the pressure, the more complex the tone.   In the case of organ
pipes, all sharp corners or irregularities along the pathway of the
wind stream as it flows to the mouth of the pipe should be removed or the tone will be apt to be windy.

The quality, and also the pitch, of orchestral instruments may
be varied by the lip and tongue position, and the pressure of
these organs on the mouthpiece of the instrument.   This technique of the lips and tongue, and their adjustment to the mouthpiece in playing wind instruments, is termed the *embouchure.*
Not only may the instrument be overblown, securing another
harmonic, by changing the embouchure, but even a single tone
may be altered in quality or slightly "lipped into pitch" in this
way.

As has already been explained, the tone of a stopped pipe
tends to have only the odd-numbered partials: fundamental,
third partial, fifth partial, and so on, while an open pipe may
possess both odd- and even-numbered ones.   Sometimes stopped
organ pipes have the stoppers perforated with a hole.   Sometimes a smaller pipe or "chimney" is set in the hole.   Naturally,
characteristics of both stopped and open pipes appear in such
cases.

It is interesting to note that bending a straight pipe into curves
or spirals, as in the brass winds, has little effect on tone quality,
so long as there are no sharp corners in the tube.   Large organ
pipes are frequently even mitered with one or two right-angle
bends, in order to fit them into small chambers, without harm-

ing the tone quality too much. Furthermore, the shape of the
cross section of a pipe, whether square or round, has no appreciable effect on tone quality either, so long as the cross section
area is unaltered.

The "scale" of the pipe, however, has a great effect on tone
quality, due to the "end correction" already explained in detail.
Air columns of large scale produce relatively pure tones, the
tone quality growing more complex as the scale is made smaller.
It is thus much easier to get the higher partials to speak by
themselves by overblowing small-scaled pipes than large. In
this respect air columns are similar to stretched strings, for the
thinner the string, the more complex the tone is likely to be,
and the easier it is, therefore, to produce higher harmonics by
themselves.

The effect of tapering a stopped pipe, such as in the oboe, has
already been mentioned. It tends to introduce the even-numbered partials, which would otherwise be weak or absent.

In brass-wind instruments, if the internal profile of the
mouthpiece cup be tapered to the tube proper without an abrupt
edge, and if the tube be given a large flare at the bell end, the
intensity of the upper partials will be reduced, rendering the
tone more mellow. Both of these effects are present in the
French horn. If the flare be made too great, however, the effective length of the air column becomes indefinite, and the tone,
as Richardson [14] says, will become dull and the natural frequencies of the tube difficult to produce. In fact, this is the very
reason why phonograph and loud-speaker horns are made with
large flare—so that they will be highly damped at their natural
resonances—for they should be able to respond more or less uniformly to all frequencies.

Vibrations are said to be damped when they die out quickly, due
to the dissipation of energy in the form of heat as the vibrating body

---

[14] Richardson, E. G., *The Acoustics of Orchestral Instruments and of the Organ*,
page 78. London: Edward Arnold & Co., 1929.

is repeatedly distorted, and to the giving up of energy to the surrounding air. It is a physical fact that the more damped the natural vibrations of a body are (the more quickly they die out) the wider is the resonant range of frequencies. Light bodies with large surfaces exposed to the air, such as the head of a drum, have their vibrations rapidly damped, but therefore are more responsive and can be made to vibrate by (in other words, can "pick up") sounds of frequencies different from their own natural frequencies. This is somewhat true of air columns in general, but particularly true of those having wide, flaring ends. On the other hand, heavy elastic bodies such as tuning forks are much less damped. An organ pipe may set a tuning fork into vibration, the sound continuing for seconds after the pipe has stopped sounding. The fork can set the pipe into vibration also, but as soon as the fork is removed or silenced the pipe will stop vibrating at once. Tuning forks can perform hundreds or even thousands of vibrations from one blow, before becoming inaudible, but are responsive only to frequencies in unison with, or extremely close to, their own natural frequency. Such bodies are said to have very sharp resonances. Two forks which resonate to each other may be rendered out of tune, so that resonance is no longer noticeable, by placing a tiny bit of wax on a prong of one of them, changing it no more than a small fraction of a tone from the other. From this it should be evident why the ideal sound pick-up, such as a fine microphone or the human ear, is very highly damped to all frequencies in the audible range.

In all the air-column instruments, relatively little change in quality is possible after the tone once speaks, as compared, say, with the great amount of change possible during the bowing of a violin tone.

Duration

The duration of the tone from an air column depends on how long the wind pressure is maintained. The primary vibrating body in an air-column instrument is always either the air itself or a reed of some sort, and all of these are highly damped bodies in comparison with, say, a piano string, which will vibrate for some seconds after it has been struck.

Instruments

The instruments in which air columns are used are:

> *Edge tones:*
>> Flute and piccolo
>> Organ flue pipes
>
> *Reeds:*
>> Cane:
>>> Single:
>>>> Clarinet, basset horn, and bass clarinet
>>>> Saxophone
>>>
>>> Double:
>>>> Oboe and English horn
>>>> Bassoon and double bassoon
>>
>> Metal:
>>> Organ reed pipes
>>
>> Lips:
>>> Trumpet, cornet, and bugle
>>> French horn
>>> Trombone
>>> Tuba

The following instruments use reeds without associated tuned air columns:

Reed organ	Accordion
Harmonium	Harmonica

C. PERCUSSION

The vibrations of stretched strings and of air columns produce, as a rule, upper partials which are harmonic or nearly so; that is, forming a harmonic series based on the fundamental. The vibrations of membranes, rods, plates, and bells, on the other hand, generally give rise to *inharmonic* upper partials, whose frequencies are not at all an even number of times the fundamental frequency, and which therefore do not coincide even approximately with the tones of the harmonic series. For this reason they are of less importance as orchestral instruments, serving principally as markers of the rhythm and for special effects. They are usually sounded by being *struck* with some sort of a stick or hammer. In many instances their tones are so complex and full of inharmonic partials, and in the case of membranes, so rapidly damped, that they seem to have no definite pitch at all. Such tones approach noise in character, and, when recorded by the oscillograph, show great irregularity from wave to wave. It is easy to understand why percussion instruments have only a limited use musically, when we remember that frequently not a single strong overtone may be consonant with the fundamental, while in other instruments the fundamental and the first five overtones lie in a major chord, while many higher overtones duplicate the tones of this chord.

Stretched Membranes

Membranes may be thought of as "two-dimensional strings," in that they must be stretched to secure sufficient elasticity to vibrate. They are usually circular, as in drums, and may vibrate in various forms, depending on how many nodal diameters or circles form. These nodes may be made visible by sprinkling a little fine sand or sawdust over the membrane. When set into

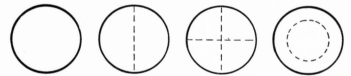

Fig. 34—Vibration of membranes.

vibration, the sand is violently agitated where the vibration-loops are located, and collects at all nodal points or lines. The figures which are revealed in this way are called *Chladni's Figures,* and show at a glance the vibration form of the membrane. Some of the simpler typical forms of membrane vibration are shown in Figure 34. In the first example, the membrane is swinging up and down as a whole. In the next examples, the dotted lines indicate nodes.

The pitch (as in a stretched string) depends on the size and the weight of the membrane, and the amount of tension it is under. The pitch lowers as the size or weight is increased, and rises as the tension is increased. Naturally, only one fundamental pitch is available without retuning, though each size of instrument has a moderate range through which it may be tuned. However, the pitch is frequently quite indefinite, because of the rapid damping of the vibration.

The loudness depends on the force of the blow (which increases the displacement as in the case of the string), and on the manner of reinforcement.

The tone quality of stretched membranes depends, in a way similar to that of stretched strings, on such factors as the dimensions, the point of striking, the material and shape of the striking point (several types of drumsticks being used), the manner of reinforcement (as, for example, in tympani or kettle-drums), and any natural or artificial irregularities in the membrane surface which would tend to determine nodal points or lines. Such nodal lines, even though not fully developed, reveal the presence of one or more inharmonic partials. And conversely, in the same way as in a stretched string, if the membrane is caused to vibrate at a point which could normally be a node, the particular overtone corresponding to that nodal division will be weakened or eliminated. Thus, if the last example in Figure 34 represents a drumhead, and the drummer strikes it at some point on the nodal circle, he will tend to eliminate this discordant overtone. Drummers know that when they find the right striking point the tone improves.

The duration of the tone depends on the elasticity of the membrane and the force of the blow.

The eardrum is an example of a *sound-receiving* membrane.

Rods, Tuning Forks

Rods are one-dimensional, like strings, but are inherently elastic, needing no stretching. Their ends are usually "loops" instead of nodes. Various vibration forms are possible depending on where the rods are struck and where supported. In transverse vibration, two such forms are illustrated in Figure 35, *a* and *b,* where the actual displacement is greatly magnified. They may also vibrate longitudinally, especially if clamped at some nodal point. In Figure 35*c,* the midpoint is a node, and the ends are "loops," the arrows indicating in magnified form

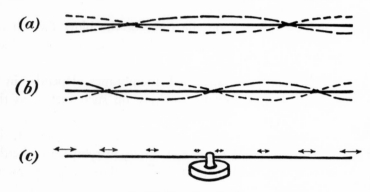

(a)

(b)

(c)

Fig. 35—Vibration of rods.

the relative amount of vibration. If upper partials are produced, additional nodes form.

Rods are also capable of torsional vibration.

The pitch depends on the dimensions, and on the characteristics of the metal.

The loudness depends on the force of the blow, and on the manner of reinforcement.

Tone quality depends on such factors as the dimensions, characteristics of the metal or other material, point of striking, material and shape of the striking point, and the manner of reinforcement. Sometimes, particularly when no resonator is used, several of the high inharmonic partials may sound at once, producing a jangling noise. If, on the other hand, the points of support be properly selected at nodal points, and the point of striking selected at a loop, a particular partial may be brought out with great purity.

The duration of the tone depends on the elasticity of the metal and the force of the blow.

The tuning fork is essentially a bent rod. If the ends of a rod vibrating as shown in Figure 35a are bent upward around its midpoint to form a U, the nodes are caused to move quite close to each other, permitting the vibrating length of the arms to be much longer than before. Naturally, this will increase the amplitude of vibration of the ends, and decrease that of the middle segment, between the two nodes. If the rod at Figure 35a is bent in this manner, the vibrating arms will swing simultaneously inward at the same time that the base of the U is forced downward, and then outward as the base of the U moves upward. In the typical tuning fork, the base is provided with a stem. The up-and-down movement of this stem is very much smaller in amplitude than that of the arms, although powerful enough to set a table top into vibration.

The tuning fork was invented in 1711 by John Shore, Handel's trumpeter, although not used as a scientific instrument until many years later. It reached perfection under Koenig of Paris. Its tone is quite pure, giving practically a sine-curve wave form. What few partials are present are usually inharmonic, quite high, and so weak as to be unheard except at the moment of striking, and are reduced still further by the use of a resonance box tuned to strengthen the fundamental. Tuning forks are usually made of cast steel, and retain their pitch accuracy with great constancy over long periods of time. They are thus useful as pitch standards, as, for example, in tuning instruments to A-440 or C-261.6. They may be tuned by filing. If the ends are filed the pitch is raised, and if the junction between the prongs is filed (preferably on the inside), the pitch is lowered. When the fork is struck very hard, the increased amplitude slows down the frequency a bit, so that as the tone gets softer a person with a keen ear can sometimes hear the pitch rise slightly. This latter pitch is the actual standard pitch, since the initial flatness does not last long.

Plates

Plates are similar to rods in that they do not require stretching, as do membranes and strings. In this respect they may be thought of as "two-dimensional rods." Their edges are usually in vibration instead of being nodal lines as in stretched membranes. They may be of various shapes, and may vibrate in various forms, as in membranes, depending on how their surface breaks up into nodes. They can be set into vibration by striking them, or by bowing them (on an edge).

Some of the simpler typical forms of vibration of a square plate, as revealed by Chladni figures, are shown in Figure 36:

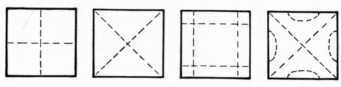

Fig. 36—Vibration of plates.

Some of the Chladni figures for very high partials form extremely intricate designs, of great beauty and symmetry. The number of vibration forms that are theoretically possible is very large in the case of plates and membranes.

The pitch depends on the dimensions of the plate, and on the characteristics of the metal or other material. The tone is often so complex that no one pitch can be heard, but just an indefinite, inharmonic jangle, as in the cymbal. If the points of support, and of striking or bowing, be properly selected, however, the fundamental or any other single partial at a time may be isolated. Particularly is this true if a tuned air resonator is associated with each plate, as in an instrument such as the celesta. In this instrument, hammers operated by levers from a small keyboard strike plates, each plate being suspended immediately above a resonant air column tuned to it.

The loudness depends on the force of blow or bowing, and on the manner of reinforcement.

The tone quality depends on such factors as the dimensions, shape, characteristics of the metal used, where and how struck or bowed, where fastened or supported, the position of natural or artificial nodes, and the manner of reinforcement.

The duration of the tone depends on the elasticity of the metal and the force of the blow.

The belly of a violin may be considered as a vibrating plate, and has been studied by means of Chladni figures. The diaphragm of a telephone receiver, being clamped at its circumference, may be considered either as a plate or a membrane.

Bells

Bells may be thought of as bent plates, as an extension of the cymbal, or as "three-dimensional tuning forks." They are usually made of metal, but may be of various materials, various shapes, and can vibrate in various vibration forms, depending on how many nodal lines or circles form. The rim is always in vibration. Glass bells may be made to vibrate so strongly by bowing them on the rim that they will shatter.

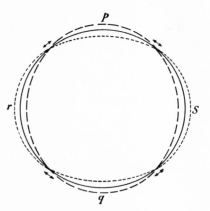

Fig. 37—Vibration of bells.

The simplest form of bell vibration, that which is responsible for the "hum-tone" heard as the sound of a bell dies away, is as shown in Figure 37, looking up at the bottom rim. The full-line circle shows the rim at rest. If the rim is given a blow at point p, this region is forced inward. At the same time point q travels inward and points r and s are forced outward. The dotted-line oval shows the new shape in magnified form. The rim then returns to its circle form, passing through this to form a new oval at right angles to the first, illustrated by the dashed line, then back to the circle and the dotted-line oval, and so on. In this type of vibration, the intersections of the circle with one oval are not quite at the same points as its intersections with the other oval. Thus there are no actual *nodes,* no point remaining completely quiet. These four pseudo-nodes on the rim are the extremities of four pseudo-nodal lines, called *nodal meridians,* which run upward from the rim to the crown of the bell. Along them, although there is no in-and-out motion, there is motion in the plane of the surface, as indicated by the arrows. This is why such a bell as a glass goblet may be set into vibration by rubbing a wet finger around the rim.

In addition to this simplest form of bell vibration, there are many others, many of them bearing no harmonic relation with each other, so that the tone of a bell is the result of an extremely complex type of vibration. More than four nodal meridians may form. Also, nodal circles may form, passing around the bell at various distances up from the rim. Tyzzer has found, for example, for a 250-pound bell, sixty-eight tones in the region from the fundamental (hum-tone) up to a frequency of 13,000, with as many as seven nodal circles in some forms of vibration and as many as thirty nodal meridians in others. Often two or more of these tones lie quite close in pitch, and this is one cause of the beating to be noticed frequently in the sound of a bell.

The pitch of a bell depends on its size, particularly its internal diameter, on the characteristics of the metal or other material, and on the shape. The greater the size, the lower the tone. However, the pitch which our ear assigns to a bell, particularly when several bells are sounded successively as in a chime, is not the pitch of the fundamental hum-tone which is heard as the sound dies away. Instead, the so-called "strike-tone" determines the heard pitch of a bell, and this is always higher than the hum-tone, and dies away more rapidly. According to Jones,[15] the strike-tone heard by the ear corresponds to no actual vibration form of the bell, but is judged an *octave below the fifth partial,* this fifth partial being frequently inharmonic, of

---

[15] Jones, Arthur Taber, *Sound,* page 352. New York: D. Van Nostrand Company. Inc., 1937.

course. In one bell, the fifth partial had a frequency of 3.43 times the fundamental, so that the strike-tone was heard as 1.71 times the fundamental. Much concerning these matters is still unknown. We do know that it is necessary to cast bells larger than needed so that they may be tuned by cutting and grinding off metal. If metal is removed from the rim, the pitch is raised. To lower the pitch, metal is removed some distance back from the rim. However, when metal is thus removed, the inter-relationship of the overtones is changed, and it becomes neces-sary to remove metal at some other point in order to retune the overtones. Too much metal may not be removed, however, for if in the tuning process the bell is left with too light a weight, the tone quality is again impaired.

The loudness depends on the force of blow.

The tone quality, which is usually of very great complexity because of the presence of many inharmonics, depends on such factors as the dimensions, shape, characteristics of metal used, thickness at various points, where and how struck, chance flaws in the metal, and so on. For church bells a special alloy is used, called *bell metal,* and containing from three to four parts of copper to one part of tin. Silver and gold, as Richardson [16] points out, are no better than this alloy for bells. The bell founder attempts to make the lower partials as prominent and as harmonic as possible, first by a proper design, and then by removing metal at various sections if necessary. In particular, he makes the bell thickest just above the rim, this thickened portion being called the *sound bow.* The ideal arrangement for the partials is thought to be such that the frequencies of the first five, beginning with the hum-tone, have the ratios 1:2:2.4:3:4, corresponding to:

for a C-bell. Some founders attempt to tune the overtones to this scheme, where it is seen that the second partial, being an

[16] Richardson, E. G., *The Acoustics of Orchestral Instruments and of the Organ* page 104. London: Edward Arnold & Co., 1929.

octave below the fifth, has therefore been made to coincide with the strike-tone. This ideal is seldom realized, however. According to T zzer, these five partials are produced by the following modes of vibration:

Vibration mode	Ideal ratios	Nodal meridians	Nodal circles
1st	1	4	0
2nd	2	4	1
3rd	2.4	6	1 (mid-way)
4th	3	6	1 (near rim)
5th	4	8	1

It is even a possibility that the nodal meridians may rotate around the bell during vibration, further complicating the result as heard by any stationary observer.

The waxing and waning of the tone of a bell may be due to the principle illustrated in the following experiment. If a teacup (a form of bell) be tapped at a point diametrically opposite its handle, or at points 90° from its handle, the pitch produced by the fundamental type of vibration is lower than when it is tapped at points 45° from the handle, because in the latter case the handle is at a node, and less weight needs to be moved. When tapped at intermediate points these two pitches may be heard together, as a discordant jangle. Similarly, large metal bells often are not entirely homogeneous and symmetrical, and their intermittent beating sound, particularly when the tone is dying out, may be caused by the combination of two neighboring but distinct rates of fundamental vibration due to this absence of uniformity. And of course, as has been mentioned, there is always the possibility of two entirely different types of vibration form having frequencies close enough together to cause beats.

The duration of the tone depends on the elasticity of the metal, the force of blow, and of course on the atmospheric conditions when heard from a distance.

Bells are used singly, in chime sets of various numbers, and in the heroic instrument called the *carillon,* which consists of a chromatic scale of many bells, usually covering at least three octaves.

Instruments

Membranes, rods, plates, and bells are employed in the following instruments:

Stretched membranes:	*Plates:*
Tympani	Celesta ⎫
Other drums, tambourines, etc.	Glockenspiel or ⎬ vibrate almost
Rods:	orchestral bells ⎭ as rods
Straight:	Cymbals
Xylophone	Gong
Hollow chimes	*Bells:*
Bent:	Carillon
Triangle	Bell chimes
Tuning fork	Single bells

D. VOICE

The human voice is unique among instruments in its power to express emotions. This is due partly to its ability to carry a definite thought content in the words spoken or sung, and partly to the fact that from the very beginnings of our racial and our individual lives, long before we knew any other instrument, we have been learning to react to voices expressing some emotion or other.

The human voice is unique also in the tremendous variations possible in its tone quality. In this respect it has a range and flexibility greater than many other instruments. In spite of this, or perhaps because of it, the production of the voice is the least understood of all instruments. Tradition and cant hold sway in this field long after they have been amended or clarified with other instruments. "Methods" are swallowed whole and fought for in an *a priori* spirit, instead of being verified or discarded as the result of patient inductive experimentation. And yet voice teachers cannot be entirely blamed for this, because the voice mechanism is not only quite a complex structure muscularly, capable of tremendous and facile variation in the relations of its parts and the character of its surfaces, but is in addition *never entirely under conscious control*. And when to these facts is added the fact that we cannot take the voice mechanism apart to see its operation, and put it together again, as we can do with any other, man-made, instrument, we understand why so much of voice teaching has always been a rather subjective, unscientific procedure. Thus, in teaching voice, circumlocution is necessary. The required setting must be secured through roundabout and subtle ways. The throat must be coaxed or surprised into its proper large shape, until a measure of control be gained over the powerful constrictor muscles. The successful vocal teacher usually has recourse to some form of imagery, which typically takes the form of "placing" the tone somewhere in the front or upper part of the head. It has been found that the attempt to do this secures the proper setting of the larynx and chief resonators in the throat, whereas if the attention is placed on these latter, a tightness usually is to be heard, the voice then being called "throaty," or "white."

Manner of Production

The voice is produced by the action of a stream of air from the lungs, which is pressed up through the windpipe against the resistance of a pair of membranes stretched together or almost together at the top of the windpipe to form the *glottis*. These, the *vocal cords,* are set into vibration, and the cavities which lie above them (the laryngeal chamber, the back of the throat, the mouth, and to some extent the head cavities), are responsible through resonance for the overtones which determine the various vowels and types of voice quality. However, as to the way that the cords vibrate and interact with the resonators, there is considerable disagreement, not only among voice teachers but among scientists as well. Two theories have been in conflict for many years: (1) the "steady-state" or harmonic theory, and (2) the "transient," "puff," or inharmonic theory.

The steady-state theory assumes that the vibration of the cords produces in the air immediately above them a complex form of vibration containing a fundamental and a large number of the members of its harmonic series, and that the effect of the resonating cavities above is to modify this complex, strengthening whichever components lie near to the natural resonant pitches of the cavities, and thus weakening the other components.

The puff theory assumes that the vocal cords act in vibration as a pair of "cushions" stretched together across the windpipe. First they are forced apart by the air pressure from the lungs, permitting a sharp, explosive puff of air to get through. Their tension then pulls them together again. The air pressure then builds up and forces another puff through, and so on. The number of puffs per second gives the frequency of the fundamental of the tone being sung. The overtones are added by the resonators, but the cavities are here assumed to be set into resonation by "shock excitation" from the sharp, impulsive air puff released from the cords once in each fundamental cycle. Their "free" vibration is then more or less damped during the period between two successive puffs, until they are "set going" again by the next puff.

In both theories the cords should usually be thought of not as stretched strings but as a double reed, periodically releasing and more or less closing off the stream of air. And in both theories, vowel and other vocal quality differences are explained largely by changes in the size and "coupling" of the resonators, which changes are learned through practice and imitation when the young child learns to talk.

The theories differ in that the steady-state theory has the cavities operating merely as selectors on an already complex tone, while the puff theory has them *producing* the overtones by being set into vibration by the puffs from below. Thus, in the steady-state theory the overtones are *harmonic and steadily maintained,* while in the puff theory the overtones are usually *inharmonic* (since the pitch of the cavities need bear no harmonic relation to that of the cord tone), and decrease in amplitude, sometimes to zero, in each fundamental cycle.

Because of the points of agreement between the two theories, their differences may be ignored in certain lines of study. Some physicists consider the differences to be merely academic, differences in representing the phenomena in physical terms instead of actual differences in the phenomena. However, it seems to the writer that the puff theory is preferable when the emphasis is on the physiological aspect, at least as an explanation of the lower register. This register, frequently called "chest," is used predominantly by all male singers, and also for the lower half of the contralto range, and the lowest tones of sopranos. For sopranos and falsetto male voices there is an increasing tendency for the puffs to become less explosive, the cords remaining open a greater part of the time of each fundamental cycle. It is as if the cords then act less as reeds and more as if they were being bowed by the air stream. And in this case the forced energizing of the upper resonators becomes less and less effective as the force of the puffs decreases. It would then be possible for the cavities to act more as selectors, were it not for the additional fact that when this occurs the cords are producing in the air next to them not a complex tone with many partials available for selection, but a very simple tone. Oscillograph records of soprano tones and male falsettos rarely show the presence of more than the third partial in any appreciable amount, and frequently nothing but the octave or just the fundamental sine curve itself.

Whichever theory we subscribe to, however, the vocal cords may be correctly described as a vibrating mechanism generating a train of waves which pass upward and are modified by the action of the resonators, and especially by the first resonators to be reached, those of the back throat. It is also true that a similar train of waves passes downward into the chest, but these are probably of little value to the tone quality, because they are largely absorbed by the spongy tissues of the lungs. And whatever vibration may be felt on the *surface* of the chest can add little to the power of the voice, as its effect on the outside air is infinitesimally small as compared with the effect of the waves issuing from the mouth. *When a voice is properly produced* this chest vibration is quite evident, and so also is a feeling of head resonance; but in most cases these would seem more truly to be *effects* of proper powerful resonation in the back throat than to be important contributing *causes* of the good quality.

Pitch

The pitch of the voice depends on the tension and the thickness of the vocal cords, and on the length of them that is permitted to vibrate, paralleling roughly in these respects the action of strings. All of these factors, as well as others concerned in voice production, are under the control of an intricate network of muscle fibres. When passing from one *register* to another as the voice ascends the pitch scale, one or more definite changes occur in the muscular action. The extreme range for the human voice is from about 60 vibrations per second for a low bass to about 1300 for a very high soprano. However, Gaspard Forster is said to have sung a tone of 44 vibrations a second, and the soprano Agujari one of 2048. The natural average difference of approximately an octave between men's and women's voices is due to the fact that the male vocal cords are longer and thicker.

Loudness

Loudness depends on the breath pressure (provided the cords can be tensed sufficiently to resist properly the breath pressure), and on the proper setting and enlarging of the resonators, particularly the back throat. A large throat permits a more vigorous action of the cords, sufficient space for resonating the tone, and a free egress through the lower pharynx and over the tongue.

Tone Quality, Placement

Tone quality is dependent on factors which may be grouped in three broad classes: (1) vibrato, (2) action of vocal cords, and (3) setting of resonators.

The importance of the vibrato to tone quality has already been discussed under that heading in Chapter 1, and illustrated in Figure 5. The vibrato adds "life" or "warmth" to the tone. Voices which contain few or no overtones, such as the coloratura soprano or male falsetto, are heard as "hooty" or "cold" if not enriched by the usually present vibrato. Voices which are normally rich with overtones but lack a vibrato are not satisfying, and may be heard as "throaty." And even voices with such an arrangement of overtones as reveals the fact that they are definitely "throaty" (produced with a tight throat) are made fairly acceptable or even pleasant if they can be given a satisfactory vibrato, even if only an artificially produced one. It usually happens, however, that a badly produced voice has no vibrato or else a bad vibrato or tremolo. When, for example, oscillograph records of voices were classified on the basis of the amount and the evenness of the vibrato discernible to the eye, the order was a close approximation to the ranking of the voices on the basis of beautiful tone quality.

The differences arising from the action of the vocal cords have already been intimated. An explosive cord action (cords remaining closed for half or more of the vibratory cycle, opening for only a relatively short, sharp, explosive puff, and quickly closing again), permits many overtones to be present. As the cord action becomes less explosive in nature, the resulting tones become less and less complex, frequently even to the point of becoming quite pure and simple tones with no observable overtones.

In addition to the effects of the vibrato and the cord action, there are almost limitless possibilities for variation of tone color among human voices—and even very great possibilities in a single voice—due to the many variations possible in the size and shape of the flexible resonating cavities; through changes in the setting of the jaws, cheeks, tongue, lips, throat muscles, and other parts; and, as pointed out by Russell, through changes in the character of their surfaces. *When the setting of the vocal*

cords and resonators that gives the best quality of tone is secured,
the voice is said to be properly "placed," and on this basic quality
are superposed the finer qualitative differences responsible for
the variations between the vowels. There is considerable evidence to indicate that the basic quality, at least in the good male
voice, is a formant somewhere in the general region of 400 to 600
cycles, caused by the resonance of a large back lower pharynx,
and that the singer attempts, with more or less success, to maintain this element throughout most if not all of the vowels. In
throaty voices this formant lies higher, perhaps as high as 1000
or 1200, due to a much smaller back throat. Speaking generally, the vowels themselves are produced by changes in the
shape of the organs *above* this important back lower resonator.
There is a rather continuous change of throat and mouth setting (and therefore of the overtones involved), as one goes from
oo through *oh, aw, ah, ă, eh, a(y), ĭ,* to *ee.* (See also the discussion of the formant theory in Chapter 1.)

The most effective "placement" is often secured by thinking
of the tone as being produced in the head, nasal passages, near
the lips, or some other "forward" position. The familiar "in
the masque" is an example. These are principally, however,
psychological illusions which aid in securing an enlarged throat,
where the main resonation takes place. The voice, in song or
speech, is never initiated elsewhere than in the larynx,[17] and the
most useful and effective resonation is almost always in that part
of the back throat immediately above the larynx.

Investigations at the Peabody Conservatory have shown that
when proper placement is secured good male voices show also a
relatively large amount of energy in a region lying between
approximately 2400 and 3200 cycles, and centering roughly
around 2800. Many female voices show a similar effect at a
somewhat higher average point. This is the "ring" in the voice,

---

[17] The "pseudo-voice" which persons who have had the larynx removed are able
to learn, through controlled passage of stomach air, if it may be called a voice, is an
exception.

or the "high formant." It is probably produced by a form of resonance in the laryngeal chamber itself, and is in direct proportion to the amount of "chest quality" being used. This high formant is present in varying amounts in all male voices, although in poorer ones it is usually less prominent, and may run up considerably higher than the above average figures. Speaking generally, the better the voice, or the louder the tone, the more prominent this formant becomes, at least during some part of the vibrato cycle. Although its amount may vary with quality or with intensity, for the most part its pitch averages around 2800-2900 cycles for men (or from about F to F♯ of the last octave of the piano), regardless of the fundamental pitch, the vowel sung, or the type of voice (whether bass, baritone, or tenor). This frequency is less prominent and sometimes almost entirely absent in speaking voices. The typical speaking voice of the majority of individuals is produced with the throat in its normal position of relative constriction, which lessens the amount of this high formant.

It is interesting and possibly significant that the natural resonant frequency of the ear canal is very close to the point we have found for the natural frequency generated in the human larynx. Figure 38

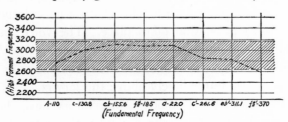

Fig. 38—Relation of meatus resonance to high formant in male voice.

shows how close this correspondence is, in the case of a good baritone. The dotted line represents the average of 41 records, using four vowels over the pitch range indicated. The shaded portion represents the area included between the boundaries of meatus resonance as given by Helmholtz (2640–3168). Many other voices show this same correspondence. It would seem to be more than just coincidence that the condition of the throat that makes possible a loud, full, "round" tone production with minimum strain to the singer should produce precisely that tone which, at least during a part of the vibrato cycle, contains a large amount of energy (sometimes well over 50%) in the relatively narrow frequency region for which his, and the listener's, ear is most sensitive. One is tempted to draw some interesting evolutionary conclusions.[18]

It must be borne in mind, however, that "2800" is not the *sole,* nor even the most important, determinant of good quality. Voices which possess it at the proper point and even which possess it in large degree, may still be of poor quality due to the lack of a suitable vibrato, or of a low enough low formant. If these are already present, the addition of a strong high frequency at the point for which the hearer's ear is most susceptible will have the effect of adding a very desirable "ring" or brilliance.

Investigations on the female voice have indicated tendencies similar to those noted in the male voice, with two exceptions: (1) the high formant centers still higher, perhaps around 3200 cycles, corresponding to a somewhat smaller larynx; and (2) some types of tone with much smaller percentage of high formant are accepted as good. The coloratura type will sometimes have practically no high formant at all, but is considered good because of its purity, and especially because of its agility. As mentioned before, soprano tones rarely contain many overtones, the high formant tends to drop out at some point as the pitch rises, and aesthetic judgments of "quality" tend to be made on the basis of other criteria than those used for lower voices. It would seem that in women a much larger part is played by the "head voice" register, which corresponds in some respects to the usually undeveloped "falsetto" in men. If the head-register tone lacks a satisfactory vibrato, it can become very objectionable indeed, especially if sustained at a high or loud pitch. It is a pure tone (lacking overtones) and must therefore get its richness through the vibrato if used for sustained work. In rapid

---

[18] A similar interesting fact is that the eye is most sensitive to those frequencies which are strongest in the radiation from the sun.

passages, however, where the individual tones are sometimes too short for even a single vibrato cycle (between one seventh and one sixth of a second on an average) to be heard, the "hooty" type of tone loses its "hoot" and can be very delightful.

Objectionable "nasality" in a voice probably is caused usually by having the entrance into the nasal pharynx opened by a relaxed velum, but not having, in addition, the size of the lower pharynx increased by the operation of the downward-pulling group of muscles. The throat may even be more constricted than before. Sometimes anatomical differences are responsible, such as an abnormally thick tongue, for example. This combination of an open nose and a constricted throat, although it results in a weaker tone, produces one with a larger *percentage* of nasal resonance, because of the small part played by a tight, small throat. With a greater degree of "throat" (at a lower resonant frequency), the same amount of "nose" means only a relatively small percentage of the total. In this better balanced tone it is then not called *nasality,* which is always from a small throat, but *head resonance.*

We can sum up and generalize by saying that the good, sustained tone quality is characterized by: (1) the vibrato, life, or warmth; (2) the low formant, "resonance," roundness, or sonority; and (3) the high formant, ring, or shimmer. Figure 39 illustrates these three characteristics. A good tone and a poor one were produced by a baritone voice. Graphs *a* and *b* are from the good tone, and *c* and *d* from the poor one. *a* and *b,* and also *c* and *d,* have been selected approximately one-thirteenth second apart in order to indicate the timbre change between extremes of the vibrato cycle. A 500-cycle timing wave is visible also. Notice in this figure: first, the lack of the timbre vibrato in the poor tone (the wave forms *c* and *d* being quite similar, and *a* and *b* quite different); second, the fact that the low characteristic, which is a third partial in the poor tone, has lowered to a second in the good tone; and lastly, that the high frequency, which is quite marked in the good tone, is almost completely

absent from the poor one. Furthermore, the good tone is able
co produce a much greater intensity than the poor one, as evi-
denced by the larger amplitude in the wave form. These tones
were sung on E♭ above Middle C (311 cycles), so that the third

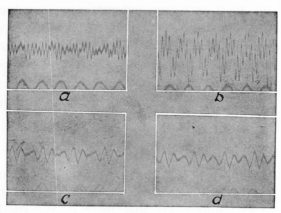

Fig. 39—Good quality contrasted with poor quality in male voice.

partial in the poor tone falls at 933. There is some evidence to
indicate that the presence of any considerable energy in the
region roughly around 900-1500 cycles, when supported by a
strong *lower* resonance, gives a tenorish quality to the voice, but
when not so supported gives it a distinctly ugly quality.

Physiological and Psychological Aspects of Good Voice Quality

These attributes of good quality are not entirely independent,
fortunately, but tend to be linked together with each other and
with a certain physiological coordination. Without considering
such important factors as the effects of variations in the shape,
condition, and moisture of the cords themselves, or the many
and complex adjustments of the intra-laryngeal muscles, it may
be said that a certain setting of the throat region tends to produce or permit all the attributes of good quality. It consists
principally in: (1) the relative relaxation and lowering of tongue
and jaw; (2) the enlargement of the pharynx, either through
permitting the larynx to lower, the sides of the throat to widen,

or the back part of the tongue to move forward; and perhaps
(3) a comfortable lifting of the soft palate, provided no undue
muscular tension results, and provided the entrance into the head
passages is not closed. This coordination involves the inhibition
of one of the most powerful, automatic, and constantly used
reflexes, the swallowing coordination, the muscles of which are
normally in a state of partial tension in many individuals. This
tension may be quite unconscious, so that for many persons, as
Stanley points out, a constricted throat may be thought to be
"relaxed." The relaxation of the swallowing coordination is
difficult for most persons, and the stiff tongue, jaw, or throat
remains a major problem.

Since the attributes of good quality all seem to be furthered
by a large throat, this should be the main concern of voice teaching, as has been emphasized by Stanley and others. It seems as
though we could almost say that there is *one* vocal fault—a
small, tight throat—and that it sometimes shows itself in the loss
of one of the attributes of quality, sometimes in the loss of
another. In Figure 40, A and B illustrate the wide differences
between the small throat and the enlarged throat. And these
diagrams do not show anything below the level of the tongue.
Additional enlargement can take place behind and below the
curve of the tongue. Vocal teachers are successful largely to the
extent that they are able, through one method or another, to
enlarge the throat. It is in the method that they differ. However, if one examines a large number of these methods, one finds
a very large percentage of them agreeing on the need for "getting
something or other *up*." This universal plea of voice teachers
to "get it up," or "forward," or "against the teeth," or "in the
masque," or "all through the head," or "away from the throat,"
helps to secure the ideal throat setting by relaxing and drawing
attention away from the powerful, and so often reflexly controlled, upward-pulling muscles of the swallowing group, which
in normal speech usually hold the throat entirely too small.
These must be permitted to relax and to be overbalanced by the

A. *Typical throat position in normal speech. Note small throat.*

B. *Typical throat position for good singing tone ("ah"). Note relaxed pillars.*

C. *Position resulting from too much "pulling down" effort. Note extremely tense rear pillars.*

D. *Position resulting from too much "pulling up" effort. Note tenseness of pillars.*

E. *Pathological throat. Enlarged and infected tonsils and swollen uvula. Open-mouth position.*

F. *Same as E, throat position for good singing tone. Note obstruction of throat-opening by tonsils, in spite of relaxed rear pillars.*

Fig. 40—Throat positions.

downward-pulling group which tends to lower the larynx and stretch the throat. If the upward-pulling muscles are unduly contracted when one attempts to sing, there is a definite sensation of strain in the throat, and a definite, objectionable, "whitish" quality to the tone.

There are innumerable variations of this imagery of head resonance. Any typical textbook on voice will furnish examples. In addition to the value of such imagery in tending, in a negative manner, to relax the swallowing muscles by drawing attention away from them, it has the very great value of tending in a positive way to gain the needed relaxation of the swallowing coordination by attacking it at a weak point. The attempt to "put it up" tends quite definitely to open the passage over the velum into the nose, and this cannot be done without securing, at least partially, the valuable relaxation which permits the throat to be enlarged and used to its best advantage. The reason for this is to be found in the peculiar nature of the physiologic structure of the back of the mouth. A detailed discussion is beyond the scope of this text, but may be found in other articles by the author.

There is no doubt that the concept of "head resonance" of some sort or another is of the greatest aid to the typical voice teacher. Almost any direction to the student to get the tone "up" somewhere or other, is of value, since with many students any mention of the word *throat* will cause a reflex *constriction* of the throat instead of an enlargement. On the other hand, repeated experiments show that, although the *attempt* to feel head resonance frequently improves the tone markedly through certain physiologic and psychologic effects, *and is therefore to be considered good pedagogy,* the actual resonating of sound in the head cavities is of very little importance, if any, in the physical production of good quality. Corroboration of this is to be found in the work of other investigators. Paget, for example, examined certain good singers whose tones, as tested by a stethoscope applied to the nostril, were found to be made with the nose-head system closed off behind the uvula.

Thus the main resonators are not in the nose or head, but in the back part of the throat, and somewhat in the mouth—the former affecting more the basic quality of the voice, and the latter being of more importance in vowel differentiation.[19] "Head resonance" is to be

---

[19] It is, however, possible to recognize most of the vowels through a stethoscope applied to the throat immediately above the larynx.

conceived rather as a *result* of the throat setting which makes powerful ringing tones possible than as an important contributing cause of that quality. It is quite possible, after the ability to secure the enlarged throat has been acquired. to learn to lift the velum just enough to close off the naso-pharynx and destroy the head resonance while still maintaining the enlarged throat and the relative relaxation of the swallowing group. And yet, one of the most effective ways of first learning how to secure that throat setting is by the use of some such imagery as "head resonance." Thus, one should not condemn this imagery.

Anything may be carried to a harmful extreme, however. In the attempt to "put it up" it is possible to use so much misdirected effort that the tongue or jaw muscles become tensed (upward-pulling coordination), even though the larynx is held down by the downward-pulling group. This condition is about as bad as when the downward-pulling group tenses in an unsuccessful attempt to lower a larynx that is held high. In both cases there is great waste of effort and loss of control. In the former case, however, because of the direction of pull, there is a tendency to pull the cords away from each other through hypertension of the tissues. The tone will then simplify, in proportion as the cord vibration loses its explosive character. It is possible that this is the explanation of the over-pure, "hooty" type of voice production, sometimes associated with the "gooseneck" appearance and arched eyebrows.

The antagonistic, simultaneous action of both coordinations is obviously bad no matter what the position of the larynx, for the typical results of incoordinated action are present: waste of effort, loss of ability to make fine or rapid adjustments, undue strain, and even pain. Even though the throat size were correct, it could not long be maintained, and the vibrato would become an irregular tremolo. In Figure 40, C and D show this antagonistic action. In both cases the "pillars," being more tense than necessary for the pitch being sung, have narrowed the width of the throat, and in addition the tone production is probably being spoiled by hypertension in the laryngeal region. These illustrations, however, must not be considered as entirely typical, since they were drawn from life, and throat positions vary greatly in different individuals.

If the various other tricks of the trade that voice teachers use to improve quality are analyzed, most or all of them will also be found to be devices for directly or indirectly enlarging the throat.

The teacher may not be aware of this, but simply knows that such devices get results. Thus, the proper taking in of breath will often loosen the interfering muscles, the jaw relaxing more and more, the deeper the breath. The throat will be stretched and the larynx lowered, because the lungs descend slightly during inspiration, drawing after them the trachea. The feeling of the *beginning* of a natural yawn, or the relaxation felt after its completion, are aids to securing a large throat. If the yawn be forced, or if it has passed into the rigid phase, this aid is of doubtful value. The ability to groove the tongue strengthens an important member of the throat enlarging set of muscles, although the grooved tongue position cannot be maintained while singing. The attempt to continue breathing out through the nose while singing, feeling the passage of the air or the resonating of the sound in the nose cavities, will aid throat enlargement through the necessary preliminary relaxation of the palate fulcrum, the fixation point from which the swallowing muscles operate when they contract the throat.

Vocal "methods" are by no means as incompatible or irreconcilable with one another as is often thought. In a very real sense most of them are seeking the same thing, and usually in much the same manner. The differences, often magnified through jealousies, are in the type of imagery used; and when methods conflict, the disagreement is almost always to be located, not in the realm of physical fact, but in this irrational realm of imagery, so necessary to the teacher while at the same time so delusive and untrustworthy. If the representatives of different methods will draw the sharp line which should separate fact from fancy, a very large and now unsuspected common ground will be found, which will give room for the growth of the sympathetic cooperation necessary for the solution of remaining problems.

It is not that fancy, in the form of the voice teacher's manifold imagery, is to be condemned. Quite the contrary. But it must be known to be imagery, valuable and varied though it is. Being imagery, it should be used merely to suggest indirectly, through its psychological effects, a certain muscular setting which is awkward for the beginner. The teacher, though using it, should bear in mind at all times the true facts, because when imagery becomes so vivid that it is transferred into the physical field, and used to explain physiologic and acoustic phenomena, it becomes extremely dubious, unreliable, and even false. It is this misuse which is largely responsible for the bitter controversies over vocal methods, as well as for their often comical explanations of the act of singing. Furthermore, since imagery is largely individual and thus variable, when it is trusted as a physical explanation, the so-called "True Method" becomes as variable as the individual temperament, instead of as stable as truth is usually expected to be.

Duration, Breath Control

The duration of a vocal tone depends on the breath capacity, and on the economy of its use in producing sound. If the breath is exhausted too rapidly, because of uneven cord surfaces, tones cannot be held long, and frequent breathing is the result. It is naturally an advantage to be able to make each breath produce tone for as long as possible, with no wastage. A breathy tone allows more air to escape through the glottis than necessary. However, a worse fault than this is an improper control of expiration.

There are two ways of controlling the expiration of breath. One is by restricting the flow at the larynx itself, with the laryngeal area acting as a valve. But this cannot be done without the assistance of the throat-constricting muscles, which, as we have seen, is very detrimental to the quality of the voice. For a powerful ringing male voice, and even for a rich contralto or a flexible coloratura soprano, the constrictors and the "pillars" should be as relaxed as possible for the particular pitch being sung, in order to permit as large a throat as possible. The breath expiration should therefore not be controlled at the throat. The correct way is through balancing the two sets of muscles which control expiration and inspiration. These are, respectively, the large abdominals, which push inward and aid in expiration, and the diaphragm, which contracts downward to enlarge the lungs in inspiration. When these are both in operation simultaneously, opposing each other in a nicely adjusted coordination without undue tension, the diaphragm "holds back" in its relaxation sufficiently to slow down the air flow to the proper point. In this way the breath may be inspired or expired at an extremely slow rate if necessary, while at the same time the throat is permitted to remain wide open except for the apposition of the cords, which need have no undue tension beyond that necessary to maintain vibration at the intended pitch and loudness. However, when this coordination is once learned it is perhaps better to think of the breathing musculature only during the act of inspiration, letting the thing take care of itself during the actual singing. A proper inspiration prepares the throat for good tone production, and *during* the actual tone production the mind can be used to better advantage in remembering "placement" sensations, or interpretation—particularly since expiration is normally the passive (relaxing) action of the diaphragm, and inspiration the active (tensing) one.

Song and Speech Contrasted

One difference between song and speech is that, in general, song prolongs the vowels and shortens the consonants, while speech does not dwell on vowels, and therefore is occupied with consonantal sounds for a larger proportion of the time. The reason that song tends to prolong the vowels is that vowels in general may be sung with an open throat and mouth, permitting power as well as beautiful quality, whereas consonants are usually produced by narrowings or more or less complete closures at one or more points between the back of the tongue and the lips. Also, since song has usually an artistic aspect, it is usually not in as much of a hurry as speech, which is almost purely utilitarian. Song can afford to sacrifice speed for beauty. Speech, on the other hand, must usually get its message across as quickly as possible, and since the understanding of it is based largely on perceiving the consonants, these are usually sufficiently emphasized while many vowels are passed over as quickly as possible. Instead of an enlarged back-throat resonator as in good singing, the result is then a more or less constant tonic constriction of the throat during speech, because of the frequent occurrence of consonants without sufficient intervening vowel time to permit enlargement. The positions of the larynx, pharynx, tongue, velum, lips, and other parts, is almost constantly changing, to a much more rapid degree than in song. The musculature is therefore kept in that degree of tonicity and constriction that will enable it to respond most effectively and rapidly to the demands of understandable consonant and vowel production. Thus speech, in English, and in most languages, tends to sacrifice beauty for rapidity. Italian, which has fewer closures, and more words ending in vowels, is a possible exception.

This fundamental distinction between song and speech is not always realized. Many authors insist that song and speech are identical in mechanism. In theory perhaps they are. In practice they most certainly diverge, at least in many persons. We have only to notice the great difference between the voice quality of many singers when they change from song to speech and the delightful "resonance" and "ring" in the speaking voice of the occasional singer who knows how to maintain the open throat in speech.

This same explanation applies to the special difficulty which presents itself to the singer, a difficulty presented by no other instrument, and one which goes far toward explaining the dearth of good voices as compared, let us say, with good violinists or good pianists. Since the voice is almost always under the necessity of singing *words,* which means it must get across to the hearer many consonant sounds, it must constantly be making throat, tongue, or mouth closures at the same time that it is attempting to keep these parts as wide open as possible for the sake of power and quality. These two things, in their very nature, are forever at odds. Frequently the result is a partial incoordination which favors either tone quality or enunciation. Only occasionally is a singer able to achieve both of these desiderata, and then he or she usually accomplishes it by learning how to make all consonants *emphatic but as short as possible,* holding off their entrance while keeping the parts enlarged on a vowel as long as possible, pronouncing the consonant rapidly, and *immediately* opening up again for the next vowel. In the interests of economy of motion, as Aikin points out, consonant-closure action should be done as much as possible with the agile tongue, and with no more cooperation from the slower-moving jaw than absolutely necessary. Naturally, in view of the importance of the large throat, diphthongs should be held on the larger vowel of the two. "Light" should be sung "lah—eet," holding the *ah* and not permitting the *ee* sound to be anticipated in the least until time to close the word.

Another difference between song and speech is that, in general, song follows a more or less strict melodic outline, sustaining for definite durations certain pitches in a certain scale, with relatively little but rapid sliding from one pitch to another; while speech has no formal melody, but slides constantly up or down depending on the sense of the words to be inflected. The sustaining of certain pitches and qualities, as in singing, makes it more difficult to understand the words, even if they are carefully pronounced. As Jones [20] points out:

When we are speaking there is a continual change from one sound to another, and it has long been recognized that the distinctness of any vowel depends in large measure on the contrast between it and other sounds that precede it or follow it. In connected speech there is usually no difficulty in recognizing different vowels, but if any chosen vowel is sung steadily for some time the lack of contrast soon makes the vowel less easy to recognize. In fact it seems to be true that a vowel is characterized, in part, by a quality which changes while the vowel is being spoken.

[20] *Op. cit.,* page 363.

The actual ranges of pitch and of loudness demanded of the singer are greater than in normal speech. The power in a sung vowel may reach a level ten thousand times as great, in physical units, as the average power in a spoken vowel during ordinary speech. The art of good singing has become highly artificial, in the sense of its being formalized and requiring much more ability than normal speech.

Whispering

Whispering occurs when the cords themselves are not brought near enough together to vibrate normally but the sounds of speech are produced, instead, through feeble excitation of the resonating cavities by the passing of the breath through one or more constricted places somewhere in the throat or mouth. The glottis could be one of these constricted places, but the constriction which is responsible for the sounds of whispering is frequently, if not usually, elsewhere in the throat or mouth.

E. NOISE

A sound either so complex, or so irregular, or both, that it seems to have no tone when heard by itself, is called a *noise*. There is, of course, no definite boundary between tone and noise. Borderline sounds are sometimes classed as tones, sometimes as noises. An extreme *ponticello* violin tone begins to shade into noise. And many noises shade into tones. If a wooden stick be dropped on a hard floor, the resulting sound would usually be classed as a noise. And yet it has a quite definite pitch, as is made very clear if several sticks, tuned to different pitches, as in the bars of the xylophone, are dropped one after the other. Quite recognizable tunes can be played by the successive noises produced by dropping such sticks. However, as Watson has worded it, "noise is more usually thought of as made up of sounds that are loud, sudden, disturbing, or disagreeable, and is more likely to be an unpitched sound than a musical sound."

Even one's attitude or mood can affect the noisiness of sounds. A recent definition of noise is, "any undesired sound." According to this concept, even the finest music may at times be noise to a person.

Noise in Percussion Instruments

Rhythm is essential to music, and noise of one sort or another is very effective in marking the rhythm. Thus, although a part of the sound made by such rhythm-marking instruments as the drums and cymbals could be called tone, a large part of it seems to our ears only noise, since the presence of inharmonic frequencies destroys the regularity of the vibration form from wave to wave. And yet we would be quite unsatisfied by music that never contained any rhythmic beats from these or similar instruments.

Another very important use for noise is in a powerful climax chord, where tone alone would never satisfy. Thus the orchestra gets its most intense effects by adding to the full volume of *tone* the *noise* produced by tremolos on drums and tympani, and on the climactic beat a crash on cymbals and gong.

Jazz music has always emphasized noise, and the modern trend in legitimate orchestral composition is also toward an increasing use of noises not heretofore used in music, sometimes in attempts to imitate the noises of modern industry and transportation, but often with no programmatic implications.

Noise Elements in All Instruments

In addition to the noise produced on the percussion instruments of the orchestra, there is a certain amount of noise present in practically every tone on any instrument, frequently at the moment the tone begins. These noises aid us in identifying the instruments in an ensemble. In the piano, there are the noises of the fingers on the keys, of the keys on their felt beds, of the hammers striking the wires. In stringed instruments, there are the noises caused by irregularities in the way the rosin particles catch the string, by the rattling of the string on the finger board, and by the finger striking the finger board. In wind instruments there are noises from the fingering of the keys. In reed instruments, there are the noises from setting the reed into vibration, from "reed quacks" or buzzing, from breaks in the tone. In flutes, there is the hissing sound of the breath. In brass instruments, there is the short preliminary noise when tone is begun. Not all of these are always present, particularly when the instrument is played by a skilled performer, but some of them can never be entirely eliminated.

Noise, therefore, is universally present. It has a very important place in music, and a real aesthetic value, when used in moderation, in helping to portray the emotional content of the music.

Noise and Health

There is some evidence to indicate that a moderate amount of noise can be an aid to concentration, to work output, or even to relaxation. Thus some persons prefer to have radio music as a background noise when they are trying to study. And, for that matter, a lullaby is frequently more of an aid to sleep than complete silence. Noise, however, particularly in modern cities, can become a great annoyance and even a positive danger to health and well-being. City dwellers live in a constant sea of noise, from traffic, building construction, whistles, bells, peddlers, newsboys, typewriters, radios, and so on, which is an important contributing cause of nervous and organic disorders, sleeplessness, and general lowered efficiency. It has been estimated that noise adds two million dollars a day to the nation's payroll through lowered office efficiency alone. Such estimates are of dubious accuracy, but there can be no doubt that noise of more than a certain intensity is detrimental. It has even been suggested that it is a contributing cause of crime. City governments are beginning to realize all this, and are taking steps to reduce noise in various ways.   Heavy traffic noise is loud enough to render inaudible a peal of thunder which would seem deafening in the country.   And the constant attempt to talk above a background of such noise can cause voices to become harsh and strident.

4

Harmony and Scales

WE come now to the questions of why certain intervals sound pleasing and others do not, and why certain rules of harmony are necessary. We cannot go far in the study of the history of music without realizing that our musical likes and dislikes are often founded on more or less vague aesthetic reasons, or perhaps on no more than prejudices. However, many of them have a sounder basis, a basis in acoustic phenomena, and it is with these that we are principally concerned here.

Relation of Consonance and Dissonance to Harmonic Series

As a matter of fact, the scientific basis of consonance and dissonance, and of the fundamental rules of harmony, is to be found in the relationships of the harmonic series, although it must be constantly borne in mind that their development has been greatly influenced by aesthetic principles as well. As the successive intervals of the harmonic series become smaller, they tend to become weaker, but more and more dissonant. The most consonant interval we know outside of the unison (which is hardly an interval), is the octave (ratio of frequencies being 1:2), and it is the first interval of the harmonic series. It is so consonant that its upper and lower tones cannot always be separated by the ear when heard together, and because of this similarity between them they have been given the same letter names. The octave is the only interval which is found in every scale, no matter in what country or what period of history it was used. Even in Chinese music, in which it is theoretically impure, it is probably produced fairly correctly in actual practice. Also, the octave was the first interval used for concerted singing, doubtless appearing originally when men and women together sang the same melody, because the natural pitch difference between the male and female voice is roughly an octave. The use of the octave in concerted singing was called *magadizing*.

The next most consonant interval is the perfect fifth (ratio 2:3), which is the second in the series. The third interval in the series is the perfect fourth (ratio 3:4), although because of its "hollow" sound and its melodic tendency to "resolve" to the major third, it no longer has the importance as a consonance that it once had. Nearly all primitive scales include these intervals as primary division points of the octave. Furthermore, the first attempts at concerted singing after the octave, were made in fifths and fourths (*organum*). Untrained singers of our own day are sometimes heard to sing at the interval of a perfect fifth from another singer.

The fundamentality of these intervals is illustrated not only by their order of appearance in the harmonic series, but also by their frequency of appearance therein. For example, among the first sixteen partials of the series (see Figure 3, page 9), the octave (1:2 relation) occurs eight times—1:2, 2:4, 3:6, 4:8, 5:10, 6:12, 7:14, and 8:16. The perfect fifth (2:3 relation) occurs five times—2:3, 4:6, 6:9, 8:12, 10:15. The perfect fourth (3:4) occurs four times—3:4, 6:8, 9:12, 12:16.

The next in the series are the major and minor thirds (ratios 4:5 and 5:6). Their inversions give, respectively, the minor sixth (5:8) and the major sixth (3:5). Beyond the thirds come major and minor seconds and still smaller and more dissonant intervals.

Even though Wallaschek has reported that some of the most primitive races of men sing in harmony, it seems to be more than a historical coincidence that the order in which intervals have been accepted for use in music performed in parts parallels as closely as it does the order in which they occur in the harmonic series. The supposition is that, since most tones are complex, man's ear had unconsciously been absorbing the sound of these intervals in the harmonic series of many of the tones he heard; and when he desired to use intervals for their own sake, they naturally appeared in musical history in the order of their appearance (and loudness) in the harmonic series. Thus, for example, for a long period of time during the classical age, pieces in a minor tonality were required to end on a major chord, the *Tierce de Picardie*. This was even extended to the ends of phrases, as in madrigals, where "false relations" often occur between the last chord of one phrase and the first of another. Later on, however, the minor third was accepted as sufficiently harmonious for a closing chord.

Since thirds have now largely superseded fourths and fifths as consonant intervals, it is interesting to conjecture whether seconds will ever become as common as thirds are now. Thus the chord of the added sixth (the presence of the major sixth degree in a final major chord, giving a major second between the fifth and the sixth degrees), which was being pioneered fifty years ago, is now a commonplace of popular music, both melodically and harmonically. Also, the Chopin *Prelude* in F major, which closes on a dominant seventh chord, may be mentioned, although this particular composer may have meant to introduce this dissonance for some imaginative or programmatic purpose. Major seconds and major sevenths above the tonic, and even more violent dissonances, are creeping into final chords now, as man pushes back the horizons of consonance in his search for new artistic experiences.

However, some theorists, notably Watt, believe that the harmonic series order has little or nothing to do with the historical order of appearance of the intervals, and that the thirds and sixths, because of certain aesthetic and psychological characteristics, will always be the most satisfactory consonances.

Additional scientific basis for the relative harmonic usefulness of the intervals may be adduced in another way. If, as we have

seen is usually the case, the tones used in music carry with them
a harmonic series, when two such tones are sounded together it
may be that certain upper partials in one series will lie close
enough (within a tone or semitone) to certain of the other series
to produce objectionable beating, which will greatly increase the
roughness of the interval. It is found that the order of musical
intervals in terms of roughness, secured in this way, also tends
to correspond to the order in which the musician places them on
purely aesthetic grounds. For example, in the case of the octave,
the partials of the upper tone all correspond to alternate partials
of the lower, adding nothing new, but only reinforcing elements
already present. Consequently, there is no beating or dissonance.
With an interval like the minor third, however, the third partial
of the upper tone falls close to the fourth partial of the lower;
and the fourth of the upper quite close to the fifth of the lower.
The resulting beating and dissonance helps to give the minor
third its veiled quality.

With more complex tone qualities such interference of partials
becomes more and more objectionable. It is thus evident that
the purer the tones used, the safer it is to employ dissonant
intervals without having the resulting chords too rough. Even
major thirds become roughened to an ear accustomed to smooth-
ness and blending, if played loudly on an instrument giving a
very complex tone, although the effect is valuable where the
emotional content of the music justifies it. Such principles have
often been put into use unconsciously by composers whose sole
criterion was, "Does it sound good?"

On the other hand, the more partials present in the tones,
the greater is the possibility of producing intervals precisely in
tune. This is because the dissonance increases markedly as such
an interval is put slightly out of tune, due to the beating of the
particular partials or fundamentals which should be in unison
with each other for that interval. For example, the presence of
the second partial in piano tones is what enables the tuner to
secure true octaves, since the second partial of any tone will beat

with the played octave of the tone if the interval is imperfect. Similarly, in the case of a true perfect fifth, the third partial of the lower tone and the second of the upper *should* exactly correspond. With complex tones which possess these partials in sufficient intensity, therefore, precise tuning of the interval is an easy matter, due to the ease of locating the relatively consonant point between two dissonant, beating, regions. If even one of the tones used is pure, or does not contain the particular partial needed for this purpose, tuning becomes more difficult. Clarinets, speaking generally, do not possess the second partial to any great degree. Therefore, if the clarinet were the upper tone of a perfect fifth, and a violin the lower one, precise tuning would be difficult, unless there were a coincidence of other, higher, partials, such as would occur if there happened to be a strong sixth in the violin and a strong fourth in the clarinet, for example. If the instruments were reversed, however, precision would be easier because the clarinet has a strong third, and the violin has second and third partials.

Evolution of Diatonic Scale (*True or "Just" Intonation*)

"It is advisable to guard at the outset against the familiar misconception that scales are made first and music afterwards. Scales are made in the process of endeavouring to make music, and continue to be altered and modified, generation after generation, even till the art has arrived at a high degree of maturity." With this warning from Parry [1] in mind, let us consider the evolution of our scales.

The modern diatonic scale has its roots in these same fundamental relationships of the harmonic series that have determined the harmonic use of intervals, although its development has again been moulded largely by aesthetic considerations. The development of this scale is thought to have been somewhat as follows.

---

[1] Parry, C. Hubert H., *The Evolution of the Art of Music*, page 20. New York: D. Appleton-Century Company, Inc., 1930.

The first "music" consisted of tonal motion only, pure melody, with no conscious thought of definite steps. Such were the rude sliding cries of the pre-savage. Next came the selection of certain points for the tones, as when the primitive flutes were pierced with several holes. Man's social contacts then systematized these chance points into primitive scales, of which there were many. Many of these scales persist in various parts of the world today. It is only in "Western music," where a harmonic development evolved, that the diatonic scale as we know it became predominant. When men and women sang simple melodies together in such primitive scales, probably thinking they were singing in unison, the natural difference in their voices of approximately an octave, together with the attraction of this interval because of its fundamentality in the harmonic series, established this interval in their minds. The drawing power of the perfect fifth and the perfect fourth then caused these intervals to appear, perhaps as division points of the octave. (Of course, they were not known by these names, since they were at first undivided into five and four tones, respectively.) It is difficult, if not impossible, to say which of them appeared first. Perhaps they appeared simultaneously, since one of them is merely the octave inversion of the other. A fourth *below* a C, for example, gives us the G which is a *fifth* above the next lower C. And there is strong evidence to show that many primitive scales were not conceived upward, as is our harmonically conceived scale, but downward. We can be fairly certain, however, that these two intervals appeared early, later to become strongly felt division points of the octave.

From then on, however, if not before, natural physical laws had less to do with the process of scale development, and aesthetic and practical considerations more. Consequently, the lines of scale development have diverged greatly according to various factors in the different racial cultures. The Hindu scales divided the octave in a different way from the Chinese, and these again differently from the Egyptian scales. Many varieties of pentatonic, hexatonic, and heptatonic scales arose. Old Egyptian flutes from the year 3000 B.C. (the Bronze Age) have a complete diatonic scale, and parts of diatonic scales have been found in instruments dating from the Stone Age. According to Parry,[2] most of the known scales of the world may be grouped in two broad classes: (1) pentatonic scales, in which semitones are rare, but in which the interval of the perfect fifth is prominent; and (2) heptatonic scales, in which semitones are common, and in which the perfect fourth is the interval which seems to have been first recognized. It must be admitted, however, that in the scales of some races one or the other, or even both, of these primary intervals are absent. The subject is a vast one, and entirely beyond the scope of this text. Here we are interested only in tracing the particular line of development that led to our diatonic scale, and upon which the entire edifice of "Western music" has been built. And the connecting link between the ages of pre-historic music and the age which produced a Bach is to be found, in the field of music, as in so many other fields, in ancient Greece.

Parry also says: "The first scale which history records as having been used by the Greeks is indeed absolutely nothing more than a group of three notes, of which those which are furthest apart make the interval of the fourth, and the remaining note is a semitone above the lower note." The effect can be secured by playing C and the A♭ and G below it, A♭ acting as a downward "leading tone" to the G. The A♭ was perhaps introduced first as an embellishment to the G, and therefore had no definite position. Later, another tone was introduced between the A♭ and the C, filling out what came to be known as a *tetrachord*. The *tone,* the interval produced by the difference between the fourth and the fifth, as we call these intervals, must have been discovered early; and along with various other types of division, attempts were made to divide up the larger intervals into tones. Various methods of tuning the

[2] *Op. cit.,* page 27.

tetrachords were tried. It was found that when two tones, approximately the size of the tone between the fourth and the fifth, were taken out of the fourth, the remaining interval was about half a tone. Thus began the subdivision of the fourths into something resembling more or less what we know as two tones and a half tone, giving various types of tetrachords, depending on the order of the tones and half tone. The combination of these various tetrachords in various ways and at various pitch levels gave rise to the old Greek modes, which were later also adapted for use by the Church. Even then there was no sense of harmony and tonality as we now know it. Performers and singers would end on almost any tone, feeling no need of ending on a "tonic."

At this time efforts were made to produce two or more melodies together, and during the centuries of this polyphonic effort, it became clear that a certain arrangement of whole and half tones was vastly superior to other arrangements in this new art. The somewhat humorous side of it, as Parry [3] says, is that this arrangement, which was arrived at only after centuries of experimentation, was one of the modes that had been known all along, but had been rather looked down upon as an inferior specimen of its kind. This mode was the old Greek Lydian mode of Aristoxenus. It had been taken possession of by the troubadours and other secular musicians of the Middle Ages, and was held in contempt by the churchmen as the "wanton mode." It was thought to incite licentiousness. It had the same arrangement of whole and half steps that our modern major scale has: whole, whole, half, whole, whole, whole, half. The half step between the seventh and eighth degrees furnished the sensitive leading tone, thereby aiding in the establishment of the sense of tonality. However, this mode, which is today known as *Pythagorean intonation,* did not have exactly the same sizes of whole and half steps (hemitones, as they were called), as the modern scale. Instead, its intervals had the following ratios:

---

[3] *Op. cit.,* page 57.

LYDIAN MODE (PYTHAGOREAN INTONATION) [4]

Interval	Ratio
1st (whole tone)	8:9
2d " "	8:9
3d (hemitone)	243:256 (approx. 18:19)
4th (whole tone)	8:9
5th " "	8:9
6th " "	8:9
7th (hemitone)	243:256

Interval from 1st tone to:	
2d	8:9
3d	64:81
4th	3:4
5th	2:3
6th	16:27
7th	128:243
8th	1:2

It was soon realized in the theory of polyphonic music, and possibly in actual practice as well, that the Pythagorean third (64:81), although quite satisfactory as a melodic interval, was somewhat inharmonious when sounded by two simultaneous tones, as when two polyphonic melodies sang a third or progressed in thirds. It was realized that if this ratio were shortened to 64:80, or, in other words, 4:5, the considerably simpler and more harmonious interval of the true major third of the harmonic series would be secured. Pythagorean intonation has imperfect (too sharp) major thirds from the first, fourth, and fifth degrees of the scale. (In other words, the third, sixth, and seventh degrees are too sharp.) If these are all shortened to true major thirds, the result is a considerably simpler series of

---

[4] Actually, Pythagoras himself probably did not know the concept of "frequency," since he did his work in terms of ratios of string length.

Some confusion may arise as to the name "Lydian," because this word implies an entirely different arrangement of whole tones and half tones in Glareanus' reclassification of the modes for ecclesiastical purposes. Those who are familiar with the names he applied to the Church modes will find his "Ionian" to correspond to the "Lydian" of Aristoxenus.

ratios, which is known by the names of the *true diatonic scale*, *true intonation,* or *just intonation,* as follows:

TRUE DIATONIC (MAJOR) SCALE (TRUE OR JUST INTONATION)

Interval	Letter names in key of C	Ratio
1st (major whole tone)	C to D	8:9
2d (minor " ")	D " E	9:10
3d (semitone)	E " F	15:16
4th (major whole tone)	F " G	8:9
5th (minor " ")	G " A	9:10
6th (major " ")	A " B	8:9
7th (semitone)	B " C	15:16

Interval from first tone to:		
2d (major whole tone)	C to D	8:9
3d (major third)	C " E	4:5
4th (perfect fourth)	C " F	3:4
5th (perfect fifth)	C " G	2:3
6th (major sixth)	C " A	3:5
7th (major seventh)	C " B	8:15
8th (perfect octave)	C " C	1:2

If these ratios are reduced to the lowest terms possible on a common base, we have the following series of numbers to represent the just scale:

$$24 : 27 : 30 : 32 : 36 : 40 : 45 : 48$$
$$do \quad re \quad mi \quad fa \quad sol \quad la \quad ti \quad do$$

It must be borne in mind that these figures represent *ratios,* not absolute values, and that this scale can be constructed on any pitch if we employ these same ratios. Thus, in the same way that we find the frequency of the octave above a tone by multiplying its frequency by 2, or that of an octave below by multiplying its frequency by $\frac{1}{2}$, so we can determine the frequency of *re* by multiplying the frequency of *do* by 27/24 (or 9/8), or that of *do* by multiplying *re* by 24/27 (or 8/9). It should be clear, therefore, that the difference of the number of vibrations of two consecutive tones a semitone or whole tone apart, or any interval of any scale, for that matter, varies widely depending on how low or high the interval is in the pitch scale, although the ratio the two frequencies bear to each other is always necessarily the same as long as the interval is unchanged. From Middle C to D will be a jump of twice as many vibrations as from C to D each an octave lower. This is illustrated by the following table giving the frequencies for four octaves of just intonation based on A-440:

C	132	264	528	1056
D	148½	297	594	1188
E	165	330	660	1320
F	176	352	704	1408
G	198	396	792	1584
A	220	440	880	1760
B	247½	495	990	1980

It is difficult at this time to know precisely to what extent just intonation remained a matter of theory or was adopted in the practice of the music of the time. Barbour feels that it is very unlikely that it was in use during the sixteenth century, the golden age of polyphony. It seems likely, however, that it was used in choral singing in final tonic chords, and perhaps in otherwise fairly static chords, where there was time for a mutual tuning adjustment to take place between singers of various parts. The same may have been true of combinations of instruments in which adjustment was possible. Whether keyboard instruments were ever tuned to make just intonation possible in practical music is open to question. Certain it is, however, that the precise relationship of the diatonic degrees determined by the series of ratios 24:27:30:32:36:40:45:48 will yield the greatest number of naturally harmonious and pleasant combinations.

We see that there are two sizes of whole tone in this scale, one with the ratio 8:9, and one 9:10. Thus, while the old Lydian mode bore considerable resemblance to the just diatonic scale, in that it contained the same order of tones and half tones, it made no distinction between major and minor whole tones, its half tones were smaller than the diatonic half tones, and its third ("Pythagorean third") was made up of two intervals of ratio 8:9. This distinction, which gave the new scale true major thirds (made up of 8:9 plus 9:10, and giving therefore a ratio of 4:5 for the just third), shifted three tones slightly from their positions in the Lydian mode. It should be mentioned that the advisability of this change of ratios was noted even by the later Greeks themselves, Didymus and Ptolemy having suggested the very alteration urged by Zarlino and others many centuries later. Whether the Greeks heard even a true major third as a consonance, however, is open to question. The relative pitch distances of the degrees in the two scales are illustrated in *a* and *b* of Figure 41.

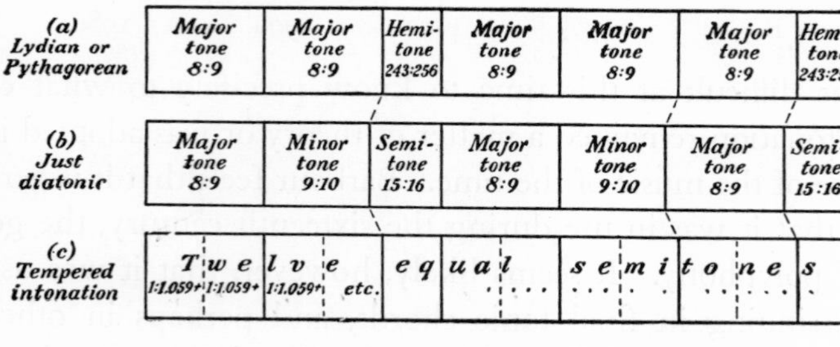

(a) Lydian or Pythagorean	Major tone 8:9	Major tone 8:9	Hemi- tone 243:256	Major tone 8:9	Major tone 8:9	Major tone 8:9	Hemi- tone 243:256
(b) Just diatonic	Major tone 8:9	Minor tone 9:10	Semi- tone 15:16	Major tone 8:9	Minor tone 9:10	Major tone 8:9	Semi- tone 15:16
(c) Tempered intonation	T w e l v e 1:1.059+ 1:1.059+ 1:1.059+ etc.			e q u a l		s e m i t o n e s	

Fig. 41—Relative sizes of intervals in Pythagorean intonation, just intonation, and equal temperament.

Some persons believe that the relationship of tones in the just diatonic scale was suggested directly by the laws of nature, perhaps because they think they sing it by natural instinct. It is true that six of its tones may be secured by using the 8th, 9th, 10th, 12th, 15th, and 16th partials from a tonic fundamental, and the other two tones by using two partials from a subdominant fundamental. Or, we may consider the scale to be derived entirely from a subdominant fundamental five octaves below the *fa* of the scale by taking the 24th, 27th, 30th, 32d, 36th, 40th, 45th, and 48th partials of that fundamental. However, it is assuming a great deal to suppose that such roundabout explanations account for the *development* of the scale. In the above case, for example, we should have to imagine that our ancestors heard partials as high as the 48th in complex tones, and that their ears were particularly struck by just those which produced a diatonic scale, neglecting the effect of those in between, and of the lower and much more prominent ones! Furthermore, we are inclined to forget the fact that certain Oriental scales, as well as primitive scales of certain races, contain intervals which do not bear any resemblance to the diatonic intervals, yet are apparently quite satisfactory to their users. And intervals which are satisfactory tend, through repetition, to become "instinctively natural." A scale with consonant intervals is unnecessary for a race who never use tones in combination, but sing everything in unison or octaves. Where polyphony or a harmonic sense develops, the scales tend to be consonant. Ellis has said, "Musical scale is not *one*, not natural, or even founded necessarily on laws of constitution of musical sound, but very diverse, very artificial and very capricious." [5]

Other persons believe that the just diatonic scale is *all* true and perfect. Unfortunately, this is not so. By reducing to lowest terms the ratios of the various triads in the just scale we get the following:

Triad on first degree	4: 5 :6
" " second "	27:32:40
" " third "	10:12:15
" " fourth "	4: 5 :6
" " fifth "	4: 5 :6
" " sixth "	10:12:15
" " seventh "	45:54:64

The triads on the tonic, subdominant, and dominant, having the ratio 4:5:6, are all true major triads, such as would be formed by the fourth, fifth, and sixth partials in a harmonic series. This is the great primary advantage of just intonation

---

[5] This is borne out by Wead, who believes that many primitive scales were determined by the instruments, instead of the instruments by the scales. These instruments were discovered perhaps by chance, possibly when burning holes in hollow bones, gourds, pottery, or reeds as part of their *decoration*. The setting of the holes is almost always equispaced in these cases, and is not in the particular decreasing ratio that would be necessary to duplicate our scale. However, since certain intervals correspond to certain in our own system, we try to interpret this primitive music according to our theory, an exceedingly dangerous and unjustified procedure. Primitive scales, according to Wead, often had intervals either increasing or decreasing in size.

over its predecessors. The despised "wanton mode" had proved the easiest of all the modes to adapt to the requirements of the new harmony which was developing, because of the ease with which its arrangement of tones and semitones permitted the alteration that gave perfect major triads on these three important harmonic reference points in the major scale. The Lydian was the only mode that had these triads even approximately major. The triads on the third and sixth degrees of the just scale are true minor triads, such as would be formed by the tenth, twelfth, and fifteenth partials in a harmonic series. No combination of tones in the Lydian mode, or as it is now called, *Pythagorean intonation,* will give these ratios of the true minor triad. However, when we come to the intervals on the second degree of the "true" scale, we find imperfection. The triad on the second degree is not true, since its fifth is too flat. If we would raise its fifth (sixth degree of the scale) we would throw it out of tune for the subdominant triad. If we lowered the second degree itself, as when tuning it for a true subdominant for the minor tonality, we would throw it out of tune for the dominant triad of the major tonality. The interval from the second to the fourth degree is not a true minor third, either, being too flat. This also cannot be remedied without spoiling other intervals. We are obliged to put up with a bad minor triad on the second degree of the scale, both the third and the fifth of this triad being wrong.[6] The triad on the seventh degree of the just scale is even more dissonant.

Thus we see that even the "true" diatonic major scale is incapable of having all of its intervals in perfect harmony, and must be considered partly as based on the relationships of the

---

[6] The older Lydian mode was superior in this respect, maintaining pure 3:2 ratios for the cadential progression of roots descending by fifths, such as E—A—D—G—C. Some theorists, Goetschius, for instance, believe this to be the more natural scale than the just intonation as a basis for harmony.

It is interesting to note that if we start with the subdominant F, and take five fifths upward, we get F—C—G—D—A, which when placed in the same octave give us a pentatonic scale: C—D—F—G—A—C, F—G—A—C—D—F, etc. Taking two more fifths, we get the remaining members of a diatonic scale.

harmonic series, and partly as a more or less conventional and artificial series of tones, yielding a large number of consonant intervals. It surely was not dictated by any imperative natural laws, although it was moulded in its development by some of the intervals of the harmonic series. And although it has its false intervals, it has no less than sixteen perfectly consonant intervals within the compass of one octave, more than double the number in the original form of the scale.

Our modern pure minor mode, starting on the sixth degree of the major, may be considered to be made up of three minor triads, one on each fundamental degree. Reference to the table on page 175 will show that the new tonic and the new dominant will be pure minor triads, since the triads on the sixth degree and the third degree of the major have the ratio 10:12:15; but that the subdominant will be impure, since the ratio is 27:32:40. In other words, if we are constructing a true scale of A minor, the old D would have to be lowered. If this is done, the ratios of the steps are as given on page 178.

The minor mode could be said to correspond roughly with the Greek Hypo-Dorian or Aeolian, except that it must always be remembered that our modern sense of tonality was unknown to the Greeks. This sense of tonality did not even take firm root until about the time of the death of Handel or the birth of Mozart. Thus, whereas the Greeks would have felt no desire to use a G♯ instead of a G in what we know as the "harmonic scale" of A minor, we feel the need of this because, hearing the A as a strong and final keynote in a definite tonality, we desire to have the G♯ as a more definite and satisfactory leading tone into the A. The alteration of this tone in this form of the scale of course would alter the above ratios accordingly, and this form of the scale is considered to be made up of minor triads on tonic and subdominant, and a major triad on the dominant. In both the pure and the harmonic minor forms there will be a pure major triad on the *sixth* degree of the minor (the old major subdominant), although this too van-

PURE MINOR SCALE IN JUST INTONATION

Interval	Letter names in A minor	Ratio
1st (major whole tone)	A to B	8:9
2d (semitone)	B " C	15:16
3d (minor whole tone)	C " D	9:10
4th (major " ")	D " E	8:9
5th (semitone)	E " F	15:16
6th (major whole tone)	F " G	8:9
7th (minor " ")	G " A	9:10

Interval from first tone to:		
2d (major whole tone)	A to B	8:9
3d (minor third)	A " C	5:6
4th (perfect fourth)	A " D	3:4
5th (perfect fifth)	A " E	2:3
6th (minor sixth)	A " F	5:8
7th (minor seventh)	A " G	5:9
8th (perfect octave)	A " A	1:2

Triad on 1st degree	A—C—E	10:12:15
" " 2d "	B—D—F	135:160:192
" " 3d "	C—E—G	4:5:6
" " 4th "	D—F—A	10:12:15
" " 5th "	E—G—B	10:12:15
" " 6th "	F—A—C	4:5:6
" " 7th "	G—B—D	108:135:160

ishes in the ascending form of the "melodic minor," where F is raised to F♯ to eliminate the melodically awkward interval of the augmented second. In the descending melodic minor, the G♯ and F♯ become G♮ and F♮—in other words, the pure minor. If G♯ and F♯ were retained, the descending scale would be indistinguishable from a major scale until the third degree from the bottom were reached.

The major and minor forms of the diatonic scale may be said to have come to maturity when the sense of tonality became fixed. This sense of tonality implies an artistic classification of the different degrees of the scale as to their functions, something which no other scale system ever attempted. No matter how much ingenuity the Chinese, Indians, Persians, Greeks, or other peoples expended in dividing their intervals and working out various modes, all of these essentially melodic conceptions seem to have stopped short of such a classification of the functions of tones in relation to a "home tone." It remained for Western music, and then only after many centuries of development, to achieve a harmonically conceived scale, a sense of tonality, and an appreciation of the functions of the scale degrees. It was in the seventeenth century, according to Parry,[7] that men began to have a distinct sense of an artistic classification of the tones of the scale. The name *note* or *tonic* of a scale "arrived finally at its decisive position as the starting-point and the resting-place of an artistic work. The establishment of the major chord on the dominant note—the fifth above the tonic—gave that note the position of being the center of contrast to the tonic; and upon the principle of progress to contrast, and back to the initial starting-point, the whole fabric of modern harmonic music is built. The other notes fell into their places by degrees."

Need for Temperament

With all of its advantages, it would seem that just intonation would have lasted a long time. Actually, it was soon changed again, for reasons of practical convenience in the composing and performance of music. As a matter of fact, Barbour believes that there is little if any available evidence that just intonation was seriously considered as a *practical* tuning system except by a few mathematicians like Kepler and Descartes. Its undoubted beauty in theoretical tuning met with serious difficulties in keyboard instruments. Such difficulties as have already been mentioned were by no means the only ones to present themselves in practical use. Two modes only had survived, the major and minor, which greatly limited artistic choice of ma-

[7] *Op. cit.*, page 58.

terial by composers. This made *modulation* a necessity, and
when music began to demand greatly increased harmonic and
melodic resources, due to the impetus of the increased artistic
activity during the Renaissance and later years, a more flexible
scale became essential.

It had long since been known that it was impossible to modulate from one tonality into any other and have a true diatonic
scale in the new tonality without adding at least one "black
note," and, in addition, altering somewhat at least one other
tone. Such additions and alterations were easy enough with
instruments such as the violin, where the pitch is adjustable,
but presented a serious problem on the keyboard instruments.
The five "whole steps" had been subdivided on the organ not
later than the fifteenth century, giving (from C major) the five
black keys. This divided the octave into twelve parts, the so-
called *chromatic* scale. However, if the original C-major scale
were in just intonation, this division would not help much,
since, when modulating three or four signatures distant, the
tones in the new tonality would be so badly out of tune as to
make music impossible without retuning (or "adjusting" in
the case of the violin). The reason for this is the fact that
there are two kinds of whole tones in the true diatonic scale, and
further, the half tones obtained by dividing either of these whole
tones are different from each other, and different from the
semitones between the third and fourth and the seventh and
eighth degrees of the original diatonic scale. If we attempt to
build a scale on the second degree, for example, we get the
wrong kind of whole tone to start with (ratio 9:10 instead of
8:9), and other errors as well. Similar errors occur in any
signature to which we try to modulate. Such pitches as F♯
and G♭, for example, are not theoretically identical. But they
are so nearly alike that by compromising a bit and putting up
with a slight degree of out-of-tuneness we may sound either
of them with the same piano key. If we had to have different
keys for these two slightly different pitches and for all the

other similar differences in the scale series, the piano would have to have many more keys than it now has, which would make it quite impracticable to play. Ellis has fixed seventy-two notes in an octave as the number essential to a theoretically complete command over all the tonalities used in modern music. Redfield believes thirty-five tones to the octave would enable us to play satisfactorily in all key signatures. But even this number would be vastly more difficult to play, and keep tuned (even during the temperature changes of a single performance), than the present twelve.

In this conflict between the ideal and the practical, the practical triumphed, and so compromises were worked out. Various methods of tuning were proposed. In some, a certain number of more commonly used scales were tuned nearly correct, and the rest were left to take care of themselves. Thus music was playable in keys up through perhaps three flats and three sharps. When only twelve tones were available in an octave, the inaccuracies of "wolves" were so bad in the remaining keys that they were not usable. One of these compromise tunings which had a widespread vogue was the *meantone tuning*. It was in conflict with another one, called *equal temperament,* until the middle of the 19th century in England. It was this latter, equal temperament, which finally won out, and which has remained to this day.

Equal Temperament

In equal temperament, the twelve semitones of the octave are all made equal (at least theoretically), and called *equal-tempered semitones*. When this is done, the frequency of each semitone is approximately 1.06 (more accurately 1.059463+) times the frequency of the one immediately below it. These tempered semitones are thus flatter than the just diatonic semitones (15:16, or 1:1.067—). (See Figure 41c.) However, two of these tempered semitones together give a whole step which is intermediate in value between the true major whole tone (8:9) and minor whole tone (9:10), though nearer to the former, making the second degree of the scale only very slightly flat. Furthermore, five and seven of these tempered semitones give, respectively, intervals quite close to the true perfect fourth and true perfect fifth. The tempered fourth is very slightly sharp, and the tempered fifth very slightly flat, but both so little as to be unobjectionable. For example, the fifth is flat only to the extent of about a fiftieth of a semitone.

It is in the major third, the major sixth, and the major seventh that tempered intonation is most inaccurate, these intervals all being perceptibly sharp as compared with just intonation. Major thirds and major sixths, for example, are sharp to the extent of about one seventh and one sixth of a semitone, respectively. These same errors are naturally reflected in the minor sixths and the minor thirds, which are, respectively, the octave inversions of major thirds and major sixths. Such differences are easily perceptible to an ear trained in just intonation, and when tempered chords are produced by sustained tones, their intervals are rougher than those of just intonation. However, as Parry [8] says concerning the intervals of primitive (and therefore melodic) scales:

An agreement in such intervals as thirds and sixths is not to be expected. They are known to be difficult intervals to learn, and difficult to place exactly in theoretic schemes; and the result is that they are infinitely variable in different scales. Some systems have major thirds, and some minor; and some have thirds that are between the two. Sixths are proportionately variable, and are often curiously dependent upon the fifth for any status at all; and of such intervals as the second and seventh, and more extreme ones, it must be confessed that they are so obviously artificial, that even in everyday practice in countries habituated to one scale they are inclined to vary in accordance with individual taste, and the lack of it.

In this connection, it is interesting to note that although the third, the sixth, and the seventh are considerably sharp in equal

---

[8] *Op. cit.,* page 21.

temperament, they are all *still sharper* in Pythagorean intonation. These differences are illustrated in Figure 41. Furthermore, although in equal temperament these three intervals all lie between their values in just intonation and in Pythagorean intonation, yet temperament places them all closer to their values in Pythagorean than to their just intonation values.

The germ of the theory of equal temperament can apparently be traced back into ancient Greece, and even into ancient Chinese civilization. According to Barbour, this theory was probably used for fretted instruments before 1500, and was put upon a correct theoretical basis during the second half of the sixteenth century,. being extended to keyboard instruments in theory, and to some extent in practice, early in the seventeenth century. The system had been proposed by Bartolo Rames in 1482. Zarlino sets forth the system in detail in 1588. Among others, Mersenne, in his *Harmonie Universelle,* 1636, gives the correct numbers for its ratios. Its advantages were made more evident by Bach's *Well-tempered Clavichord,* written in 1722. The new tuning was long a controversial subject, however, and it was not until the middle of the nineteenth century that its reign could be said to be complete.

Although musicians often repeat glibly that the tempered scale is imperfect, few understand the necessary cause of that imperfection, even with such works available as those of Helmholtz, Ellis, and many others. The cause lies in the mathematical relations of the ratios involved. In the keyboard as we know it, if one starts with any tone, say a C, and continues to step off any interval whatsoever, he will eventually arrive again on another C, perhaps only one octave, perhaps many octaves above the original C. In the case of the major third, only one octave is needed: C to E, E to G♯ (A♭), and A♭ to the next C. The minor and major second, the minor and major third, and the augmented fourth, are all enharmonically divisible in this way into one octave. The minor sixth requires two octaves, the major sixth three octaves, the perfect fourth and the minor seventh five octaves, the perfect fifth seven, and the major seventh eleven octaves before such a return to the starting tone takes place. This is because of the indivisibility of the number of semitones in certain intervals into the number of semitones in the octave interval, and is determined by finding the least common multiple of those numbers. The process of stepping off the same interval obviously involves multiplying the starting frequency by the interval ratio an increasing number of times. Thus, for a true major third.

C 261.6
E ....(261.6 × 5/4) 327
G♯ (A♭)......(261.6 × 5/4 × 5/4) 409
C above........(261.6 × 5/4 × 5/4 × 5/4) 511

Since all octaves should double the frequency, which would demand here an upper C of 523.2, the discrepancy between three true major thirds, which bring us only to 511, and a true octave, which demands 523.2, is obvious. Three true thirds just simply do not go evenly into an octave. What we call major thirds on the keyboard are obviously too sharp. The reason lies in the nature of numbers themselves, and it can be shown that this same thing is true of every other interval. To state it mathematically, the expansion of the octave ratio is incommensurable with the expansions of the ratios of all other intervals. This means that we can never hope to arrive at a true octave of a tone by stepping off any true interval except the octave interval itself. In other words, a twelve-tone division of the octave is necessarily imperfect because of the nature of the number series itself.

Equal Temperament Contrasted with Just Intonation and Pythagorean Intonation

This method of dividing the octave into twelve equal semitones distributes the errors among the various tonalities, so that no interval in any key sounds too· much out of tune, while at the same time preserving for us the possibility of free modulation on which the whole development of modern harmony has been built. In this connection, the following passage from Parry [9] is worth quoting:

An ideally tuned scale is as much of a dream as the philosopher's stone, and no one who clearly understands the meaning of art wants it. The scale as we now have it (equal temperament) is as perfect as our system requires. It is completely organised for an infinite variety of contrast, both in the matter of direct expression—by discord and concord—and for the purposes of formal design. The instincts of human creatures for thousands of years have, as it were,

---

[9] *Op. cit.,* page 60.

sifted it and tested it till they have got a thing which is most subtly adapted to the purposes of artistic expression. It has afforded Bach, Beethoven, Schubert, Wagner, and Brahms ample opportunities to produce works which in their respective lines are as wonderful as it is conceivable for any artistic works to be. A scale system may fairly be tested by what can be done with it. It will probably be a good many centuries before any new system is justified by such a mass of great artistic works as the one which the instincts and efforts of our ancestors have gradually evolved for our advantage.

Equal temperament enables us to play equally well, or perhaps we should say equally badly, in all keys. Because of the universality of the influence of keyboard instruments on all musical art for many centuries, the system has been imposed to an almost exclusive degree on all forms of music, so much so that the distinction between the greater and the lesser whole tone (major and minor whole tone) has again been lost (if in truth it ever was appreciated except in a philosophic way). The universal influence of temperament is further illustrated in the fact that musicians with fine ears will frequently declare certain just intervals to be out of tune. It is said that chamber music ensembles and *a cappella* choirs, who practice habitually without the hindrance of a piano or organ, are able to break this universal bondage of the tempered scale, and are occasionally heard to perform in just intonation, particularly on closing, static, chords. The resulting blending and absence of roughness is very striking, though sometimes insipid, to an ear accustomed to the imperfections of tempered harmony. As a matter of fact, however, there is considerable doubt as to whether the *"a cappella* tradition"* which such groups seek to recover was in just intonation, since much of this early music was probably not unaccompanied. Arnold Schering contends strongly that it was accompanied, supported by viols and lutes in equal temperament or by organs in a variety of meantone tuning which Barbour feels would have given little opportunity for the singers to practice just intonation. Furthermore, certain modern *a cappella* groups are habitually and purposely trained to sing certain in-

tervals more or less altered, and often neither in just intonation
nor in equal temperament, for aesthetic reasons or for the purpose of maintaining their pitch without flatting. Particularly
are the major thirds on tonic and dominant made sharper. This
may be done without artistic harm, because the interval of the
third (and also its inversion, the sixth), is infinitely variable.
Primitive scales, and even modern scales, indicate this interval
to be by no means fundamental. Furthermore, as Barbour has
pointed out, just intonation does not have the paramount importance that it would have if music were a static rather than
above everything a dynamic art. In the former case, the purity
of the single chord would be a prime desideratum. During the
movement of the music, however, the intervals frequently (and
in the case of string performers, *usually*, according to Greene)
incline to those of Pythagorean intonation. If a viola and violin
are tuned by perfect fifths to the same A, the low C-string of
the viola will make with the E of the violin an interval of two
octaves and a Pythagorean third. String technique and tradition generally seek the sound of these high thirds, except in
held chords, and sometimes even then. Similarly, many choral
directors feel that the most effective safeguard against flatting
is to raise the third and seventh degrees (except sometimes in
relatively final—static—chords), attempting to make them not
only sharper than true, but even sharper than the already too
sharp tempered thirds and sevenths, approaching the Pythagorean intonation used by string players. As has been mentioned, the third, sixth, and seventh degrees of tempered intonation lie closer to their positions in the old Pythagorean
intonation than to those of just intonation, and Pythagorean
intonation has shown a remarkable and recurring vitality
through the centuries, both in the theory of tuning schemes and
in the actual musical practices of the day, according to Barbour.

But, even if we grant that the ears of performer and listener
are "unspoiled" by either Pythagorean or tempered intonation,
and are quite capable of hearing the relatively small deviations

of their intervals from those of the harmonic series and the "true scale" derived therefrom, the musical performer and the musical listener will usually be intent on the broader musical outlines, and will therefore tend to correct what they hear (often an unconscious process), into what they desire to hear. This process plays a tremendous role in the reactions of many persons. Because of the constant movement of the music, the interested listener allows slightly incorrect intonations to pass unnoticed, as an interested reader fails to detect typographic errors. Furthermore, the human ear is an organ which, though accurate and sensitive beyond imagination, is still "human" in the sense of being subject to infinitely complex physiological and psychological factors instead of relatively predictable physical factors. For example, the fatiguing effect of one tone will distort the apparent pitch of a succeeding one, sometimes to extents considerably greater than the relatively small inaccuracies of equal temperament. And as we have seen on page 21, the perceived pitch may vary with the loudness of the tone. And as accurate as the ear is, it is yet "adjustable," and is considerably lenient toward whatever dissonance it has heard often enough to become familiar with. The vitality and longevity of certain non-harmonic primitive scales illustrate this. And if we have learned to tolerate and even enjoy the extreme dissonances which characterize the modern idioms, perhaps we are more able to tolerate the slightly imperfect intervals of equal temperament.

In addition to all of this, aesthetic and psychologic considerations often cause performers to vary intervals to greater degrees than the inaccuracies of either tempered intonation or Pythagorean intonation. Thus violinists, even though they may invoke the "true scale," actually often markedly increase major and augmented intervals and diminish minor and diminished intervals. They take decorating tones, appoggiaturas and embellishments very close to the essential tones. They make the leading tone even more sensitive by taking it higher than its true pitch, in order to anticipate more effectively, as it were, the resolution. And the effectiveness of the *true* seventh (seventh harmonic, lower than the tempered flatted seventh degree) as a leading tone to the third of the subdominant key, is doubtless due at least as much to the aesthetic satisfaction of hearing this active tone very near to its resolution as it is due to the result of its position in the harmonic series. As Professor Clapp of the University of Iowa has said in Stewart's *Introductory Acoustics:*

> While these alterations are thus away from, not toward, the natural scale (just intonation), they are aesthetically eminently justified, since in our contemporary music the contrast between major and minor, and the "tendency" of certain tones to progress to certain others . . . are of relatively great psychological importance. To distinguish this practice of emphasizing "tendency" from a true attempt to approximate the scale of nature, I suggest that performers should speak of an "artistic" or "harmonic" scale, rather than make an inaccurate use of the terms "pure" scale and "natural" scale.

If small variations from a mathematically exact tempo give life and zest to a performance, it is not hard to understand that slight variations from theoretically correct pitches add interest also, especially when there is melodic or aesthetic justification for them. As Barton has said, "We must remember that the right of science to dictate ceases where aesthetics begins." It is possible for an interval to be aesthetically dissonant, while mathematically consonant, and vice versa. And even in the preliminary tuning of an orchestra to the oboe A, the violinists, and even other players, frequently tune a bit sharp. If this is for the sake of gaining brilliance, it is aesthetically justified. It is questionable whether an orchestra is ever really tuned, in the physical sense of the word, even just before it starts the opening chord of the performance.

We see, therefore, that the perfection of "true" or just intonation in any scheme permitting modulation is a practically unattainable ideal. Instead, we see that the vast structure of classic, romantic, modern, and ultramodern music has been made possible by the adoption of equal temperament with its ratios standing somewhat closer to those of Pythagorean than to those of just intonation. We see performers altering intervals for various reasons on those instruments where variance is possible, and we see that the variations tend often closer to Pythagorean intonation than to just or even to tempered intonation. We conclude therefore that just intonation is not only well-nigh impossible of attainment, but in view of certain aesthetic factors often undesirable as well. Thus Pierce found that just intervals were reacted to as insipid, and the listeners preferred the more incisive thirds of equal temperament. All of these facts, plus that of the continual voluntary and involuntary variations of pitch, particularly those produced in the vibratos of all good voices, string players, and many players of other instruments, which carry the pitch over bands five- and tenfold as wide as the differences between just and tempered intonation, are not realized by the zealous purists of just intonation.[10] The almost hypnotic charm that the just ratios have had over many scientists and some musicians in the last half century stems largely from the researches of Helmholtz, and his development of the theory that dissonance is caused by the beating of partials. On percussive instruments such as the piano, where the intensity, especially the intensity of the overtones, drops rapidly after tone production, and where as a result of the percussiveness the tones usually succeed each other rapidly, the beats are so transient as to be unobjectionable. In the case of instruments such as the voice and the violin, where a variation of the pitch, intensity, and overtone relationship by the vibrato is almost invariably present, the beating is so complex, so "regularly irregular," as to be unobjectionable or even pleasant. And, as has been noted on page 24, even in the case of tones which can be steadily sustained, the presence of a number of sources *not* precisely in

---

[10] Choral conductors who seek to eliminate the normal vibrato for the sake of securing just intonation may sacrifice as well the greater beauty of well-produced and "warm" voice quality, which is always associated with a moderate amount of vibrato.

tune with each other, producing a "pitch fringe," may give rise
to a complex, multitudinous beating which has a charm of its
own.

From all, of this evidence, and judging not from theory but
from practice, which always antedates theory, the greatest effectiveness of the just ratios lies in their use in final, held, chords,
in those instruments where the tone can be fairly evenly sustained. With an octave of only twelve semitones just intonation
is impossible to maintain over the simplest modulation. And
while tempering the scale was once called "vulgar temperament" and has been called by Professor Horace Lamb "tam-
pering with the scale," it has nevertheless been the means of
advancing the art of music to an incalculable extent.

This is an appropriate place to mention the oft-renewed controversy as to the relative pitch of corresponding sharp and flat notes.
For example, is F♯ higher or lower than G♭? If we were to adopt
equal temperament without reservations, as on keyboard instruments
containing only twelve tones to the octave, the question would become
meaningless, since F♯ and G♭ are identical in both theory and practice. The fact that there ever is a controversy over the question reflects the fact that in the minds of most musicians, as well as in the
technique of the instruments in which small pitch variations are possible, some other tuning system still disputes the field with equal
temperament. And, as Pole[11] points out, the position of tones depends on what tuning system has been used in deriving them. Let
us start, for example, with eight tones forming a major scale in just
intonation, and derive seven sharped tones by taking true major
thirds up from these original tones or from already-derived sharps.
Similarly, let us derive seven flatted tones by taking true major thirds
down from the original tones or from already-derived flats. We then
find that the flats are *always* higher than the corresponding sharps
(that is, G♭ is higher than F♯, E♭ higher than D♯, and so on).
This is shown in the first column of the table below, which gives
the ratios to the base 1 of all of these tones. The only transposition
in the alphabetic order is where B♯ and E♯ come, as would be
expected, above C♭ and F♭, respectively. Every other sharped tone is
below its enharmonic flatted neighbor.

---

[11] Pole, William, *The Philosophy of Music*, Chapter XII. New York: Harcourt.
Brace & Company, Inc., 1924.

But this is in direct opposition to all the tradition and technique of string instruments, which as we have seen tends toward the other tuning system, Pythagorean intonation. Many other instruments also, including the human voice, when actually used in the making of music tend often toward Pythagorean intonation. And in Pythagorean theory, in which the sharps and flats are calculated by taking successive true fifths or true fourths up or down from C, using always as the frequency of the keynote the one last computed for that note, it will be found, as Redfield points out, that *no* sharp note is *ever* as flat as its corresponding flat note (that is, F♯ is always higher than G♭, D♯ always higher than E♭, and so on). This is shown in the second column below, where the alphabetic order is entirely changed, and where B♯ and E♯ are even above C♮ and F♮, respectively:

DERIVED FROM JUST INTONATION		PYTHAGOREAN	
		B♯ — 2.027	
C — 2.000	....	C — 2.000	
B♯ — 1.953		B — 1.898	
C♭ — 1.920		C♭ — 1.873	
B — 1.875		A♯ — 1.802	
B♭ — 1.800		B♭ — 1.778	
A♯ — 1.758		A — 1.688	
A — 1.667		G♯ — 1.602	
A♭ — 1.600		A♭ — 1.580	
G♯ — 1.563		G — 1.500	
G — 1.500		F♯ — 1.424	
G♭ — 1.440		G♭ — 1.405	
F♯ — 1.406		E♯ — 1.352	
F — 1.333		F — 1.333	
E♯ — 1.302		E — 1.266	
F♭ — 1.280		F♭ — 1.249	
E — 1.250		D♯ — 1.201	
E♭ — 1.200		E♭ — 1.185	
D♯ — 1.172		D — 1.125	
D — 1.125		C♯ — 1.068	
D♭ — 1.067		D♭ — 1.053	
C♯ — 1.042		B♯ — 1.014	
C — 1.000	....	C — 1.000	
B♯ — .977			

Thus we see that this controversy is yet another indication of the fact that "true intonation" does not hold undisputed claim in the fields of either musical theory or practice. Neither, for that matter, does equal temperament or Pythagorean intonation. Before we answer the question dogmatically in one way or the other, we must agree on our instrument and our tuning theory, for there is more than one way to derive the sharps or flats, depending on the criteria set up, the intervals chosen, the method of calculation, and so on. The ultimate justification of any method in a specific case lies in how closely it recognizes the actual significance of the harmonic and melodic con-- text in which the tone is used. And even this significance is not constant, as we have seen, but subject to variable aesthetic factors (as in the case of the very high leading tone), and to a hearer's habits of listening.

Tuning Procedure in Equal Temperament

Pianos and organs are tuned in tempered intonation by tun- ing the tones of one of the middle octaves first. This is called "laying the temperament," and can be fairly accurately done by tuning a series of intervals (such as ascending fifths and de- scending fourths, for example: C-G-D-A-E-B-F#-C#- etc.), slightly sharp or flat, so that each interval beats at a certain rate, according to tables which have been calculated. The fifths are all slightly contracted and the fourths slightly expanded. However, the fourths and fifths beat quite slowly in the mid- range of pitch, and, furthermore, their beats in the case of the piano soon become inaudible because of the unsustained tone of the piano as compared with the organ. Therefore, as the work proceeds, the fourths and fifths are checked by the thirds and sixths, which have faster beat rates and therefore furnish a rather accurate check. For example, when the preceding series reaches A by an ascending fifth, a descending fourth, and an- other ascending fifth, the major sixth, C to A, can be used as a check test on the accuracy of the work. It should beat at a certain rate which is known to the tuner. When the A is cor- rect, and the E is secured from it by a descending fourth, this E may be checked by the beat rate of the major third, C to E. Various tuning schemes are used by different tuners, but all em- ploy these principles. And in the tuning by fourths and fifths of a whole octave, all the major and minor thirds and sixths be--

come available as test intervals, in a way well illustrated by White.

Thus the "tuning" of a tempered instrument is in reality a process of controlled *mistuning*. Since it is at least as difficult to secure with exactitude a certain definite degree of mistuning as it is to tune an interval accurately true (free of beats), it is seldom that instruments are correctly tempered. As a matter of fact, few tuners, if any, attain approximate theoretical perfection of tempering, which can only be achieved by adjusting the various beat rates to close limits, preferably with the aid of some tuning device other than the rough criteria of tuning "slightly" sharp, or putting "about one wave" (estimated) in an interval. Accurate tuning requires both a good ear and a fine muscular control of the tuning hammer. On the other hand, as has been described, if we had sufficient tones in each octave to make just intonation possible in any key, although it would perhaps be easier to tune them (by intervals free of beats), the instrument would not long keep correctly these many slight pitch differences, and would be immeasurably harder to play.

The laying of the temperament in the piano is done at first on only one of the three wires present for each unison, the remaining wires being damped by wedges or felt strips. After the temperament is set these unisons are trued up—freed of beats. Then the remaining tones of the instrument are secured by tuning octaves, also free of beats, up and down from the tempered tones in this middle octave. The fundamentality of the octave, being as it is the first interval in the harmonic series, makes it necessary for all octaves in the mid-range to be quite well in tune. The ear, through its capacity to make illusory corrections in what it hears, can learn to tolerate tempered thirds and sixths, but demands its octaves pure, at least in the mid-range. As has already been mentioned, however, tuners sometimes "stretch" the octaves in the extreme upper and lower ranges, because of the lack of correspondence between frequency and pitch in these regions. Thus the uppermost tones of a piano are sharped, and the lowermost flatted, because of the limitations of the human ear.

In the case of the organ, when one stop has been placed in tempered intonation, others may be tuned to it by tuning unisons or octaves free of beats. In the "mixture stops," which for the sake of gaining brilliance sound one or more members of the harmonic series in addition to the fundamental for each key depressed, the temperament is set as usual for the fundamentals, but the pipes giving harmonic series intervals associated with each fundamental are tuned true (no beats with the fundamentals). And because of the variations of tempered from just intonation, which are marked in the case of the major third, these stops are more effective when they do not contain thirds, tenths, or seventeenths, because of their frequent clashing when the corresponding tempered tones are played, as will occur in many chords.

There are two types of simple tests which the tuner uses, or which may be applied to ascertain whether or not a tuner has done a good job, aside from the obvious fact that on the piano the two or three strings of each unison should give no beats with each other, and on any instrument, the octaves should not beat except perhaps at the upper and lower extremes, as already noted.

The first type of test depends on the fact that the rate of beats in any perfect fifth (seven semitones) up from a given tone should be the same as the rate in the perfect fourth (five semitones) down from that tone, provided the outer tones make a true octave (no beats). Thus if any octave is played, and found true, and it be then divided into a fourth and a fifth so that the fifth is the higher interval, the beating rates in these two should be alike. This will not work if the fourth is the higher interval. A similar result is obtained if the test intervals are the minor third and the major sixth within an octave, as for example C to E♭, and E♭ to C above. These tests depend on the beating of upper partials, and therefore should be of particular value in the low bass regions of the piano, where the fundamental is quite weak. Only the second test would actually be of value here, however, because the beat rates of fifths and fourths are too slow in the bass region to be readily timed.

The other type of test is based on the fact that, since an interval is defined as a *ratio* of frequencies, and a beat rate is a *difference* of frequencies, the same mistuned interval will produce different beat rates according to its position in the frequency range. The higher its position, the higher the beat rate. Thus, as discussed by Harker, if an octave is divided into three major thirds, and these are played in ascending order, they should produce a regularly increasing beat rate. Thus the three major thirds between A-220 and A-440 beat as follows when correctly tuned:

A to C♯	8.73 beats per second
C♯ to E♯..............	11.00 " " "
F (E♯) to A	13.86 " " "

These are too rapid to count accurately, but the general impression of their increasing rapidity is sufficiently accurate for a rough check on the tuning. By the same principle, any interval whatsoever should increase its beat rate in a regular fashion as it is produced successively up the chromatic scale. Other check tests are described by White.

The following table, from Redfield, gives the frequencies of a tempered scale compared with those of a just scale, both based on A-440. In theory, each tempered pitch is 1.059463+ times the frequency of the tempered semitone below it:

	JUST	TEMPERED	ERROR
A	— 440	440	0
G♯	— 412.5	415.30	+ 2.80
F♯	— 366.66	369.99	+ 3.33
E	— 330	329.63	— 0.37
D	— 293.33	293.66	+ 0.33
C♯	— 275	277.18	+ 2.18
B	— 247.5	246.94	— 0.56
A	— 220	220	0

Characteristics of Different Tonalities

It is often maintained that the various tonalities have quite definite and specific characteristics, so that certain kinds of compositions are more effective in certain keys, and so that a listener can recognize the key of a piece by its particular "color" or "mood." If the instrument is correctly tempered there are no cues available through differences in intervals, as was the case with the modes. It is of course possible that the various keys *are* actually different because of inaccurate tempering, which would possibly bias some tonalities in the direction of just intonation, and make others more discordant. Thus the various keys would acquire a certain individuality, tending to resemble modes. This has been pointed out by Harker, who says, "The procedure for tuning having become more or less standardized, some measure of consistency in these pseudo-modal variants of the scale is to be anticipated," particularly since "musicians appear to agree that the modification in musical effect consequent upon transposition is much less marked on the organ or harmonium which, in virtue of their sustaining power, can be made to conform much more closely to equal temperament."

If the instrument is fairly correctly tempered, however, some other explanation must be sought. Some have found such an explanation in the different leverages of the white and the black digitals on the piano, which of course have different distributions in the various keys. It is thought to be difficult to produce identically the same effect as regards time of contact, force, displacement, and so on, when the levers are of different length. This explanation is at least partially discredited, however, by the fact that in modern pianos the leverages and the touchweights are equalized for the black and white digitals. Perhaps a more likely explanation is the fact that black digitals are struck with straighter fingers than white ones, which may modify the tone intensity somewhat, or at least the performer's reaction to the tone. Thus, for example, the digitals of all but one of the sharp-key tonics (counting through six sharps) are white keys, which would usually be struck with more curved fingers, while those of all but one of the flat-key tonics are black keys, which being shorter would be struck with straighter fingers. The more curved the finger is, the shorter is its lever distance from the joint, and the greater the force that can be transmitted to the hammer mechanism, which gives a possible explanation for the common reputation of sharp keys as more brilliant, flat keys as softer, mellower, and more harmonious.[12] This explanation gains plausibility if it is true, as one author has said, that these differences are lessened or destroyed when the music is performed on an instrument not depending on strength of key stroke, such as the organ, where the only cue is in sufficient memory of absolute pitch to recall to mind the tonality and its previously associated "color." Another writer, however, has said that piano pieces retain their emotional qualities when played on a player piano, on which the mechanical difference between playing white and black digitals disappears. Here too, though, the *previously* associated characteristics can be influencing our reaction.

We see from this, however, the intimate connection which the *physiology* of the technique has on the reaction to certain instruments. Thus, even the degree of facility with which certain keys may be played, on the piano, violin, or other instruments, may color their effect on the player, and even their effect on the hearer.

In the case of the violin, certain keys acquire distinguishing characteristics through the number of open strings used, since open strings have a different quality from stopped ones, and cannot easily be given a vibrato. For example, the keys of G major or D major on a violin frequently use open strings, as compared with the keys of G♭, A♭, D♭, or E♭.

---

[12] In this connection it is interesting to note that if two pianos are tuned absolutely to the same pitch, musicians who play them successively sometimes declare the softer-toned one to be flatter than the other.

Somewhat similar arguments might apply to wind instruments.

Of course, musical associations play an enormous part in all of this. It is questionable whether the whole explanation of the characteristics of the various tonalities, or at least the most important explanation, does not lie in the *psychological* field. Since the symbol ♯ means to raise something, and ♭ to lower something, these symbols, especially when several occur together in a signature, cannot help but have respectively a brightening, elevating effect, or a darkening, lowering, or even depressing effect on the emotional tone of the person who sees them. It may be below the level of consciousness, but it is nevertheless real. And many times (but by no means always), the composer will select his key accordingly. Some enthusiasts even insist, and probably correctly, that a piece played in F♯ major is quite differently heard and felt than when played on the same instrument in G♭ major, using of course the same digitals. Such differences are primarily mental. The performer, thinking the piece in one key or the other, is affected, frequently unconsciously, by previously experienced pieces in that same key, and this mental set predisposes his reaction to the new piece, or even modifies his performance of it, as well as the character of his bodily movements while playing. A listener, perhaps aware of the signature of the piece, or perhaps only imagining it to be in one signature or another, could be affected by his own resulting mental set even if the performance were unaffected by the mental set of the player.

Still another explanation of key characteristics may be found in a recognition by the listener, frequently quite faulty and unconscious, of the absolute pitch of the various tonalities, together with the association of previously experienced pieces in these tonalities. And if a piece has been experienced often enough to "set" it at a certain absolute pitch level, it will obviously be brightened if raised a bit, and probably changed markedly in character if raised still more.

5

Hearing

WHEN we feel someone's pulse we feel a succession of pulsations in his wrist which are produced by variations in the pressure of the blood as it responds to the periodic pumping beats of the heart. This furnishes a sort of "slow-motion picture" of the kind of periodic atmospheric pressure variations to which our ear responds when in contact with musically agitated air, except that in the latter case the pulsations are carried through the air, are incredibly faster and more complex, and yet at the same time incredibly feeble in actual power. Of the five primary senses with which man is endowed, four of them: *taste, smell, vision,* and *touch,* are common to all vertebrate animals, and even detectable in much humbler forms of life; but *hearing,* according to Beatty,[1] is a comparative newcomer among the senses. "It occurs but rarely among the multitudinous tribes of the insect world, and exists only in the most rudimentary form among fishes."

Mechanism of Hearing

The mechanism of hearing consists of three parts: the outer, the middle, and the inner ear. The outer ear includes the external parts and the ear canal, which extends about an inch and a quarter into the head, terminating at the eardrum, or *tympanic membrane,* a thin membrane about a three-hundredth of an

---

[1] Beatty, R. T., *Hearing in Man and Animals,* Preface, page v. London: George Bell & Sons, Ltd., 1932.

inch thick. The middle ear contains a chain of three small bones, called the *hammer, anvil,* and *stirrup,* and collectively called the *ossicles.* When sound waves strike the drum, setting it into sympathetic resonant vibration, these three bones pass the vibrations from the drum to the *oval window* into the inner ear, at the same time forming a lever system which while decreasing the size of the movement increases the pressure variations from thirty to sixty times. The inner ear, called the *cochlea* from its resemblance to a small snail shell, is a spiral cavity about a quarter of an inch in diameter, located in one of the hardest regions of the skull bone. It is filled with a liquid, and contains the *basilar membrane, tectorial membrane, organ of Corti,* and other extremely small and delicate membranes and fibers, the action of which is not fully understood, but the result of which is the stimulation of a great number of tiny hair cells. These are stimulated by about 24,000 little fibers, sensitive to various parts of the pitch range. Thus, hearing may be considered a highly specialized form of the sense of touch. In this connection it is interesting to note that sounds may be discriminated in a rough way through a development of the sense of touch in the finger tips. Professor Gault's work with the *teletactor* for the deaf is an illustration. Since hearing is a specialized form of the sense of touch, the ear may become fatigued in the same way that any neural end organ may be fatigued. Thus, airplane passengers may find themselves deafened for a time after completing their journey, unless the cabin has been well insulated, a problem which is claiming the attention of the transport lines.

This deafening, however, is quite different from permanent deafness. It is entirely different, also, from the fullness or ringing of the ear produced by differences in altitude. This latter, which can be noticed when riding in an elevator, or even when riding over hilly country in an automobile, is caused by a difference of air pressure on each side of the eardrum. Normally the pressure in the middle ear balances the pressure on the outside of the drum, but in a fairly rapid change of altitude there is not sufficient time for an adjustment. This adjustment usually occurs when one swallows or yawns, which opens the Eustachian tube (from the middle ear to the throat) and permits a neutralization of pressures.

Pitch Limits and Sensitivity

Since the sense of hearing is a psycho-physiological response, it is natural to suppose that it is only effective between certain definite limits. Thus, in the matter of pitch, our ears are only sensitive to vibrations lying within a certain range of frequency. This range is somewhat variable among individuals, and even for the same individual from time to time, but its average for normal persons with no hearing loss may be taken roughly as being from 20 to 20,000 vibrations per second. This is a range of about 10 octaves, roughly from about E♭ below the lowest C on the piano to the third E♭ above the highest C on the piano. The range of the piano, 7¼ octaves, is from A-27½ to C-4186. This is about the extent of the useful range for fundamental pitches in music, although it is exceeded by some pipe organs. Of course, a fundamental at 4186 may have in its harmonic series three overtones lying within the audible range, since its third overtone (fourth partial) has a frequency of 16,744, which is still below 20,000. In most cases these very high overtones add little in the way of quality differentiation, lying as they do so near, and, for some persons, even beyond the upper limit of hearing. However, the overtones lying in the frequency range from 4,000 to at least 10,000 are of great importance in enabling us to recognize and to identify the quality of certain instruments.

Below the lower frequency limit of hearing, we feel the individual vibrations. If a series of puffs or clicks be produced very slowly we even have time to note periods of silence between them. But as they are repeated beyond some certain degree of rapidity, as Peirce observed, each hearer loses the intervals of silence and the sound appears continuous. The frequency of repetition necessary for the production of a continued sound from single impulses is around 20 per second, or in exceptional cases perhaps as low as 16 per second. (Pipe organs equipped with a "32-foot stop" can produce a tone of about 16 vibrations per second, corresponding to an octave below the lowest C on the piano.) In this connection it is interesting to note that somewhere around this same frequency separate visual impressions coalesce to form a satisfactory continuous impression. Moving pictures create their illusion of continuous motion when about 16 frames are presented to the eye each second, although because of the objectionable flickering, modern motion-picture projectors present 24 frames to the eye each second.

In the case of the ear, however, we often do not feel that the individual puffs coalesce into a satisfactory tone until there are 40 or more per second. In the case of the lowest tones of the organ, as Bragg says, it is a question whether we *hear* them, or whether we only *feel* the shaking of the pews. Perhaps, in fact, we are deceived by hearing the overtones when we think we are hearing a very low fundamental.

With regard to the upper limit of audibility, we again find considerable variation. This limit tends to be higher in children, decreasing slowly with advancing age. It is sometimes sharply defined, the interval of a single tone being sufficient to produce the change from evident sound to silence. Old persons can often not hear the high squeak of a bat, nor the sounds of certain insects. Certain animals can hear higher sounds than human ears can. Possibly insects may communicate with each other by sounds entirely beyond our range of hearing.

Subsonic or *infrasonic* vibrations of the air (those having frequencies below approximately 20 per second), and *supersonics* or *ultrasonics* (above approximately 20,000 per second), are not heard as sound by human ears. Thus, they have little importance for us in this text, although certain lower forms of life are greatly affected by them, even sometimes, in the case of supersonics, to the point of paralysis or death. Supersonics are used by ships at sea for echo sounding, submarine detection, and so on.

The ear is very sensitive to small changes in the pitch of successive tones, except toward the upper and lower limits of hearing. With pure tones, a variation of one fortieth of a tone may often be detected in the mid-range by a musical ear.[2] As the tones become more complex, within limits, still finer discriminations are possible, as the presence of the overtones aids the judgment. If pure tones at 262 and 263 are being listened to, the ear has only this one region in which to judge. If overtones are present, the ear's judgment is fortified by many more pairs of tones. The tenth partials, for example, give 2620 and 2630, and in this region the ear's pitch discrimination is much keener than in the range of Middle C. Not only is *discrimination* fine in the mid-part of the range, but many musicians develop excellent "absolute pitch" memory for tones in this mid-range. Toward the extremes of pitch, discrimination and memory become rapidly more difficult, even in distinguishing such wide differences as that between a major third and a major sixth. Even the trained ear of a piano tuner is often inaccurate in the uppermost and the lowest octaves of that instrument, which are still well within the pitch limits of hearing, and tuners and players disagree on the amount of "octave stretching" proper in these regions.

Loudness Limits and Sensitivity

In the case of loudness, we again find definite limits to the sense of hearing. Our ears are sensitive only to vibrations lying within a certain range of intensities. Those that are too soft are not audible, whereas those that are too loud cause a tickling

---

[2] Of course, if the tones are sounded simultaneously, the beats enable us to perceive far finer differences.

or prickling sensation, or even pain, and thus are more *felt* than heard. However, between these extremes, which are called respectively the *threshold of audibility,* and the *threshold of feeling or pain,* there is a tremendous range of variation.

The loudest sound that a full orchestra can produce (which is still far below the pain threshold), appears, according to Sivian, Dunn, and White, to be at least ten million times more intense in physical energy than the softest violin tone used with an audience (by no means the softest tone one can hear). This is a range of response far beyond that of any comparable mechanical instrument, and over a considerable part of this intensity range, as Wegel has said, the ear differentiates with certainty between complex sounds so nearly alike that no existing physical apparatus can separate them. But even so, the ear is by no means as sensitive to changes in intensity as it is to changes in frequency.

The following table, given by Jeans,[3] listing the results of recent experiments at the Bell Laboratories, gives some idea of the differences in the energy given out in the sound of various instruments:

| | *Energy* |
Origin of Sound	*(Watts)*
Orchestra of seventy-five performers, at loudest......	70
Bass drum at loudest	25
Pipe organ at loudest	13
Trombone at loudest	6
Piano at loudest	0.4
Trumpet at loudest	0.3
Orchestra of seventy-five performers, at average.....	0.09
Piccolo at loudest	0.08
Clarinet at loudest	0.05
Human voice { Bass singing *ff*	0.03
Alto singing *pp*	0.001
Average speaking voice	0.000024
Violin at softest used in a concert	0.0000038

    [3] Jeans, Sir James, *Science and Music,* page 229. New York: The Macmillan Company, 1937.

It is interesting to note in passing how very small is the energy of even a loud sound. According to Jeans:[4]

A fair-sized pipe organ may need a 10,000 watt motor to blow it; of this energy only 13 watts reappears as sound, while the other 9987 watts is wasted in friction and heat. A strong man soon tires of playing a piano at its loudest, his energy output being perhaps 200 watts; of this only 0.4 watts goes into sound. A thousand basses singing *fortissimo* only give out enough energy to keep one 30 watt lamp alight; if they turned dynamos with equal vigour, 6000 such lamps could be kept alight.

The physical terms *intensity* or *energy* must again not be confused with the psychological experience of *loudness*. As we have already seen, with regard to the sense of pitch, a musical pitch interval of, say, a semitone, is determined not by the difference between its frequencies but by their *ratio*. Thus the semitone between 150 and 160 sounds to be of the same size as that between 300 and 320, since, although the frequency difference has been doubled, the ratio in each case is 15:16. All the sense organs seem to follow within limits this psychological rule, called the *Weber-Fechner law,* which states that equal increments of sensation are associated with *equal ratios,* or *equal increments of the logarithm of the stimulus.* In the case of loudness, the sensation of *loudness-difference* depends not on the difference in intensities involved, but on their *ratio*. The important thing, for example, is not the total amount of sound energy crossing the footlights but the ratio of this energy to the energy of the audience noise and other noise over which it must be heard.

Thus our ears respond approximately logarithmically to the physical energy in a sound wave, so that, fortunately, it is impossible for us to hear any sound as ten million times *louder* than another. Because of this, a new unit of loudness, measured on a logarithmic scale, has become useful in recent years. If one sound has ten times the physical energy of another one,

4 *Ibid.*

the logarithm of the intensity ratio is 1, and the first sound is said to be 1 *bel* above the second. The name is coined from the name of Alexander Graham Bell, the inventor of the telephone. If the intensity of the first is 100 times that of the, second, it is said to be 2 bels above the second, since the logarithm of the intensity ratio is 2. A handier unit is usually used, called the *decibel* (one tenth of a bel), abbreviated *db*. The sound of the first tone would then be 10 db above the second when the intensity ratio is 10, 20 db when the ratio is 100, 30 db when it is 1000, and so on. The number of db is found by taking 10 times the common logarithm of the ratio of the intensities involved. It so happens that the decibel is approximately equal to the smallest change in loudness that is perceptible to the average listener.

Since the decibel deals with ratios, small differences in db naturally correspond to great differences in the energies involved, as shown in the following table:

Intensity level in db	*Intensity ratios above threshold of audibility*
0 (threshold)	
10	10
20	100
30	1,000
40	10,000
50	100,000
60	1,000,000
70	10,000,000
80	100,000,000
90	1,000,000,000
100	10,000,000,000

Thus we see that a sound at 100 db intensity (such as would be heard from an average speaker when the ear is placed at half an inch from his mouth), has ten billion times the energy that would be needed for sound perception at the threshold of audibility.

A quiet city garden may be as quiet as 20 db above the

threshold of audibility; an average office may be 45 to 50 db above this threshold. Ordinary conversation at three feet is at 65 db, while a noisy restaurant may reach 70 db, and very loud radio music in the home 80. The roar of a lion eighteen feet distant has been measured at 87 db. A subway may reach 95, and a boiler factory 95 to 100. These various sounds, it is true, are not strictly comparable in loudness unless they are of the same pitch, because loudness varies with pitch. Also, a faint sound may be heard through a louder one in the same pitch region if the difference in intensities is not more than 12 db; and if the pitches are different, the difference in intensities may be still greater before the fainter one is completely masked. However, it is easy to understand why ordinary conversation at three feet, with a level at 65 db, is impossible in a subway or a boiler factory, and is difficult, to say the least, when it must compete with loud radio music. A very loud auto horn at twenty feet may be as high as 100 db. An airplane motor at 1600 revolutions per minute, heard at a distance of eighteen feet from the propeller, or the noise of hammer blows on a steel plate, heard at a distance of two feet, rise to around 115 db, getting close to the upper limit, the threshold of pain. Naturally, for a sound to be heard, it should rise more or less above the noise level at the listener's position, unless it has some distinctive character. The total range of loudness from the least audible sound in an absolutely quiet place to the most intense sound that can be experienced without injury to the hearing mechanism is about 120 db. The range from the softest violin tone used with an audience to the loudest sound from the full orchestra, representing an energy ratio of 10,000,000 to 1, is a range of 70 db—a range which might occur, say, from 25 db above the threshold to 95 above. It is thus evident that concert music as produced today does not utilize much more than half of the whole intensity range of which the ear is capable in the treble. As far as our ears are concerned, concert music could usually be made softer without dropping below the noise of the

hall, and could be considerably louder without reaching the
threshold of feeling. This has in fact been tried, through electrical manipulation, with remarkable effects. Pitch and quality
distortions are likely to occur at high intensities, however.

Both the frequency and the intensity limits of hearing may be
conveniently shown on one diagram, for which we are indebted
to the researches of Wegel, Fletcher, Munson, Mills, and others
in the Bell Telephone Laboratories. One of the latest forms
of this diagram is that shown in Figure 42, taken from a com-

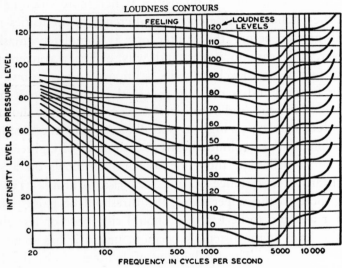

Fig. 42—Equal loudness contours between the threshold of audibility and the
threshold of feeling.
(Courtesy Bell Telephone Laboratories, New York)

mittee report on "American Tentative Standards for Noise Measurements," in the *Journal of the Acoustical Society* for October,
1936. If some arbitrary low standard of intensity be chosen, and
then if the intensities of sounds above this standard which are
necessary to make them just audible be plotted at various frequencies, the curve marked "O" will be secured. This is the
threshold of audibility curve. It is obvious that the sensitivity
of the ear varies with the frequency. According to this diagram,
it is at its most sensitive point somewhere between 3000 and

4000. For many of the purposes to which this diagram is put, the intensity level of a just-audible tone at a frequency of 1000 is taken as the standard zero level, as has been done in Figure 42. On this basis, a just-audible tone at 32 cycles will lie more than 60 db higher, and therefore will require more than a million times the energy of a just-audible tone at 1000. This is borne out by the fact that an organ pipe producing a vibration of 32 cycles, which pipe is about 16 feet long and requires a heavy supply of air, still sounds no louder, if as loud, as a little pipe six inches long which can be blown by a child.

These tremendous differences in sensitivity as the frequency is varied are further illustrated by the following table, which Jeans [5] has prepared from data secured by Fletcher and Munson:

Tone	Frequency	Pressure variation at which note is first heard (in bars) [6]	Energy required (in terms of minimum)
CCCC (32-foot pipe of organ, close to lower limit of hearing)	16	100	1,500,000,000,000
AAA (bottom note of piano)	27	1	150,000,000
CCC (lowest C on piano)	32	0.4	25,000,000
CC	64	0.025	100,000
C	128	0.005	3,800
c^1 (Middle C)	256	0.001	150
c^2	512	0.0004	25
c^3	1,024	0.0002	6
c^4	2,048	0.0001	1½
f^4 (maximum sensitivity)	2,734	0.00008	1
c^5 (top of piano)	4,096	0.0001	1½
c^6	8,192	0.0005	38
c^7	16,384	0.01	15,000
Close to upper limit of hearing	20,000	500	38,000,000,000,000

[5] Op. cit., page 220.

[6] The bar is a standard unit of pressure, equal to one megadyne per square centimeter.

Referring again to Figure 42, if we imagine a tone to be kept at a constant intensity level of 50 db while its frequency is raised from 20 to 5000, we can see that its sensation level would be zero until it reached a frequency of 55, when it would become just audible. Its sensation level would continue to rise until at a frequency of 1000 it was 50 db above the threshold of audibility. At 5000 it would be still higher. The sensitivity of the ear is assuredly dependent on the frequency being listened for.

A further complication enters here. It is found that raising two tones a certain sensation level above the threshold does not leave them equally *loud*. Loudness level must be determined by comparing a tone with a standard reference tone of known intensity, and varying the tone until it sounds equally loud to the reference tone. When this is done, a series of equal loudness curves may be drawn, as shown in Figure 42, known as *contours of equal loudness level*, such that every point on any one curve has a loudness level equal to the number marked on the curve. It is seen that at the particular frequency of 1000, the loudness levels correspond with the intensity levels, but this is not true at other frequencies. For example, a tone at a frequency of 100 needs to be lifted only 40 db in sensation level above the threshold to reach a loudness level of 70, whereas at a frequency of 1000 it would have to be raised 70 db to reach a loudness level of 70.

The shape of the loudness contours gives us the explanation for the effect of the overtone structure of a tone on its loudness. Suppose we have two complex tones, each with a fundamental of 100 and with equal total intensities. Let the first have its energy divided equally between the fundamental and the second partial, 200, and let the second tone have its energy divided equally between its fundamental and its tenth partial, 1000. Because of the shape of the loudness contours, the fundamentals and even the second partial will make only a small contribution to the total *loudness,* whereas the tenth partial will have a large effect, causing the second tone to sound considerably louder than the first, even though no greater energy is involved. This is an extreme case, of course, but it illustrates the fact that the loudness of a tone can be increased or decreased by modifying the overtone structure even if the fundamental frequency and total intensity are unchanged. This is yet another illustration of the fact that loudness is a psychological, sensational, attribute of tones, not dependent in any simple way on the physical amplitude of the vibration.

A study of the shape of the threshold of audibility curve will indicate that an auditorium should be treated with materials which are somewhat more absorbent at high frequencies than at low; otherwise, as a reverberating sound dies away, the low frequencies drop sooner below the threshold of audibility, while the highs are still heard. All frequencies should drop evenly in *loudness* to the point of inaudibility. (See the article by MacNair, listed in the bibliography.) But of course, if too much absorption occurs at the high frequencies, a loss of brilliance will result, and also a distortion of tonal balance, since tone qualities with many overtones are modified to a greater extent than the purer qualities. Instruments whose quality depends on high overtones will of course suffer under such conditions. (See the footnote on page 227.)

The topmost curve in Figure 42, marked "120," may be taken as the threshold of feeling or pain. It is at times possible to hear above this, but seldom without discomfort. If the threshold of feeling and the threshold of audibility could be plotted for still lower and still higher frequencies than has been done in Figure 42 (something which it is difficult to do with certainty), it is probable that they would meet each other at points somewhere in the neighborhood of 20 and 20,000 cycles, thereby enclosing an "auditory sensation area" within which must lie every sound which we can hear. These curves, however, are idealized average curves. Individual ears, even those which have no deafness at any point, may vary these thresholds quite appreciably above or below the indicated curves. The individual audiogram is more likely to be zigzag instead of curvilinear.

The sensitivity of the ear at the lower limit, the threshold of audibility, is remarkable.   In the most sensitive frequency range, with average listeners whose threshold has not been raised by partial deafness, if the atmospheric pressure be periodically changed by about *one third of a billionth* of its total value, such a change will be sensed by the ear as sound.   A tone of this strength gives rise to a movement of the air particles back and forth by less than a billionth of an inch, and even in spite of there being a thousand or more vibrations a second the maximum speed attained by the air particles at the midpoints of their swings is less than the rate of a quarter of an inch a day.   (See the textbook by Colby [7] for an interesting presentation of this material.)   For an average sound the pressure variations are about one millionth of normal atmospheric pressure.   Tones produced by periodic variations of atmospheric pressure of as much as a thousandth are extremely loud, and those caused by a pressure variation as great as one per cent (one hundredth) are so intense as to injure the hearing mechanism.   The actual power output in a normal voice is approximately one five-millionth of that taken by a 40-watt electric bulb.   According to Beatty,[8] the smallest intensity perceptible to the ear has a power of the same magnitude as the power which is received as light through transparent air from a candle eight miles away. The recently adopted standard reference intensity for acoustic measurements is represented by that fraction of a watt per square centimeter which is indicated by the numeral 1 with sixteen ciphers after it, and this is only slightly under the intensity which marks the threshold of audibility for the *average* ear in its most sensitive frequency range, and undoubtedly is actually audible to keen ears.

From all of this we see that there are definite limits to the sense of hearing.   Tones which are too soft, too loud, too low, or too high, will not be heard.   Even so, there are a great

[7] Colby, M. Y., *Sound Waves and Acoustics.* Henry Holt & Company, Inc., 1938.

[8] Beatty, R. T., *Hearing in Man and Animals,* page 69. London: George Bell & Sons, Ltd., 1932.

number of distinguishable tones left within these limits. Fletcher reports that the total number of simple tones distinguishable from each other either by loudness or pitch differences or both is over half a million. How many more distinguishable complex tones there are, containing anywhere from two to perhaps forty partials, is left to the imagination.

Duration Limits and Sensitivity

Tones which are sustained for a very long time tend to be heard incorrectly through fatigue of the hearing mechanism. Such fatigue may perhaps even deafen a person temporarily for certain pitches.

Tones which are too short are not heard, or at least are not heard sufficiently well to give the sensation of pitch. The length of time necessary to perceive pitch has in the past been variously estimated from a tenth of a second down to a thousandth of a second, depending partly on the pitch used. Recent experimental work seems to confirm the shorter times, indicating that in some cases the pitch of tones of extremely short duration may still be rather accurately placed. Professor Gray, of the University of Louisiana, has devised equipment to interrupt a telephone circuit in such a manner as to permit a very small section of a tone to be heard in the telephone receiver. His subjects have been able to judge the pitch of tone sections which were shorter than a single vibration of the fundamental frequency, doubtless by the aid of the overtone spacing.

Recently, Lifshitz has discovered that the apparent duration of a sound varies with its loudness.

Binaural Sense

Another faculty that our ears perform with fair ease is that of telling us from what direction a sound comes. This is possible because we have *two* ears—*binaural hearing*. The nearer ear may hear the sound a trifle louder than the other (as in the case of higher frequencies, which are not diffracted around the

head as easily as lower frequencies). A more likely explanation with regard to the lower frequencies (up to perhaps 1000
or 1200 cycles), is that the nearer ear hears the sound a trifle
sooner and therefore somewhat "out of phase" with the other.
According to Beatty,[9] "if sound arrives simultaneously at the
two ears, we ascribe it to a source either directly in front or
directly behind" (and we sometimes have difficulty in deciding
whether it is from front or back, unless aided by reflections
from walls). However, "if it reaches one ear later than the
other by as little as a ten-thousandth of a second, the source
is judged to have moved appreciably to one side or the other."
In some cases, differences of the order of a hundred-thousandth
of a second may be perceptible. The degrees of these differences help to determine the sound as coming from a certain
direction. Thus, the person who is deaf in one ear is handi-
capped not only in the loudness of sounds heard, but also in
appreciating their direction. But even in his case, his ear may
be aided in these judgments by reflections of sounds from walls
or other objects.

The illusion of "auditory perspective" in reproduced sound depends
on the ability of the ear to sense the direction of a sound. The old-
fashioned stereoscope introduced the illusion of perspective into a
picture by permitting one to view simultaneously two pictures, each
with a single eye, photographed from points slightly separated as are
the human eyes. In a similar way in the field of sound, by using
two or more microphones and a corresponding number of loud-
speakers, a similar illusion may be created. For example, if orchestral
music is transmitted by means of three microphones, at right, left,
and center of the stage, connected separately to three loud-speakers
at corresponding points on a distant stage, the sound is reconstructed
in its proper spatial relation. The violins seem to be on the left, since
they are heard louder and slightly sooner from that loud-speaker. If
a person walks from left to right across the stage while singing, his
transmitted sounds are heard less and less from the left-hand speaker,
and more and more from the right-hand one, which gives the hearers
the exact auditory illusion of his walking across the stage.

[9] *Op. cit.*, page 155.

Naturally, if one's ears were farther apart than the diameter of the head, one could sense the direction of sound with greater accuracy. This principle has been used in devices which make use of two horns separated by several feet, placed on opposite ends of a rotatable bracket, the sounds collected in each horn being led by tubes to separate ears. By rotating the bracket until the sounds appear equally strong and instantaneous in both ears, the direction of a distant airplane motor, for example, may be fairly accurately known. The principal error in this case, however, is due to the fact that the source has moved ahead during the seconds the sound has taken to arrive at the horns. If two such stations are in telephonic communication, they may plot the intersection of their two directions to learn fairly accurately the actual position of the sound, as in wartime sound ranging in the location of enemy cannon. The same principle may be responsible for the fact that the ears of a grasshopper are found on its forelegs instead of on the narrower head, as has been pointed out by Beatty.

In the case of complex sounds, our ability to localize them may be further aided by the difference in quality at the two ears produced by unequal diffraction of the components when we are facing anywhere other than straight toward the sound. Localization may also be aided by the variation in quality that depends on the location of the source in its particular environment, as pointed out by Stewart.[10] Thus, in the familiar surroundings of our homes, we can tell which room a sound comes from by the character and degree of its associated reverberation.

Deafness

When the individual's threshold of hearing is raised above normal for any reason, he is to that extent deafened. In a certain sense the term may be used to apply to the deafening effect produced on all normal listeners by the presence of a high noise

---

[10] Stewart, G. W., *Introductory Acoustics*, page 147. New York: D. Van Nostrand Company, Inc., 1933.

level around them. The average city dweller is subjected to a
noise level nearly always at least 30 db above his threshold of
audibility, unless he pulls blankets over his head. For most of
his working day this level is never less than 50 db and may
rise intermittently as high as 90 or more. This is an entirely
different state of affairs from that which his ancestors, from
whom he inherited his nervous system, were subjected to. Persons in a boiler factory must speak very loudly to each other
to be heard above the noise level. They are for the moment
"deafened" though possessing normal hearing.

However, the term *deafness* usually refers to a pathological
condition of some sort in the hearing mechanism, whether an
inherited or non-inherited deficiency from birth, or a physiological or neurological deterioration from injury, illness, or
other cause. It may be caused by injury or degeneration of any
of the organs from the eardrum to the cochlea and its associated nerves. Sometimes it is temporary, but usually permanent.
It may be complete or only partial. Deafness is usually not
uniform over the pitch range. It may be at the lower end, the
upper end, or somewhere between. A person may be quite
deaf to pitches in a certain limited region, and able to hear
normally in the remainder of the pitch range. It is a fact that
nearly all fundamental speech sounds which enable us to understand words have one or more of their "characteristics" in the
higher frequency regions. This is particularly true of consonants. If a person speaks with every vowel changed to "uh,"
but pronounces every consonant, he can still be fairly easily
understood. Therefore, since the characteristic differences in
speech sounds that make for intelligibility lie in the higher frequencies, the person who is deafened to these higher frequencies is indeed unfortunate. The importance of this region may
be realized by the fact reported by the Bell Laboratories that
if all frequencies above 500 are cut out, only 5 per cent of words
may be understood, even though still loud. The best hear-

ing aids are designed to strengthen electrically the particular pitch region for which the individual is deafened, applying the strengthened vibrations to the eardrum via the air in the ear canal, as in a telephone, or, in the case of impaired drum or ossicles, directly to the mastoid bone behind the ear, whence they travel via "bone conduction" to the cochlea.

Deafness has an important bearing on speech. We learn to speak principally through hearing speech sounds from others. When deafness comes on, the continual check that hearing normally imposes on our own speech processes is gone, and speech may become progressively more slovenly and "dead" in its monotonous and careless intonation. In the case of children who are congenitally deaf, the learning of speech is extremely difficult. When a child of school age becomes gradually deaf, the mind also may give up its arduous labor in assigning meanings to sounds so imperfectly distinguished from each other, unless the teacher is infinitely patient and understanding with the individual case. Many cases of apparent low mentality are in reality cases of partial deafness.

Distortions of Hearing

Since the sense of hearing is a psycho-physiological response, it is not only limited to certain ranges but subject to certain distortions as well. Throughout the text, mention has been made of various of these distortions, such, for example, as the distortions and confusion which can occur in pitch judgments toward the upper and lower extremes of the pitch range, and toward the upper extreme of the loudness range. Mention has also been made of the partial deafness resulting from long exposure to noise, such as that of an airplane. In addition to the deafness, pitch distortions may occur here, due to fatigue effects. Thus, a continuous tone of a certain pitch may affect a considerable region of hair cells on either side of the part responsive to that pitch, so that distortions will be noticed for a time in other parts of the pitch scale, some tones being judged higher than they are, and others lower.

Apparently the passage of sound directly to the cochlea through the skull in "bone conduction" introduces certain distortions. Thus, in an individual possessed of normal hearing, a vibrating tuning fork heard through the skull bone by clamping the teeth on its base, will sometimes appear slightly higher in pitch than when heard normally. Also, violinists (whose tones may be heard either through the ear canal, membrane, and middle ear in the usual way, or by transmission directly to the cochlea through the chin rest of the instrument and the bones of the chin and head), sometimes complain of the difficulty of discriminating pitch, whereas when listening to another player they have no such difficulty. Is this difficulty due perhaps to bone conduction? A similar thing occurs also with singers, who often can hear very fine pitch errors in others and yet be unaware of making similar or greater ones themselves.

A type of distortion is produced in the middle ear. The nature of the bones of the middle ear is such that when any pure tone louder than a moderately soft intensity is produced, the action of these bones is such as to introduce the octave and higher harmonics as well. The louder the tone, the greater is this type of distortion, and the more prominent become the higher harmonics. The effect lessens as the pitch rises. In the case of a very loud tone of low or medium pitch, even though it may be produced physically by sound waves of pure simple harmonic motion, the psychological experience resulting from its physiological reception in the cochlea is equivalent to that of a fundamental plus a long series of overtones. If it be complex to start with, it is made even more complex in the ear. Furthermore, these same bones in the middle ear are sometimes the cause of difference tones. All difference tones which cannot be found to have any existence in the air (cannot be "picked up" by resonators), and which sound as if they were being produced inside of our ears, are probably introduced by the mode of vibration of these middle ear bones.[11] And this is perhaps why, when a poor radio set is unable to transmit frequencies below Middle C, for instance, we still seem to hear the low viola and 'cello tones in their correct octaves, their fundamentals being produced by the difference tones between adjacent harmonics. The diaphragm of a telephone does not transmit frequencies appreciably under 300 cycles, and yet we seem to hear by telephone the fundamental pitch of women's and men's voices, which lie in the neighborhood of 256 and 128, respectively, the fundamentals probably being supplied as difference tones. Thus, if a fundamental at 100 had third, fourth, and fifth partials (300 400, 500), the difference tones introduced by the ear bones, between 300 and 400, and between 400 and 500, would supply a frequency of 100, the same as that of the missing fundamental. Also, the difference tone between 300 and 500 would supply a frequency at 200, that of the missing octave. Thus, not only are strong fundamentals supplied with partials by the structure of the ear, but missing fundamentals and other low partials tend to be supplied by the ear as difference tones between the partials which *are* present, provided these latter are truly harmonic. Radio will not transmit fundamentals of kettledrums lying below its cutoff point, because the overtones of drums are not harmonic, and would not give difference tones of the same frequency as the fundamental. Perhaps the fundamentals of the lowest tones of the piano, an instrument which does produce harmonic overtones, are perceived in part subjectively, since the ratio of the fundamental to the total tone is low, even in a grand piano. And the acoustic justification for the use of difference tones to "fake" 32-foot stops in an organ is to be found in this phenomenon. The reality of these subjective tones can easily be demonstrated. In an experiment performed at the Bell Laboratories, two loud pure tones were sounded in front of an eardrum, and were found to produce at least sixteen sub-

---

[11] Recent evidence seems to indicate that ear distortion may be produced in the inner ear as well as, or perhaps instead of, in the middle ear. See, for example, the work of Wever and Bray.

jective tones, counting harmonics of each single tone as well as various difference and summation tones, in the range investigated (o to 4300). Thus, when sound is electrically amplified to much higher levels than originally, the total complex heard is considerably changed. The composer and conductor of the future may have to consider this.

Another type of useful distortion, already mentioned elsewhere, is the ear's tendency to hear a single central pitch when a group of neighboring pitches are sounded simultaneously (as when a number of performers attempt to play or sing in unison), or when the vibrato carries the tone rapidly enough back and forth over a pitch band.

Mention should also be made here of the fact that the different members of an audience do not usually hear exactly the same sounds from the stage. This is not due to the physiology of the ear, but to the fact that the standing-wave "interference" pattern for a certain pitch may cause it to be loud for a hearer in one seat, but soft for a hearer as short a distance away as the next seat. For another pitch, conditions will be reversed. Furthermore, sound is projected from many instruments in considerably different strengths in different directions. Much more is sent out in whatever direction the belly of a violin is facing than in the direction of the sides. In the case of brass instruments, much more sound energy, especially in the higher frequencies, is sent out in the direction the bell points than in other directions. Swaying movements of the performer will then naturally change the loudness of a sustained tone for any certain listener, particularly for one near the stage. Still another complication is found in the fact that persons near the stage experience less distortion from atmospheric absorption of frequencies than do those in the back. According to Mills, these effects may be responsible for differences of as much as 30 db between the sounds heard in different seats. If such differences occur between partials, the tone quality is changed, and the critic's difficulties increased. These matters can help to explain the differences in reaction to be heard after any concert, entirely apart from the fact that one's hearing ability at various pitches —his "audiogram"—is almost sure to be slightly different from his neighbor's. Thus, not only do we differ from each other in our aesthetic reactions to a musical performance, but we are all likely not even hearing exactly the same thing in the beginning. Music critics might occasionally profit by knowing these phenomena of auditorium sound, as well as their own audiograms.

Analysis of Complex Sounds

In spite of the various limitations and distortions to which the sense of hearing is subject, the normal human ear has a marvellous capacity for analyzing complex sounds. We cannot easily say what colors are present in a mixture of many pigments, nor what ingredients have been put into a mixture of many flavors, but with little difficulty we can pick out and focus our attention successively on different instruments contributing to an orchestral ensemble of extreme complexity. Pole [12] has expressed this in a striking way:

> The only means the ear has of becoming aware of all these simultaneous sounds is by the peculiar mode of condensation and rarefaction of some particles of air at the end of a tube [the ear canal] about the size [thickness] of a knitting needle, forming a single air wave, which, though so small, is of such complex structure as to contain in itself some element representing every sound going on in the room. And yet when this wave meets the nerves, they, ignoring the complexity, single out each individual component element by itself, and convey to the mind of the auditor, without any effort on his part, not only the notes and tones of every instrument and class of voice in the orchestra, but the character of every accidental noise in the room, almost as distinctly as if each single sound or noise were heard alone!

Through past experience we attach meaning to these various component vibrations. And we can even do more than this.

[12] Pole, William, *The Philosophy of Music*, page 27. New York: Harcourt, Brace & Company, Inc., 1924.

With attentive listening we can often distinguish certain of the overtones in a complex tone produced by a single instrument. However, the ear is usually unable to keep them apart for long. They fuse with the fundamental, and we hear one pitch of some characteristic quality rather than several simple pitches.

6

Electronic Recording, Reproducing, and Synthesizing of Sound

Limitations of Early Phonographs

In 1877 Edison produced the first phonograph record. His apparatus (which was first intended as a scientific instrument) consisted essentially of a sound-receiving diaphragm with a stylus attached, which made indentations on a tin-foil sheet wrapped around a moving cylinder. These indentations copied the sound waves of the voice or music being recorded, and although they made a very imperfect copy, the sound was intelligibly reproduced when the stylus was made to retrace the indentations. Edison made further improvements and produced a commercial machine. Alexander Graham Bell and C. S. Tainter introduced separate machines for recording and reproducing. In 1894 the Berliner machine was produced, which introduced disc records, and in which the movement of the recording stylus was from side to side in the groove instead of up and down. From then on many attempts were made to improve the reproduction. Horns, which were necessary to secure sufficient volume, introduced new problems because of their resonances, and efforts were made to equalize the resonances of horn, diaphragm, and so on, so as to secure as undistorted reproduction as possible.

These early methods, however, were seriously limited because of the small amount of energy available from sound for cutting a record. If an orchestra was being recorded the players would have to sit very close together and play rather loudly into the horn of the recording instrument. Modern methods make use of electrical recording and electrical reproduction.

Electronic Recording and Reproduction

In these methods, the sound to be recorded is picked up electrically by a microphone and amplified thousands of times if necessary by means of the type of electron tubes used in radio sets. The resulting amplified currents are then applied to the record-cutting mechanism, or to the device which "photographs the sound" on a moving-picture film. Similar electrical methods are used for transforming these electrical variations back into sound waves, and for amplifying them to any extent desired. Thus in the making of a phonograph record, or of a sound picture, the performers no longer need be cramped, nor under the necessity of performing loudly, for the softest whisper can be caught, and amplified as much as necessary. Great improvements in disc record materials, in disc-driving mechanisms, in photographic emulsions and techniques, and in microphones and amplifiers, have made possible an astonishing fidelity in recording and reproducing methods, provided sufficient care be taken with the loud-speaker. Commercial lateral-cut phonograph discs can record sound, according to Mills, from about 40 to about 5500 cycles, with a practically uniform response from 300 to 5500. Below 300 the response is deliberately weakened in order to save the record grooves from cutting into each other, owing to the fact that the amplitudes of low-frequency tones are greater than those of high-frequency tones of equal acoustic power. At the upper frequencies, also, in the usual commercial record the response is purposely tapered off above 4000 or 4500, in order to reduce "needle scratch." This characteristic background noise, which is most noticeable in the silent portions of a record, results from the practice of mixing an abrasive with the material of the disc in order to "grind in" the needle of the reproducing head. The penalizing of higher frequencies of course affects the music quality as well as reducing the scratch noise. Vertical-cut ("hill-and-dale") discs of the most recent type, such as are used for radio transcriptions and music distribution systems of the better sort, can record up to 9000, while at the same time not being under the necessity of lessening the low frequencies. Scratch noise is also reduced, and these records can preserve an intensity range of 50 or more decibels. Film recording has its own problems of background noise, partially caused by irregularities in the grain of the film emulsion. This noise is about 45 db below the peaks of music, however, as compared with needle scratch on lateral-cut discs, which is only about 30 db below the music. The frequency range which can be recorded on film is about as great as that on vertical-cut discs.

It is not necessary to have the intermediate step of preserving the sound impulses on some more or less permanent material for future reproduction, such as by a space pattern on a wax disc, or by a chemical pattern in a film emulsion. This step may be omitted, and the sound immediately reproduced in amplified form, either as in a public address system in the same room or wired to a distant auditorium, or as in the radio, where it is transmitted to a distance by radio waves. These allied developments have been so greatly improved that the electrical variations delivered, say, to the loud-speaker of a good receiving set from a near-by high-quality broadcasting station are a fairly accurate copy of the original sound waves, and if the station is transmitting from its own studio and not from a program circuit a frequency range up to 7500 or more and a fair intensity range can be transmitted. The trouble here also is in this last link, the loud-speaker.

Limitations of Loud-Speakers

Although progress is continually being made, particularly in the use of separate units for various pitch ranges, it still seems almost impossible to build an inexpensive speaker that has, with its associated circuits, sufficiently wide frequency and volume ranges. An ideal speaker should give a uniform response throughout the whole audible pitch range. Practically, however, a response range from 40 to 15,000 would reproduce everything that could possibly be distinguished by the average listener. Many listeners, of course, would be satisfied with even less complete reproduction. Reference to Figure 42 will show that the very low and very high frequencies must be quite strongly produced in an instrument to be audible. In the usual musical instruments they are but weakly produced. Thus, a fairly uniform range from 60 to, say, 10,000 cycles would be very good indeed, the last octave, from 10,000 to 20,000, adding but little. It is true that the highest tone commonly used in music has a frequency of only 4186, but a higher range than this is necessary to secure faithful reproduction of the overtones that give the characteristic musical tone qualities. In addition to such an extended pitch range, a large volume range is necessary if we are to secure faithful reproduction of all impulsive sounds, such as pistol shots, hammering, the slamming of a door, the beginning of piano tones, and so on. Ordinary commercial radios, with perhaps circuit limitations as well as speaker limitations, cut off at their upper end at from 3000 to 6000 cycles, with a few expensive sets going to 8000. Many of them are so limited in volume range that the initial percussive phases of loud piano tones "rattle" with distortion, although the continuant phases are rather soft. The volume range is limited at the lower end by radio's "background noise"—static—and at the upper end by loud-speaker limitations and by the fact that radio tubes overload and distort their output beyond a certain point. The difference between these levels is in the best sets as much as 50 db, but in most sets only about 30 db, representing a power ratio of about 1000 to 1. How can such an instrument respond to such differences as that between a very soft violin solo and a very loud passage of a large orchestra, which, as we have noted on page 207, has been found to be a difference of 70 db, representing power differences in the ratio of 10,000,000 to 1? Vertical disc recording and film recording, for that matter, will only handle ratios from about 30,000 to 1, which, however, is satisfactory for a program heard in a home or small auditorium.

Limitations in the frequency range not only impair the tone quality of music, but may seriously interfere with speech. In speech, the lower frequencies are more important in securing volume and the higher frequencies in securing clearness of speech. If an electrical speaker permits the lower components to come through and damps off the treble, voices still sound rather natural in loudness and general quality, but the words cannot be understood. This effect is increased if we hear it through a partition, which usually damps the highs very much more than the lows. If the treble is present and the bass lost, the voices lose greatly in loudness and naturalness, but are still understandable, as in the telephone. This, as has been mentioned in the preceding chapter, is because so many of the speech sounds have one or more "characteristics" in the higher frequency regions.[1]

Another limitation of the electrical speaker, though of less importance because of the tolerance of the ear for moderate distortions of quality, is the difficulty of building an inexpensive instrument that is free from resonance peaks of its own. Such resonance peaks exaggerate certain frequencies out of proportion to the rest. When this effect is pronounced, the distortions are quite apparent. The tone becomes "tinny" if it is a high that is exaggerated, and dull or "mouthy" if it is a low. These same effects will be produced however, respectively, by systems which have an insufficient response at the low end or at the high end.

All phases of the reproduction of music, from the microphone to the loud-speaker, and including the acoustic conditions

---

[1] Thus, in improving over-reverberant lecture rooms, sound-absorbing materials should be sought which do not cut down the reverberation time of higher frequencies too greatly. The vowel "ee," which contains high frequencies, is modified toward "oo" in many reverberant halls because of the greater absorption of high frequencies than lows. Choirs in reverberant churches are thus perhaps not always to be blamed for poor diction.

of both the recording and the reproducing rooms, have been greatly improved, and probably will continue to be, partly through the insistence of moving picture audiences in demanding better and better reproduction. The theatre with a reputation for "poor acoustics" loses patronage. However, there is no certainty that further improvement will come. The general public, which, after all, supports the radio industry directly or indirectly, as it does every industry, seems astonishingly satisfied by inferior home radios. The majority of radio listeners seem to be satisfied with frequency ranges from 100 to 3000 or 4000, and volume ranges between the noise level of hum and the peaks of sound of around 30 db or a little more. Mills [2] says, "They object to the shrillness of higher frequencies even though these exist in the actual music and they prefer the more 'mellow' tones. That is a serious matter. Thousands of persons are getting accustomed to music which lacks all naturalness or brilliancy. They neither demand nor care for a faithful reproduction." The danger here is that the electrical transmission of music will be standardized on a low aesthetic level, and the few discriminating listeners will be unable to secure the reproduction they desire. As a matter of fact, many chain program circuits transmit only 5000 cycles. There is no articulate demand for any more from the radio listeners. Thus the better radio sets, which transmit from about 50 to 4500 cycles, and have a range of about 40 db, reproduce about everything normally broadcasted; and there is little use or advantage for the best sets, which handle from about 40 to 8000 cycles with a range of about 50 db. The ever-present "tone control" is an indication both of the imperfection of the set, which if reproducing correctly would require no distortion in one direction or another, and of the lack of a critical ear on the part of the listening public.

[2] Mills, J., *A Fugue in Cycles and Bels,* page 221. New York, D. Van Nostrand Company, Inc., 1935.

Electronic Instruments

In addition to the use of electrical methods for recording and *re*-producing sound, such methods are now being put to use in the creation of sounds. New musical instruments with remarkable versatility are being produced. Some of them produce sound by electrical modification and amplification of the tone of some legitimate instrument, or of the tone of a small metal reed. Others synthesize new qualities electrically by building up various overtones in various strengths, and amplifying the result, sometimes with further modification.

Owing in part to their limitations, these instruments are not yet being warmly received by musicians in general. Enthusiasm for them is scattered, and frequently interspersed with condemnation. Some of the limitations are as follows.

Instruments which synthesize complex tone qualities by building up overtones are often not provided with a sufficient number of overtones to give satisfactory complex qualities. All electronic instruments are subject to the danger of restricted ranges of frequency and volume resulting from circuit and speaker limitations, as in the case of the electrical phonographs and radios described in the preceding section. Furthermore, electronic instruments, strange as it may seem, are sometimes too perfect. Aesthetically, we seem to get more pleasure out of tones which are not too precisely in tune, nor too abruptly commenced or stopped, nor having too perfect a vibrato. In an ensemble, a "pitch fringe" is desirable around the true pitch; so also an "agogic fringe" around the true beat instant. And in the case of the vibrato, an "irregular regularity" is far more desirable than an exact regularity, which, as in the case of the organ tremolo, for example, sometimes becomes unbearable after a while. The charm of these fringes and irregularities, and of similar variations from the true or exact, stems from the aesthetic principle of uncertainty, and is similar to the charm we experience from a charcoal drawing as compared with the exactness of a photograph.

Since it has become possible to amplify loud-speaker sound without limit, it is necessary to be aware of, and, if necessary, to guard against such distortions of pitch and tone quality as are produced at such intensities, as discussed on pages 21 and 217ff.

Undoubtedly these electronic instruments will be continually improved, however, and may even in the future displace some of our present instruments, particularly if a great composer arises to write a great literature in their own particular idiom. And to offset their disadvantages, they have certain definite advantages. For example, one of the most popular electronic organs cannot get out of tune, is easily portable, and yet can produce very low tones without the need of expensive, long, heavy pipes, which now carry so much of the cost of organ building. It is no criticism at all to say that the sounds of *high-quality* systems for the electrical creation or reproduction of music are unmusical because they are "phonographic" or "mechanical." We know rather accurately beyond just what ranges of intensity and pitch the ear is incapable of hearing or discriminating, and apparatus can be built and has been built, although expensive, which will completely reproduce these ranges, so that the finest musicians' ears can be completely deceived as to whether the music is "real," "canned," or "synthetic."

Certainly these developments should be considered in a tolerant light. Sneers for the scientist have been popular among musicians ever since the beginning. Every advance in the mechanics of a musical instrument has probably been met by a storm of protest. But progress comes sooner through cooperation than otherwise. The question should not be, "Who dares thus to defile Art?", but, "What values do the various electrical methods for creating sound have for the future of music?"

Bibliography

IT is almost impossible to keep textbook bibliographies free
from significant omissions, considering the wealth of material
available in any field which has crystallized sufficiently to make
a textbook necessary.   Therefore the following bibliography,
containing, among others, most of the works consulted or quoted
in the preparation of this text, makes no pretensions to exhaus-
tiveness.   It is restricted with three exceptions to works available
in English.   Certain older representative references have been
included, but many more have been omitted, since their material
is usually covered by more up-to-date publications.   The dating
is not uniform, in that some works are listed with their original
date of publication to emphasize priority, whereas others are
given according to recent revisions to emphasize up-to-dateness.
The bibliography includes an arbitrary selection of articles from
the indices of the *Journal of the Acoustical Society of America,*
covering various phases of modern acoustics, and indicating the
wide ramifications to which this field is spreading.   Many more
might have been inserted.

Abbott, R. B., "Response Measurement and Harmonic Analysis of
   Violin Tones," *J. Acoust. Soc. Amer.,* VII, 1935, pp. 111-116.
Acoustical Society of America.   Many other articles from the *Journal
   of the Acoustical Society* not listed separately in this bibliography.
   Consult indices of the journal.
Aikin, W. A., *The Voice.*   New York: Longmans, Green & Com-
   pany, 1910.
Audsley, G. A., *The Art of Organ Building.*   2 vols.   New York:
   Dodd, Mead & Company, Inc., 1905.

Bagenal, H., and A. Wood, *Planning for Good Acoustics*. New York: E. P. Dutton & Co., Inc., 1932.

Barbour, J. M., "Equal Temperament: Its History from Ramis (1482) to Rameau (1737)." Ph.D. Thesis, Cornell University, 1932.

————, "The Persistence of the Pythagorean Tuning System," *Scripta Mathematica,* I (No. 4, June, 1933), pp. 286-304.

Barnes, W. H., *The Contemporary American Organ*. 3d ed. New York: J. Fischer & Brother, 1937.

Bartholomew, W. T., "A Physical Definition of 'Good Voice-Quality' in the Male Voice," *J. Acoust. Soc. Amer.,* VI (1934), pp. 25-33.

————, "The Role of Imagery in Voice Teaching," *Proceedings of the Music Teachers National Association,* 1935 volume.

————, "A Survey of Recent Voice Research," *Proceedings of the Music Teachers National Association,* 1937 volume.

Barton, E. H., *A Textbook on Sound*. New York: The Macmillan Company, 1908.

Beatty, R. T., *Hearing in Man and Animals*. London: George Bell & Sons, Ltd., 1932.

Böhm, T., *The Flute and Flute Playing in Acoustical, Technical, and Artistic Aspects*. 2d English ed., revised and enlarged, translated and annotated by D. C. Miller. Cleveland: Dayton C. Miller, 1922.

Boner, C. P., "Acoustic Spectra of Organ Pipes," *J. Acoust. Soc. Amer.,* X (1938), pp. 32-40.

Bragg, W. H., *The World of Sound*. New York: E. P. Dutton & Co., Inc., 1920.

Broadhouse, J., *Musical Acoustics*. New York: Charles Scribner's Sons, 5th impression, 1926.

Buck, P. C., *Acoustics for Musicians*. New York: Oxford University Press, 1918.

Chávez, C., *Toward a New Music; Music and Electricity*. New York: W. W. Norton & Company, Inc., 1937.

Cheslock, L., "Violin Vibrato," *Peabody Conservatory Research Studies in Music,* No. 1, 1931.

Colby, M. Y., *Sound Waves and Acoustics*. New York: Henry Holt & Company, Inc., 1938.

Curry, R., *Mechanism of the Human Voice*. New York: Longmans, Green & Company, 1940.

Davis, A. H., *Modern Acoustics*. New York: The Macmillan Company, 1934.

————, and G. W. C. Kaye, *The Acoustics of Buildings*. London: George Bell & Sons, Ltd., 1927.

Dodds, G., and J. D. Lickley, *The Control of the Breath*. New York: Oxford University Press, 1925.

Drew, W. S., *Singing, the Art and the Craft*. New York: Oxford University Press, 1937.

Ellis, A. J., "On the Musical Scales of Various Nations," *J. Soc. Arts*, 1885.

Elson, A., *The Book of Musical Knowledge*. Boston: Houghton Mifflin Company, 1927.

Fletcher, H., "Loudness, Pitch and the Timbre of Musical Tones and Their Relation to the Intensity, the Frequency, and the Overtone Structure," *J. Acoust. Soc. Amer.* VI (1934), pp. 59-69.

——, *Speech and Hearing*. New York: D. Van Nostrand Company, Inc., 1929.

Garcia, M., "Observations on the Human Voice," *Philos. Mag.*, X, 1855.

Gault, R. H., "An Interpretation of Vibro-Tactile Phenomena," *J. Acoust. Soc. Amer.*, V (1934), pp. 252-254.

Ghosh, R. N., "Theory of the Clarinet," *J. Acoust. Soc. Amer.*, IX (1938), pp. 255-264.

Giltay, J. W., *Bow Instruments, Their Form and Construction*. New York: Charles Scribner's Sons, 1923.

Glover, C. W., *Practical Acoustics for the Constructor*. Cleveland: The Sherwood Press, Inc., 1933.

Greene, P. C., "Violin Performance with Reference to Tempered, Natural, and Pythagorean Intonation," *University of Iowa Studies in the Psychology of Music*, IV, 1937.

Hamilton, C. G., *Sound and Its Relation to Music*. Philadelphia: Oliver Ditson Company, Inc., 1912.

Harker, G. F. H., "Principles Underlying the Tuning of Keyboard Instruments to Equal Temperament," *J. Acoust. Soc. Amer.*, VIII (1937), pp. 243-256.

Hart, H. C., M. W. Fuller, and W. S. Lusby, "Precision Study of Piano Touch and Tone," *J. Acoust. Soc. Amer.*, VI (1934), pp. 80-94.

Helmholtz, H. L. F. von, "On the Sensations of Tone as a Physiological Basis for the Theory of Music." Translated, thoroughly revised and corrected, rendered conformable to the 4th (and last) German edition of 1877, etc., by A. J. Ellis. 3d ed. 1895, Longmans, Green & Company.

Hermann-Goldap, E., Über die Klangfarber einiger Orchesterinstrumente," *Ann. d. Physik*, XXIII (1907), pp. 979-985.

Humphreys, W. J., *Physics of the Air*. (Section on meteorological acoustics.) 2d ed., revised. New York: McGraw-Hill Book Company, Inc., 1929.

Jeans, J., *Science and Music*. New York: The Macmillan Company, 1937.

Johnstone, A. E., *Instruments of the Modern Symphony Orchestra and Band*. Revised and augmented edition by Edwin J. Stringham. New York: Carl Fischer, Inc., 1930.

Jones, A. T., *Sound*. New York: D. Van Nostrand Company, Inc., 1937.

———, "The Strike Note of Bells," *J. Acoust. Soc. Amer.*, VIII (1937), pp. 199-203.

Kaufmann, W., "Über die Bewegungen geschlagener Saiten," *Ann. d. Physik*, Vol. 54 (1895), pp. 675-712.

Knudsen, V. O., "Some Cultural Applications of Modern Acoustics," *J. Acoust. Soc. Amer.*, IX (1938), pp. 175-184.

Kock, W. E., "Certain Subjective Phenomena Accompanying a Frequency Vibrato," *J. Acoust. Soc. Amer.*, VIII (1936), pp. 23-25.

Kwalwasser, J., "The Vibrato," University of Iowa Studies in Psychology, No. IX, *Psychol. Monog.*, 1926.

Lemon, H. B., and H. I. Schlesinger, *Sound: a guide for use with the educational sound pictures "Sound waves and their sources" and "Fundamentals of acoustics."* Chicago: University of Chicago Press, 1934.

Lewis, D., "Vocal Resonance," *J. Acoust. Soc. Amer.*, VIII (1936), pp. 91-99.

———, and M. Cowan, "The Influence of Intensity on the Pitch of Violin and 'Cello Tones," *J. Acoust. Soc. Amer.*, VIII (1936), pp. 20-22.

Lifshitz, S., "Apparent Duration of Sound Perception and Musical Optimum Reverberation," *J. Acoust. Soc. Amer.*, VII (1936), pp. 213-221.

Lloyd, Ll. S., *Music and Sound*. New York: Oxford University Press, 1937.

London Physical Society, *Report of a discussion on audition*. London: London Physical Society, 1931.

Loomis, A., and H. W. Schwartz, *How Music Is Made*. Elkhart, Ind.: C. G. Conn, Ltd., 1927.

MacNair, W. A., "Optimum Reverberation Time for Auditoriums," *J. Acoust. Soc. Amer.*, I (1930), pp. 242-248.

Mason, D. G., *The Orchestral Instruments and What They Do*. New York: H. W. Gray Company, Inc., 1909.

McLachlan, N. W., *The New Acoustics*. New York: Oxford University Press, 1936.

———, *Noise*. New York: Oxford University Press, 1935.

Meinel, H., "Violin Tone," *Elektrische nachrichten-technik*, XIV (1937), pp. 119-134.

Metfessel, M., "Sonance As a Form of Tonal Fusion," *Psychol. Rev.*, Vol. 33 (1926), pp. 459-466.

Metzger, W., "The Mode of Vibration of the Vocal Cords." University of Iowa Studies in Psychology, No. XI, *Psychol. Monog.*, 1928.

Miller, D. C., *Anecdotal History of the Science of Sound*. New York: The Macmillan Company, 1935.

———, *The Science of Musical Sounds*. New York: The Macmillan Company, 1916.

———, *Sound Waves: Their Shape and Speed*. New York: The Macmillan Company, 1937.

Mills, J., *A Fugue in Cycles and Bels*. New York: D. Van Nostrand Company, Inc., 1935.

Morse, P. McC., *Vibration and Sound*. New York: McGraw-Hill Book Company, Inc., 1936.

Mott, F. W., *The Brain and the Voice in Speech and Song*. New York: Harper & Brothers, 1910.

New York City Noise Abatement Commission, *City Noise*. New York: 1930.

Niemoeller, A. F., *Handbook of Hearing Aids*. New York: Harvest House, 1940.

Ogden, R. M., *Hearing*. New York: Harcourt, Brace & Company, Inc., 1924.

Olson, H. F., *Elements of Acoustical Engineering*. New York: D. Van Nostrand Company, Inc., 1940.

Ortmann, O., "On the Melodic Relativity of Tones," *Psychol. Monog.*, 1926.

———, *The Physical Basis of Piano Touch and Tone*. New York: E. P. Dutton & Co., Inc., 1925.

———, *The Physiological Mechanics of Piano Technique*. New York: E. P. Dutton & Co., Inc., 1929.

———, "The Sensorial Basis of Music Appreciation," *J. Compar. Psychol*, II (1922), pp. 227-256.

Paget, R., *Human Speech*. New York: Harcourt, Brace & Company, Inc., 1930.

Parry, C. H. H., *The Evolution of the Art of Music*. (1st edition, 1893.) Edited with additional chapters by H. C. Colles. New York: D. Appleton-Century Company, Inc., 1930.

Peirce, B., *An Elementary Treatise on Sound*. Boston: James Munroe & Co., 1836. (Contains a very large bibliography on various aspects of sound from Greek philosophers up to 1836.)

Petran, L. A., "An Experimental Study of Pitch Recognition," *Psychol. Monog.*, 1932.

———, "Pitch Discrimination Near the Upper and Lower Thresholds of Audition," *Amer. J. Psychol.*, XLV (1933), pp. 248-262.

Pierce, E. H., "A Colossal Experiment in Just Intonation," *Mus. Quart.*, July, 1924.

Pohl, R. W., *Physical Principles of Mechanics and Acoustics*. Authorized translation by W. M. Deans. London: Blackie & Son, Ltd., 1932.

Pole, W., *The Philosophy of Music*. 6th ed. New York: Harcourt, Brace & Company, Inc., 1924.

Redfield, J., "Certain Anomalies in the Theory of Air Column Behaviour in Orchestral Wind Instruments," *J. Acoust. Soc. Amer.*, VI (1934), pp. 34-36.

———, *Music, a Science and an Art*. New York: Alfred A. Knopf, 1928.

Richards, G. J., "On the Motion of an Elliptic Cylinder Through a Viscous Fluid," *Phil. Trans. Roy. Soc.*, Oct., 1934.

Richardson, E. G., *The Acoustics of Orchestral Instruments and of the Organ*. London: Edward Arnold & Co., 1929.

———, *An Introduction to Acoustics of Buildings*. London: Edward Arnold & Co., 1933.

———, *The Prevention and Insulation of Noise*. London: E. & F. N. Spon, Ltd., 1932.

———, *Sound, a Physical Textbook*. 2d ed. New York: Longmans, Green & Company, 1935.

Rothschild, D. A., Timbre Analysis of the Vibrato. *University of Iowa Studies in the Psychology of Music*, I. Iowa City: University of Iowa Press, 1932.

Russell, G. O., *Speech and Voice*. New York: The Macmillan Company, 1931.

Sabine, P. E., *Acoustics and Architecture*. New York: McGraw-Hill Book Company, Inc., 1932.

Sabine, W. C., *Collected Papers on Acoustics*. Cambridge: Harvard Univ. Press, 1922.

Sacia, C. F., "Speech Power and Energy," *Bell Syst. Tech. J.,* IV (Oct., 1925).

Saunders, F. A., "The Mechanical Action of Violins," *J. Acoust. Soc. Amer.,* IX (1937), pp. 81-98.

Schoen, M., "The Pitch Factor in Artistic Singing," University of Iowa Studies in Psychology, No. VIII, *Psychol. Monog.,* 1922.

Schwartz, H. W., *The Story of Musical Instruments.* New York: Doubleday, Doran & Company, Inc., 1938.

Scripture, E. W., *Researches in Experimental Phonetics.* Washington, D. C.: Carnegie Institute, 1906.

Seashore, C. E., *Psychology of the Vibrato in Voice and Instrument.* Iowa City: University of Iowa Press, 1936.

Sivian, L. J., H. K. Dunn, and S. D. White, "Absolute Amplitudes and Spectra of Certain Musical Instruments and Orchestras," *J. Acoust. Soc. Amer.,* II (1931), pp. 330-371.

Slocum, S. E., *Noise and Vibration Engineering.* New York: D. Van Nostrand Company, Inc., 1931.

Smith, H., *The Making of Sound in the Organ and in the Orchestra.* London: William Reeves, Bookseller, Ltd., 1911.

Snow, W. B., "Change of Pitch with Loudness at Low Frequencies," *J. Acoust. Soc. Amer.,* VIII (1936), pp. 14-19.

Spain, H., *Equal Temperament in Theory and Practice.* New York: H. W. Gray Company, Inc. (no date).

Stanley, D., *The Science of Voice.* New York: Carl Fischer, Inc., 1929.

————, and J. P. Maxfield, *The Voice, Its Production and Reproduction.* New York: Pitman Pub. Corp., 1933.

Stetson, R. H., "The Breathing Movements in Singing," *Arch. Néerl. de Phon. Exper.,* 1931.

Stevens, S. S., and H. Davis, *Hearing, Its Psychology and Physiology.* New York: John Wiley & Sons, Inc., 1938.

Stewart, G. W., *Introductory Acoustics.* D. Van Nostrand Company, Inc., 1933.

————, and R. B. Lindsay, *Acoustics.* New York: D. Van Nostrand Company, Inc., 1930.

Taylor, Sedley, *Sound and Music.* London: Macmillan & Co., Ltd., 1873.

Tiffin, J., "Some Aspects of the Psychophysics of the Vibrato," University of Iowa Studies in Psychology, No. XIV, *Psychol. Monog.,* 1931.

Tyndall, J., *Sound.* London: Longmans, Green & Company, 1867.

Tyzzer, F. G., "Characteristics of Bell Vibrations," *J. Frank. Inst.,* Vol. 210, No. 1 (1930), pp. 55-66.

Wagner, A. H., "An Experimental Study in Control of the Vocal Vibrato," University of Iowa Studies in Psychology, No. XIII, *Psychol. Monog.,* 1930.

Wallaschek, R., *Primitive Music.* London: Longmans, Green & Company, 1893. (Very extensive bibliography.)

Watson, F. R., *Acoustics of Buildings.* 2d ed., revised. New York: John Wiley & Sons, Inc., 1930.

————, *Sound.* New York: John Wiley & Sons, Inc., 1935.

Watt, H. J., *The Foundations of Music.* New York: The Macmillan Company, 1919.

————, *The Psychology of Sound.* New York: The Macmillan Company, 1917.

Wead, C. K., *Contributions to the History of Musical Scales.* Washington, D. C.: Smithsonian Institute, 1900.

Wegel, R. L., "The Physical Characteristics of Audition and Dynamical Analysis of the External Ear," *Bell Syst. Tech. J.,* I (1922), pp. 56-68.

West, W., *Acoustical Engineering.* New York: Pitman Pub. Corp., 1932.

Westerman, K. N., "The Physiology of Vibrato," *Music Educators Journal,* March, 1938.

Wever, E. G., and C. W. Bray, "Distortion in the Ear as Shown by the Electrical Responses of the Cochlea," *J. Acoust. Soc. Amer.,* IX (1938), pp. 227-233.

White, W. B., *Piano Tuning and Allied Arts.* Boston: Tuners Supply Co., 1938.

————, "Practical Tests for Determining the Accuracy of Pianoforte Tuning," *J. Acoust. Soc. Amer.,* IX (1937), pp. 47-50.

Wolf, S. K., D. Stanley, and W. J. Sette, "Quantitative Studies on the Singing Voice," *J. Acoust. Soc. Amer.,* VI (1935), pp. 255-266.

Wood, A. B., *A Textbook of Sound.* New York: The Macmillan Company, 1930.

Wood, Alexander, *The Physical Basis of Music.* New York: The Macmillan Company, 1913.

————, *Sound Waves and Their Uses.* London: Blackie & Son, Ltd., 1930.

Yasser, J., *A Theory of Evolving Tonality.* New York: American Library of Musicology, 1932.

Zahm, J. A., *Sound and Music.* Chicago: A. C. McClurg & Co., 1892.

Index

A

Absorption, 67-76, 211, 220, 227
Acoustics defined, 2
Aeolian tones, 108
Aesthetics, 25, 60, 75, 76, 147, 161, 162, 165-168, 186-189, 192, 221, 229
Air columns, 103-129
Air waves, 33, 51, 55 (see also Sound waves)
Amplitude, 7, 19-21, 33, 59, 91, 95, 96, 98, 102, 149, 211, 224
Angle:
  of incidence, 64
  of reflection, 64
Auditory perspective, 214
Auditory sensation area, 208-213

B

Bar, 209
Bassoon, 129
Beats, 25, 57-61, 84, 118, 138, 166, 167, 189, 192-195, 203
Beat tone, 61, 63
Bell metal, 137
Bells, 15, 135-139
Binaural sense, 213-215
Bone conduction, 45, 217, 218
Bowed strings, 88, 89, 92, 97
Bow pressure, 88, 97-100, 102
Bow speed, 97-99
Brass winds, 15, 41, 110, 115-117, 123, 124, 126, 127, 220
Breath control, 155, 156
Bugle, 116

C

Carillon, 139
Carrying power, 36
Celesta, 134, 139
'Cello (see Violoncello)
Chamber music, 69, 72, 76, 185
"Chest register," 142, 146
Chimes, 15, 119, 139
Chladni's figures, 130, 134, 135
Choral singing, 41, 173, 185, 186, 189, 227
Chromatic scale, 180
Church modes, 170, 171

C (continued)

Clarinet, 14, 37, 110, 115, 117, 119, 125, 129, 167, 204
Cochlea, 45, 200, 216-218
Complex sounds, analysis of, 221, 222
Complex vibration, 10, 12, 13, 48-51, 136
Compression (see Wave motion, compressional)
Consonance, 163-167, 174-177, 188
Consonants, 156-158, 216
Coupled systems, 60, 61, 110, 141
Cymbals, 139, 160

D

Dead spots, 56, 57, 66, 67
Deafness, 200, 213-217
Decibel, 69, 206-210, 216, 225-228
Diatonic scale evolution, 167-179
Difference tones, 61-63, 218-220
Diffraction, 77-80, 213, 215
Diffusion, 34-36
Dissonance, 98, 163-167, 176, 187-189
Distortions in hearing, 187, 217-221, 230
Doppler effect, 82-84
Double bass, 103
Drums, 128, 130, 131, 139, 160, 204, 219
Duration limits and sensitivity, in hearing, 213
Duration of tones, 103, 128, 131, 133, 135, 138, 155

E

Ear, 35, 128, 187, 194 (see also Hearing)
Echoes, 63-66, 68, 72, 74
Eddies, 108, 109
Edge tones, 107-109, 122, 124
Elasticity, 3, 44, 85, 88, 103, 105, 130, 131, 135, 138
Electronic instruments, 229, 230
Embouchure, 126
End correction, 121-123, 127
English horn, 129
Equal temperament, 174, 181-196

F

Falsetto, 5, 15, 142, 144, 147
f-holes, 102
Flute, 12, 15, 108, 115, 120, 124, 129, 161, 168

Formant, 15-19, 145-149
French horn, 9, 115, 124, 127, 129
Frequency, 5, 7, 19-22, 24, 33, 43, 79, 94, 95, 107, 110, 116-122, 172, 173, 201, 202, 208-211, 224-230
Frequency ratios, 9, 163, 164, 171-178, 180-184, 189-191, 195, 205
Fundamental, 8-14, 16-20, 49, 53-55, 63, 65, 86, 91, 92, 97-99, 111, 114-118, 120, 122, 123, 126, 174, 194, 195, 201, 202, 210, 211, 219, 222

G

Glockenspiel, 139
Gong, 139
"Good acoustics," 74-76
Greek modes, 170, 171, 177

H

Harmonic analysis, 53, 54
Harmonic series, 7, 9, 90, 91, 95, 98, 113-117, 122, 123, 141, 163-168, 177, 187, 188, 193, 194, 201
Harmonics, 90-95, 97-100 (see also Partials, harmonic)
Harp, 37, 94, 97, 100, 103
"Head register," 147
Hearing:
    analysis of complex sounds, 221, 222
    bone conduction in, 45, 217, 218
    distortions in, 187, 217-221, 230
    duration limits and sensitivity, 213
    loudness limits and sensitivity, 35, 203-213
    mechanism, 47, 62, 146, 199-201, 207
    pitch limits and sensitivity, 194, 201-203, 208, 209, 211
Helmholtz resonator, 38, 53
Huyghens' principle, 77

I

Inharmonics (see Partials, inharmonic)
Instruments, electronic, 229, 230
Insulation, sound, 72-74
Intensity, 21, 69, 203-212, 225, 230
Interference, 56-58, 220
Intervals, 8, 9, 83, 94, 118, 162-195
Intonation:
    just (true), 172-196
    Pythagorean (see Pythagorean intonation)
Italian opera, 76

J

Just (true) intonation, 172-196

L

Lateral cut discs, 224, 225
Liturgical music, 70
Loop, 7, 86, 92, 104-107, 111-113, 117, 121, 123, 131, 132
Loudness, 7, 19-21, 23, 72, 95, 96, 131-133, 137, 143, 203-214, 216-218, 220
Loudness contours, 208-210
Loudness limits and sensitivity, in hearing, 35, 203-213
Loud-speakers, 41, 127, 214, 224-230
Lydian mode, 170, 171, 173, 174, 176 (see also Pythagorean intonation)

M

Magadizing, 164
Meantone tuning, 181, 185
Membranes, 130, 131
Middle C, 6, 7, 9, 17, 22, 44, 102, 117, 121, 125, 173, 203, 209, 219
Minor mode, 177, 178
Mixture stops, 13, 194
Mode:
    church, 170, 171
    Greek, 170, 171, 177
    Lydian (see Lydian mode)
    minor, 177, 178
Momentum, 3, 85, 105
Music:
    chamber, 69, 72, 76, 185
    liturgical, 70
    Wagnerian, 76
Mute, 96, 97, 124

N

Natural period, 5, 102, 109, 110
Needle scratch, 224, 225
Node, 7, 11, 86, 90-92, 97, 98, 104-107, 111-113, 123, 130-136, 138
Noise, 14, 15, 20, 130, 159-162, 207
    effect on health, 161, 162, 215, 216
Noise elements in all instruments, 160, 161

O

Oboe, 12, 19, 52, 110, 113, 115, 117, 119, 125, 127, 129
Orchestra, 24, 41, 160, 204, 207, 214, 221, 224, 226
Organ:
    electronic, 229, 230
    pipe, 13, 15, 25, 39, 53, 54, 60, 62, 63, 70, 75, 76, 106-111, 114, 117-128, 180, 185, 192, 194, 196, 197, 201, 202, 204, 205, 209, 219, 229
    reed, 111, 129

Organum, 164
Oscillograph, 47-51, 59
Ossicles, 200, 217-219
Overblowing, 114, 115, 122, 126, 127
Overtones, 7-9, 99, 100, 115, 117, 118, 122, 130, 131, 141, 144, 201-203, 210, 211, 218, 222, 226, 229 (*see also* Partials)

P

Partials:
    harmonic, 7-9, 11, 48-51, 53, 54, 87-95, 97-100, 112-118, 121-123, 126, 127, 166, 167, 174-176, 194, 219
    inharmonic, 11, 15, 51, 98, 129-139, 141, 160
Peabody Conservatory of Music, 73, 145
Percussion, 129-139, 160
Period, 33 (*see also* Natural period)
Phase, 54, 57, 214
Phonograph, 47, 52, 127, 223, 224, 229, 230
Piano, 9-11, 14, 15, 45, 54, 89-91, 94-96, 98-100, 103, 160, 181, 185, 189, 196, 197, 204, 205, 209, 219, 226
    tuning, 21, 192-195
Pipe organ (*see* Organ, pipe)
Pipes:
    open, 111-115, 117, 118, 121, 124-126
    "scale" of, 115, 122-124, 127
    stopped, 107, 111-115, 117, 118, 122, 124-127
Pitch, 6, 19-21, 23-25, 60, 78, 83, 94, 95, 102, 112, 116-123, 130, 132-134, 136, 137, 143, 159, 186, 187, 190-193, 198, 201-203, 207, 213, 216-222, 225, 226, 230
    nomenclature, 9, 121
Pitch fringe, 24, 190, 229
Pitch limits and sensitivity, in hearing, 194, 201-203, 208, 209, 211
Plates, 134, 135
Plucked strings, 87, 88, 92, 97
Pressure amplitude, 33
Pythagorean intonation, 170, 171, 173, 174, 176, 183, 186, 187, 189, 191

R

Radio, 207, 219, 225, 226, 228, 229
Rarefaction, 30-32, 47, 48, 51, 52, 54-58, 104-107, 111
Recording, 46-53, 223-225, 227, 228
Reed organ, 111, 129
Reeds, 110, 111, 115, 117-120, 124-126, 128, 129, 141, 142, 161, 229

Reflection, 63-76, 104-106, 109, 111, 214
Refraction, 79-82
Reinforcement, 37-39, 89, 96, 97, 100, 109, 124, 131, 132, 134, 135
Reproduction of sound, 223-230
Resonance, 11, 14, 27, 28, 37-39, 60, 61, 74, 102, 109, 110, 118, 122, 128, 141-145, 148, 152-154, 157, 159, 223, 227
Reverberation, 25, 67-72, 74-76, 215
Reverberation time, 69-72, 74-76, 227
Rods, 131-133

S

Saxophone, 115, 129
Scale:
    chromatic, 180
    diatonic, 167-179
Silent zones, 82
Simple harmonic motion, 4, 5, 13, 49, 51, 87
Sine curve, 5, 49, 133, 142
Sound defined, 2
Sound insulation, 72-74
Sound pictures, 224
Sound shadows, 77, 78
Sound waves:
    in various media, 44-46
    over great distances, 41-43
    velocity, 30, 39-41, 44, 79-81, 107, 118, 119
Sounds, analysis of complex, 221, 222
Speech, 68-70, 146, 156-159, 216, 217, 227
Standing waves:
    compressional, 104-107, 109, 118, 220
    transverse, 86, 92-94, 104, 132
Stretched strings, 15, 85-103
String quartet, 69 (*see also* Chamber music)
Struck strings, 89, 90, 92, 97
Subjective tones, 218-220
Subsonics, 202, 203
Summation tones, 63, 220
Superposition, 54-56, 86, 94, 104, 105, 111
Supersonics, 202, 203
Sympathetic vibration, 27, 96

T

Temperament:
    equal, 174, 181-196
    need for, 179-181
Tetrachord, 169, 170
Threshold:
    of audibility, 204, 206-212, 215
    of feeling or pain, 204, 207, 208, 211

Tonality, 170, 177-180, 196-198

Tone quality, 12-21, 34-36, 50, 96-102, 131-133, 135, 137, 138, 143-149, 220, 226-230

Tones:
  Aeolian, 108
  beat, 61, 63
  difference, 61-63, 218-220
  duration (*see* Duration of tones)
  edge, 107-109, 122, 124
  subjective, 218-220
  summation, 63, 220

Torsional vibration, 89, 94, 132

Traveling waves, 85-88, 104

Tremolo, 25, 26, 70, 144, 153, 229

Tremulant, 25 (*see also* Tremolo)

Triangle, 139

Trombone, 9, 115, 117, 129, 204

True intonation (*see* Just intonation)

Trumpet, 124, 129, 204

Tuba, 41, 129

Tuning:
  meantone, 181, 185
  piano (*see* Piano)

Tuning fork, 5, 13, 15, 18, 28, 57-59, 74, 128, 133, 139, 218

Tympani, 131, 139, 160, 219

Tympanic membrane, 199

U

Una corda, 96, 97

V

Valves, 115-117

Velocity of sound (*see* Sound waves, velocity)

Vertical cut discs, 225, 227

Vibration:
  complex, 10, 12, 13, 48-51, 136
  damped, 127, 128, 131
  defined, 2
  sympathetic, 27, 96 (*see also* Resonance)
  torsional, 89, 94, 132

Vibration form, 12, 14, 15, 19-23, 53-55, 90-94, 96, 98, 114, 124, 130, 132, 138, 160

Vibrato, 21-26, 60, 100, 144, 146-149, 153, 189, 197, 220, 229

Viola, 103, 219

Violin, 19, 37, 38, 45, 54, 60, 89, 91, 92, 94-96, 99-103, 135, 159, 167, 180, 187, 189, 197, 204, 207, 214, 218, 220, 226

Violin A (A-440), 6, 43, 44, 49, 119, 133, 173, 195

Violoncello, 96-103, 219

Vocal cords, 110, 140-144, 149, 153, 155, 156, 159

Voice, 15, 19, 22-24, 36, 139-159, 189, 204, 218
  physiological and psychological aspects, 149-155
  "placement," 140, 143, 145, 150, 152, 153, 156

Voix celeste, 60, 61

Vowels, 14, 18, 22, 141, 145, 146, 152, 156-159, 216, 227

W

Wagnerian music, 76

Water waves, 28, 29

Wave-length, 43, 44, 64, 78, 79, 106, 107, 112, 121

Wave motion:
  compressional (longitudinal), 30-33, 44, 46, 48-51
  transverse, 28, 29, 46

Waves:
  air, 33, 51, 55
  sound (*see* Sound waves)
  traveling, 85-88, 104
  water, 28, 29

Weber-Fechner law, 205

Whispering, 159

Whispering galleries, 66, 67

Wind gradients, 80-82

Wind pressure, 109, 116-118, 121, 124, 126, 128, 143

Wolf note, 102

Wood winds, 15, 115-117, 123, 124

X

Xylophone, 139, 159